EXPERIMENTS IN MODERN LIVING
SCIENTISTS' HOUSES IN CANBERRA 1950–1970

EXPERIMENTS IN MODERN LIVING
SCIENTISTS' HOUSES IN CANBERRA 1950–1970
MILTON CAMERON

E PRESS

Published by ANU E Press
The Australian National University
Canberra ACT 0200, Australia
Email: anuepress@anu.edu.au
This title is also available online at http://epress.anu.edu.au

---

National Library of Australia Cataloguing-in-Publication entry

Author: Cameron, Milton.

Title: Experiments in modern living : scientists' houses in Canberra, 1950 - 1970 / Milton Cameron.

ISBN: 9781921862694 (pbk.) 9781921862700 (ebook)

Notes: Includes bibliographical references and index.

Subjects: Scientists--Homes and haunts--Australian Capital Territory--Canberra.
            Architecture, Modern Architecture--Australian Capital Territory--Canberra.
            Canberra (A.C.T.)--Buildings, structures, etc

Dewey Number: 720.99471

All rights reserved. No part of this publication may be reproduced, stored in a retrieval system or transmitted in any form or by any means, electronic, mechanical, photocopying or otherwise, without the prior permission of the publisher.

Cover design by Sarah Evans.
Front cover photograph of Fenner House by Ben Wrigley, 2012.

This edition © 2012 ANU E Press; revised August 2012

Contents

Acknowledgments vii

Illustrations xi

Abbreviations xv

Introduction: Domestic Voyeurism 1

1. Age of the Masters: Establishing a scientific and
   intellectual community in Canberra, 1946–1968 7

2. Paradigm Shift:
   Boyd and the Fenner House 43

3. Promoting the New Paradigm:
   Seidler and the Zwar House 77

4. Form Follows Formula:
   Grounds, Boyd and the Philip House 101

5. Where Science Meets Art:
   Bischoff and the Gascoigne House 131

6. The Origins of Form:
   Grounds, Bischoff and the Frankel House 161

Afterword: Before and After Science 189

Bibliography 195

Index 207

Acknowledgments

When I first started researching Canberra houses I was impressed by the level of interest the topic generated. Many people volunteered information and provided useful contacts. When I combined their recollections with my own primary research and oral history interviews, I felt like I was assembling a puzzle—a giant, mid-twentieth-century puzzle of Canberra's history—whose components were houses, architects, clients, scientific institutions and dates.

Most of all I am indebted to the clients and the architects who commissioned and designed the houses discussed in the following pages. Clients Frank Fenner, John Zwar and Ben Gascoigne, and architect Colin Griffiths from Harry Seidler's office, were generous with their time and gave excellent firsthand accounts of those events—more than half a century ago—that shaped their houses. Without their enthusiasm, and willingness to answer my many questions, this study would not have been possible. The book is further indebted to the many other clients and architects who have long departed but whose voices can still be heard in the extensive personal correspondence and records they left behind.

I would also like to thank many family members of those original protagonists. The Gascoigne family—Hester, Thomas ('Toss') and Martin—were most helpful in recalling details of the lives, and houses, of Ben and Rosalie. Hester and Toss deserve a special mention for their personal interest in my project, for their generosity in offering information and contacts regarding other houses and other clients, and in facilitating the interviews with Ben. Martin Gascoigne located suitable images from the Rosalie Gascoigne Archives. Candida Griffiths (nee Philip) gave a detailed account of the history of the Philip House, together with the other houses in the Vasey Crescent Group. The fact that she is an architect herself made her contribution especially pertinent. Phoebe Bischoff was most helpful, and deserves credit for having the foresight to donate Theo Bischoff's documents to the ACT Heritage Library for the ongoing benefit of researchers such as myself.

Where family members were not available, colleagues of the original clients—or people who worked in the same institutions—proved helpful. Without the help of Brendan Lepschi, a CSIRO scientist and another person who is interested in early modern houses, the chapter on the Zwar House would not have eventuated. Lepschi introduced me to John Zwar, permitted me to refer to his own research and provided excellent photographs of the now-demolished Zwar House. The many lunchtime conversations that Lloyd Evans conducted with Otto Frankel—all of which he recorded in note form and left in the Basser Library at the Australian Academy of Science—helped to fill in details of the Frankel houses.

Canberra would not be what it is today—and neither would this book—without its various national institutions, many of which brought the principal protagonists to the city. Fortunately, many of these same institutions now house their records for posterity. From these, I obtained a significant amount of primary research material. My thanks go to the many librarians and archivists who helped me in my searches. In particular, I would like to thank Rosanne Walker from the Basser Library at the Australian Academy of Science. Rosanne showed me where to find the Fellows' files, and left me to sit at a long desk where I was watched over by portraits of Florey, Oliphant, Fenner, Philip, Gascoigne and Frankel. The staff of the Petherick Reading Room at the National Library of Australia, where much of this book was written, were helpful at all times. I would like to thank Andrew Sergeant in particular for his personal attention. Antoinette Buchanan, of the ACT Heritage Library, assisted with locating files and documents from the Theo Bischoff Collection; Pennie Pemberton at the ANU Archives helped to locate information regarding university staff houses; while archivists at the National Archives of Australia sourced a wide variety of information from their repository. Sophie Clement from the ACT Chapter of the Australian Institute of Architects helped to confirm details of some houses.

A number of people from locations outside Canberra helped. Dirk Meinecke from Harry Seidler and Associates, Sydney, provided information regarding the Zwar House; Robert Woodley of the Pictures Collection, State Library of New South Wales, assisted me to access documents from the Harry Seidler Archives; while staff at the Australian Manuscripts Collection of the State Library of Victoria provided files and drawings from the Grounds, Romberg and Boyd records.

The many people who assisted by sharing their knowledge of Canberra houses include Roger Benjamin, Catherine Townsend, Bruce Townsend, Enrico Taglietti, Roger Pegrum, Derek Wrigley, Peter Freeman, Geoff Ashley, Dennis Formiatti, Karina Harris, Neil Hobbs, Lyn Gascoigne, Pam Macdonald, Joy Warren, Graham O'Loughlin, Lenore Coltheart, Barry Smith, Ann Moyal, Susan-Mary Withycombe, Rosemary Birch, Peter Conroy and Mark McKenna. Other people I would like to thank include Andrew Benjamin, Brian McGrath, Betty McGrath, Paul McGrath, Atsuko Takeda, Rebecca Smith, Ted Cremean, Claire Toepfer, Rod MacIver, Tom Sutton and Sarah Evans.

This book began life as a PhD dissertation at the University of New South Wales, where I received excellent advice from my supervisor, Harry Margalit. I am particularly grateful for Harry's timely, straightforward and honest advice, all of which helped to keep the project on the right track. I am also grateful to my co-supervisor, Paul Hogben, for his considered and detailed comments. My former colleagues at the University of Canberra were helpful during the early days of my search for a suitable research topic. In particular, I would like to thank Craig Bremner, Gevork Hartoonian, visiting academic Ranulph Glanville and Andrew Metcalf, who also provided information from his own records of Canberra architecture. Stephen Frith, current owner of the Frankel House, pointed out details of that house.

Those people whose assistance was critical in the conversion of my dissertation into book format include Ian Chubb, Steve Dovers, Harriet Edquist, Philip Goad, Marilyn Fenner, Victoria Grounds, Penleigh Boyd, Tony Lee (Robin Boyd Foundation), Eric Sierins, Bill Lyristakis, Karen May and Duncan Beard. Ben Wrigley's excellent photographs bring to light the architectural qualities of the houses, and contribute much to the visual character of the book.

Last, but certainly not the least, I would like to thank my own family. My mother and father, Marie and Murray, are long gone, but their influence lives on. Their passions for designing and building led to my career in architecture, but the most valuable lesson they taught me was to follow my own interests. My daughters, Venetia and Naomi, have grown up considerably since I first started thinking about Canberra houses, and now enjoy pointing out houses that their dad might like. But above all others, I am indebted to my partner, Ann McGrath, for her patience, support and advice over the years. Without her there would be no book. An academic who is involved in writing and publishing in her day job, Ann was often asked for similar advice after she came home in the evenings. I promise not to discuss footnotes after 10 pm ever again.

Illustrations

Figure i Map of Canberra, c. 1962 Image: drawn by the author, November 2009. Drawing influenced by map of Los Angeles in Elizabeth Smith, *Case Study Houses: The complete Case Study House program 1945–1966*	xvi
Figure ii 'The Lantern' (Verge House), Red Hill Photograph: the author, 2012	2
Figure 1.1 Coombs and Chifley in front of Palm House at Kew Gardens, London, 1946 Photograph: National Archives of Australia. NAA: M2153, 22/4	10
Figure 1.2 Oliphant, Hancock and Florey inspect the university site, Easter 1948. Lewis was not invited Photograph: Oliphant Papers, Barr Smith Library, University of Adelaide	13
Figure 1.3 University House, The Australian National University, 1954 Photograph: National Archives of Australia. NAA: A1200, L17793	18
Figure 1.4 The four medical professors—Eccles, Albert, Fenner and Ennor—study plans for the John Curtin School of Medical Research, Canberra, August 1950 Photograph: Australian News and Information Bureau, The Australian National University Collection	21
Figure 1.5 Birch House, central courtyard with swimming pool Photograph: Max Dupain, 1968. Max Dupain & Associates Archives	24
Figure 1.6 Model of the Australian Academy of Science, Canberra Photograph: Wolfgang Sievers, 1963. National Library of Australia. nla.pic-vn4474852	27
Figure 1.7 'Margaret and Otto Honeymoon, 1940, Lake Wanaka, New Zealand' Photograph: Manuscript Collection, Adolph Basser Library, Australian Academy of Science. Frankel, Sir O. H., FAA (1900–2007), MS 106, Box 13	29
Figure 1.8 'Otto's two wives Margaret Anderson and Tillie Donsbach in the Port Hills' Photograph: Manuscript Collection, Adolph Basser Library, Australian Academy of Science. Frankel, Sir O. H., FAA (1900–2007), MS 106, Box 13	30
Figure 1.9 Frankel House, Opawa, Christchurch, c. 1940 Photograph: Manuscript Collection, Adolph Basser Library, Australian Academy of Science. Frankel, Sir O. H., FAA (1900–2007), MS 106, Box 13	32
Figure 1.10 Phytotron hothouse, Commonwealth Scientific and Industrial Research Organisation, Canberra, 1962 Photograph: National Archives of Australia. NAA: A1200, L42101	35
Figure 1.11 Benjamin House, view from north-west Photograph: Wolfgang Sievers, 1958. National Library of Australia. nla.pic-vn4503045	39
Figure 2.1 Fenner House, view from north-east Photograph: from 'House at Red Hill, Canberra', *Architecture and Arts* 13 (August 1954)	43
Figure 2.2 Fenner House, floor plan Image: redrawn by the author from Robin Boyd. Courtesy of the Robin Boyd Foundation	44

Figure 2.3 Fenner House, view from west. The diurnal block is on the left; the nocturnal block on the right Photograph: from 'House at Red Hill, Canberra', *Architecture and Arts* 13 (August 1954)	45
Figure 2.4 Fenner House, view from west Photograph: from 'House at Red Hill, Canberra', *Architecture and Arts* 13 (August 1954)	45
Figure 2.5 Viewing Canberra Medallion on wall of Fenner House, 1956. From left: Karl Schreiner (holding screwdriver), Vicki Fenner, Mrs Schreiner, John Scollay (ACT Chapter, RAIA), Frank Fenner, Marilyn Fenner and Bobbie Fenner. Boyd was in the United States at the time Photograph: Manuscript Collection, Adolph Basser Library, Australian Academy of Science. Fenner, F. J., FAA (1914–2010), MS 143, Box 3	46
Figure 2.6 Fenner House, view from north-west Photograph: Ben Wrigley, 2012	47
Figure 2.7 Manning Clark House, entrance hall showing ladder to study Photograph: the author, 2010	53
Figure 2.8 Frank Fenner, diary entry for 12 July, 1953 Image: Fenner, 'Collins' Trip Book, 1953. Manuscript Collection, Adolph Basser Library, Australian Academy of Science. Fenner, F. J., FAA (1914–2010), MS 143, Box 22. Courtesy of Marilyn Fenner	57
Figure 2.9 Frank Fenner, diary entry for 22 August, 1953 Image: Fenner, 'Collins' Trip Book, 1953. Manuscript Collection, Adolph Basser Library, Australian Academy of Science. Fenner, F. J., FAA (1914–2010), MS 143, Box 22. Courtesy of Marilyn Fenner	58
Figure 2.10 Lever House, New York Photograph: J. Alex Langley, from Banham, *Age of the Masters: A Personal View of Modern Architecture*, 113	59
Figure 2.11 Aerial view of the John Curtin School of Medical Research, The Australian National University, 1957 Photograph: National Archives of Australia. NAA: A1200, L23558	63
Figure 2.12 Marcel Breuer, 'binuclear' house proposal, 1943 Image: from Blake, *Marcel Breuer: Sun and Shadow, the Philosophy of an Architect*, 149	66
Figure 2.13 Fenner House, view from north-east Photograph: Ben Wrigley, 2012	68
Figure 2.14 Fenner House, kitchen Photograph: Ben Wrigley, 2012	69
Figure 2.15 Fenner House, living room Photograph: Ben Wrigley, 2012	76
Figure 2.16 Fenner House, dining room Photograph: Ben Wrigley, 2012	76
Figure 3.1 Zwar House 1955, south-east view from Yapunyah Street Photograph: Brendan Lepschi, 2005	77
Figure 3.2 Bowden House, view from south-west, 1954 Photograph: Max Dupain, from Seidler, *Houses, Interiors and Projects*, 53	79
Figure 3.3 Harry Seidler's Point Piper Studio at night Photograph: from *Art and Design*, no. 1, 1949, 26	80
Figure 3.4 Zwar House, floor plan Image: redrawn by the author from Harry Seidler	82

Figure 3.5 Zwar House, cross-section Image: from 'John Zwar House, Lot 68 Yapunyah O'Connor ACT', drawn by Colin Griffiths for Harry Seidler, 4 August, 1955. John Zwar Collection	84
Figure 3.6 Portrait of Harry Seidler with Walter Gropius Photograph: Max Dupain, 1954. National Library of Australia. nla.pic-an12660573	86
Figure 3.7 Zwar House, view from south Photograph: Brendan Lepschi, 2005	97
Figure 3.8 Zwar House, view from dining area Photograph: Brendan Lepschi, 2005	97
Figure 4.1 Philip House, view from north-east Photograph: Ben Wrigley, 2011	101
Figure 4.2 Vasey Crescent Group, site plan Image: redrawn by the author from Grounds, Romberg and Boyd. Courtesy of Victoria Grounds and the Robin Boyd Foundation	106
Figure 4.3 Philip House, living room, looking east Photograph: Candida Griffiths (daughter of Frances Philip and John Philip)	108
Figure 4.4 Philip House, living room, looking south-west Photograph: Candida Griffiths	111
Figure 4.5 Philip House, floor plans Image: redrawn by the author from Grounds, Romberg and Boyd. Courtesy of Victoria Grounds and the Robin Boyd Foundation	112
Figure 4.6 Frances Philip, Painting: Philip House from north, 1988 Image: Candida Griffiths Collection	124
Figure 4.7 Frances Philip, Painting: Philip House and children, 1965. Left to right: Peregrine, Candida and Julian Image: Candida Griffiths Collection	129
Figure 5.1 Gascoigne House, view from north Photograph: Bill Lyristakis, 2010	131
Figure 5.2 'Residence 19', Mount Stromlo Observarory, 1926. This would become the Gascoignes' first house Photograph: National Archives of Australia. NAA: A3560, 1820	136
Figure 5.3 Rosalie Gascoigne, *Loose Leaf*, 1991. Sawn 'Schweppes' soft drink crates Image: Rosalie Gascoigne Archives	140
Figure 5.4 Gascoigne House, floor plan Image: redrawn by the author from Theo Bischoff. Courtesy of Phoebe Bischoff	150
Figure 5.5 Rosalie Gascoigne with *Ikebana*, Gascoigne House, c. 1969 Photograph: National Archives of Australia. NAA: A1501, A9510	152
Figure 5.6 Gascoigne House, hall with artworks by Rosalie Gascoigne, c. 1975 Photograph: Rosalie Gascoigne Archives	154
Figure 5.7 Gascoigne House, living room with various artworks, c. 1975 Photograph: Rosalie Gascoigne Archives	157
Figure 6.1 Frankel House, Opawa, Christchurch, c. 1940 Photograph: Manuscript Collection, Adolph Basser Library, Australian Academy of Science. Frankel, Sir O. H., FAA (1900–2007), MS 106, Box 13	161
Figure 6.2 Frankel House, Cobby Street, Campbell, view from south-west Photograph: Ben Wrigley, 2011	162
Figure 6.3 Frankel House, Nicholson Crescent, Acton, 1955 Photograph: National Archives of Australia. NAA: A1200, L19496	163

Figure 6.4 Hans Sedlmayr, the five 'genetic elements' of Borromini's architecture Image: redrawn by George Hersey after Sedlmayr and Borromini, from Hersey, *The Monumental Impulse: Architecture's Biological Roots*, The MIT Press, 161	167
Figure 6.5 Frankel House, preliminary floor plan, October 1969. Service functions to the left, living zone in the centre, bedrooms on the right. Cobby Street is to the bottom of the sheet Image: ACT Heritage Library, Bischoff, Theo – Architectural Records, 0159. Courtesy of Victoria Grounds and Phoebe Bischoff	175
Figure 6.6 Frankel House, revised plan, December 1969 Image: ACT Heritage Library, Bischoff, Theo – Architectural Records, 0159. Courtesy of Victoria Grounds and Phoebe Bischoff	177
Figure 6.7 Frankel House, view from dining room Photograph: Ben Wrigley, 2011	184

Abbreviations

AAS	Australian Academy of Science
AAT	Anglo-Australian Telescope
ACT	Australian Capital Territory
ACTHL	Australian Capital Territory Heritage Library
ANU	The Australian National University
BOAC	British Overseas Airways Corporation
CEBS	Commonwealth Experimental Building Station
CIAM	International Congress for Modern Architecture
CSIR	Council for Scientific and Industrial Research
CSIRO	Commonwealth Scientific and Industrial Research Organisation
CSO	Commonwealth Solar Observatory
CUC	Canberra University College
FCAC	Federal Capital Advisory Committee
FCC	Federal Capital Commission
IBP	International Biological Program
JCSMR	John Curtin School of Medical Research
MARS	Modern Architecture Research Society
MIT	Massachusetts Institute of Technology
MSO	Mount Stromlo Observatory
NAA	National Archives of Australia
NCDC	National Capital Development Commission
NCPDC	National Capital Planning and Development Committee
NLA	National Library of Australia
NSW	New South Wales
NT	Northern Territory
RAIA	Royal Australian Institute of Architects
RSTCA	Register of Significant Twentieth Century Architecture
SHS	Small Homes Service
SLV	State Library of Victoria
SOM	Skidmore, Owings and Merrill
TAA	Trans-Australia Airlines
WRI	Wheat Research Institute (New Zealand)

Experiments in Modern Living

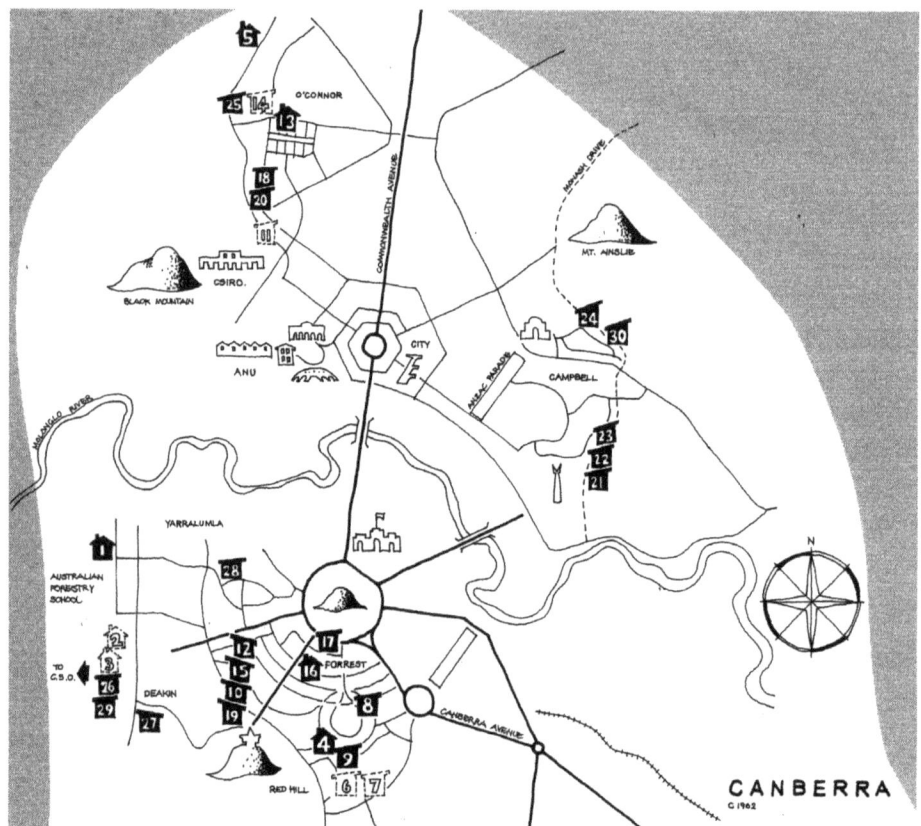

Figure i Map of Canberra, c. 1962. Drawn by the author, November 2009. Drawing influenced by map of Los Angeles in Elizabeth Smith, *Case Study Houses: The complete Case Study House program 1945–1966*

Select Inventory

Address	Client	Occupation	Architect	Date Complete	Comments	Map Reference
Westridge House, Banks Street, Yarralumla	Charles & Ruth Lane Poole	Forester & interior decorator	Harold Desbrowe-Annear	1928	Sympathetically extended	1
Director's Residence, Commonwealth Solar Observatory	Geoffrey & Doris Duffield	Astronomer	Henry Rolland	1928	Almost totally destroyed by fire	2
Residence 26, Commonwealth Solar Observatory	Ben & Rosalie Gascoigne	Astronomer & artist	Federal Capital Commission	c 1928	1st house. Destroyed by fire	3
Dial House, 2 Moresby Street, Red Hill	Robin & Pattie Tillyard	Entomologist	Ken Oliphant	1930	Modified	4
Weetangera Road (now 199 Dryandra Street), O'Connor	Sir Mark & Lady Rosa Oliphant	Nuclear physicist	Moir & Sutherland	1951	Mostly original	5
28 Monaro Crescent (corner Vancouver Street), Red Hill	Sir John & Lady Irene Eccles	Neurophysiologist (Nobel Prize winner)	Eccles, with Tom Haseler	1952	Demolished	6
3 Vancouver Street, Red Hill	Sir Hugh & Lady Violet Ennor	Biochemist & dress designer	Hocking & Warren	1953	Demolished	7
11 Tasmania Circle, Forrest	Manning & Dymphna Clark	Australian historian	Robin Boyd	1953	Excellent, open to public	8
1 Torres Street (corner Monaro Crescent), Red Hill	Frank & Bobbie Fenner	Microbiologist/virologist	Robin Boyd	1954	Excellent	9
4 Bedford Street, Deakin	Dr. Hilary & Barbara Roche	Medical researcher	Robin Boyd	1955	Excellent	10
40 Nicholson Crescent, Acton	Sir Otto & Lady Margaret Frankel	Geneticist/plant breeder & artist	Oscar Bayne	1955	1st house. Demolished	11
11 Northcote Street, Deakin	Ivor & Caroline Bowden	Public servant	Harry Seidler	1955	Excellent	12
2 Todd Street, O'Connor	John & Heather Zwar	Plant physiologist & artist		c 1955	1st house. Excellent	13

Experiments in Modern Living

Address	Client	Occupation	Architect	Date Complete	Comments	Map Reference
12 Yapunyah Street, O'Connor	John & Heather Zwar	Plant physiologist & artist	Harry Seidler	1956	Demolished	14
10 Gawler Crescent, Deakin	Bruce & Audrey Benjamin	Philosopher	Alex Jelinek	1956	Excellent	15
58 National Circuit, (corner Melbourne Avenue), Deakin	Doug & Dawn Waterhouse	Entomologist	Moir & Sutherland	1958	Excellent	16
6 Somers Crescent, Forrest	Keith & Mary Boardman	Research chemist	John Scollay	1959	Excellent	17
6 Hobbs Street, O'Connor	George & Valeska Stewart	CSIRO scientist	Rudi Krastins	1959	Appears original	18
22 Dugan Street, Deakin	Ben & Rosalie Gascoigne	Astronomer & artist		c 1959	2nd house. Appears original	19
8 Hobbs Street, O'Connor	Ralph & June Slatyer	Ecologist	Rudi Krastins	1961	Appears original	20
42 Vasey Crescent, Campbell	John & Frances Philip	Environmental physicist & artist	Sir Roy Grounds	1961	Excellent	21
44 Vasey Crescent, Campbell	Bruce & Penny Griffing	Geneticist	Sir Roy Grounds	1961	Excellent	22
46 Vasey Crescent, Campbell	Gordon & Catherine Blakers	Public servant	Sir Roy Grounds	1961	Excellent	23
24 Cobby Street, Campbell	John & Phyllis Nicholson	Population ecologist	Sir Roy Grounds	1965	Substantially altered	24
144 Dryandra Street, O'Connor	Philip & Moira Trudinger	Plant physiologist	Sir Roy Grounds	1965	Excellent	25
86 Morgan Crescent, Curtin	Ian & Kathleen Marshall	Microbiologist & laboratory technician	Theo Bischoff	1966	Second storey added	26
38 Beauchamp Street, Deakin	John & Kerry Lovering	Geologist	Ancher, Mortlock & Woolley	1967	Excellent	27
3 Arkana Street, Yarralumla	Sir Arthur & Lady Jesse Birch	Research chemist & artist	Bunning&Madden (Noel Potter)	1968	Excellent	28
3 Anstey Street, Pearce	Ben & Rosalie Gascoigne	Astronomer & artist	Theo Bischoff	1969	Excellent	29
4 Cobby Street, Campbell	Sir Otto & Lady Margaret Frankel	Geneticist/plant breeder & artist	Sir Roy Grounds	1971	2nd house. Excellent	30

Introduction: Domestic Voyeurism[1]

In 2003 I started looking for a house in Canberra. This was not a detective search for a missing house by Robin Boyd, Harry Seidler or Roy Grounds—an attempt to uncover a long lost masterpiece and reveal it to the world. It was a much more prosaic investigation. I was trying to find a house for my family to live in. Like all those looking to buy a house in Australia's capital city, I faithfully scanned the real estate section of *The Canberra Times* each Saturday morning and prepared a list of houses to visit. Over the next two years, we visited many open houses in the inner northern suburbs of O'Connor, Ainslie and Campbell, and in Forrest, Deakin and Red Hill to the south. Some were further out—Aranda in the north, and Curtin and Pearce in the south. Many advertising brochures were collected, compared and filed away for future reference.

On the whole the houses were a mixed bunch, as one might expect. But every now and then a real gem showed up. Unfortunately, they were usually well out of our price range. A house attributed to Boyd, at 44 Vasey Crescent, Campbell, was one example. So was the house at 32 Holmes Crescent, Campbell, designed by Frederick Theodore ('Theo') Bischoff—a former student of Boyd who had moved from Melbourne and established his own office in Canberra. Another Boyd house—'The Lantern', at 204 Monaro Crescent, Red Hill—was more affordable, but quite impractical for our needs. A few other significant houses came onto the market, including one at 4 Yapunyah Street, O'Connor, attributed to Seidler.

Most of the houses we inspected were located in the same inner suburbs that, 50 years previously, had been settled by new residents arriving to take up positions in the burgeoning national capital. By the turn of the twenty-first century, these suburbs were in a state of flux. The house sites that had once been on the fringes of Canberra were now set in prime, inner-city locations and were heavily in demand. Many of the original houses they contained— considered substandard by current standards—were being demolished to make way for much larger versions.[2]

---

1 'Domestic Voyeurism' follows Beatriz Colomina's essay on Adolf Loos and Charles Le Corbusier entitled 'The Split Wall: Domestic Voyeurism', in Beatriz Colomina, ed., *Sexuality and Space* (Princeton, NJ: Princeton Architectural Press, 1992), 73–128.
2 It is not intended to give the impression that all significant houses were facing demolition. Many have been retained and some are subject to heritage legislation. Some important houses, however—including Bob Warren's Ennor House, Oscar Bayne's first Frankel House and Seidler's Zwar House—have been demolished.

Figure ii 'The Lantern' (Verge House), Red Hill

Photograph: the author, 2012

These random intrusions into other people's domestic spaces opened up an aperture through which it was possible to view certain aspects of Canberra's social history—aspects that would otherwise have remained hidden from view. Walter Benjamin wrote that 'to live is to leave traces', and likened these clues to evidence in a good detective story.[3] While inspecting these houses, it was impossible not to notice the traces of everyday life that their inhabitants had accumulated over decades of living and working. This was especially so because the houses contained evidence of lives that had been particularly rich in artistic, intellectual and cultural experience. Modern sculptures sat in the gardens, and bookshelves were strewn with scholarly books. Hung on the walls of modest houses, virtually hidden from the street by Australian native gardens, were original modernist paintings and prints by some of Australia's most celebrated artists. The owners of one house had obviously been friends with the painter Arthur Boyd: a photograph amongst his paintings depicted a group of people standing alongside the artist. Many of these houses contained a study, on the walls of which were black-and-white photographs of graduation ceremonies, or of people standing in front of university buildings in various international locations.

---

3 Walter Benjamin, 'Paris: Capital of the Nineteenth Century', in *Reflections, Essays, Aphorisms, Autobiographical Writings*, Translated by Edmund Jephcott (New York: Helen and Kurt Wolff, 1978), 155.

It soon became apparent that a high proportion of the vendors of these houses were scientists or academics—often professors—who had retired from The Australian National University (ANU), or from the Commonwealth Scientific and Industrial Research Organisation (CSIRO). To those who were interested in buying the houses, this fact was not as important as other details—such as the gross permissible building envelope or best location for a swimming pool. But to me, the stories of those original inhabitants—how they came to live in Canberra, where they worked and the circumstances under which they commissioned architects to design their houses—became an obsession. It appeared that this was one aspect of Canberra's history—and of the nation's history—that had been left out of the discourse. While Canberra's demographic reputation has generally been that of a public service town, supplemented with periodic influxes of politicians, these houses contained, within their built structure and contents, evidence of another form of settlement—that of a highly educated, cultured and well-travelled intelligentsia.

I found that the occupants of these houses—and others in Canberra—had been responsible for some truly remarkable achievements. These included founding Australia's conservation and forestry policy; developing microwave technology for radar—the one weapon that Hitler conceded had prevented German victory in the Atlantic; working with J. Robert Oppenheimer on the Manhattan Project; leading world research in nuclear physics, winning a Nobel Prize for physiological research; making major contributions to galactic evolutionary theory; curing the world of smallpox; inventing a chemical process that allowed the manufacture of the contraceptive pill; inventing insect repellent (later manufactured as 'Aerogard'); calculating the thermodynamics of water movement to maximise water efficiency in dry lands; founding an international movement for the conservation of genetic plant resources; and writing what was once considered by many Australians to be the definitive version of European history in Australia.[4]

But it was their connection to the houses that became most important to me. My search for a house had taken a different turn; no longer looking for one, I was now looking for many. I compiled as many data as I could about Canberra's clients, architects and houses, and prepared an inventory of architect-designed houses that were built in Canberra during the 1950s and 1960s.[5] To the various lists and guides that were then available, I added details from a variety of other sources: articles from *The Canberra Times*, discussions with residents who had

---

4   The scientists and their respective fields were Charles Lane Poole (forestry), Sir Mark Oliphant and Sir Ernest Titterton (nuclear physics), Sir John ('Jack') Eccles (neurophysiology), Ben Gascoigne (astronomy), Frank Fenner (microbiology and virology), Sir Arthur Birch (chemistry), Doug Waterhouse (entomology), John Philip (environmental physics) and Sir Otto Frankel (genetics and plant breeding). The historian was Manning Clark.
5   The Select Inventory (p. xvii) is an abbreviated version that covers the houses that are relevant to the book.

grown up in Canberra, and visual observation of houses from suburban streets. *The Canberra Times* articles, most of which were written by Ann Whitelaw under the title 'Homes and Building', were particularly helpful. In many of her descriptions of the houses, she mentioned the occupations of the clients. I began to include a 'client occupation' column on my inventory, and was able to correlate Whitelaw's information with further details obtained from the ACT Electoral Roll, from which it was possible to confirm names, occupations, street addresses and dates of occupation. Publications on the establishment of The Australian National University and the CSIRO, plus histories of the John Curtin School of Medical Research and the Mount Stromlo Observatory, provided more names to be matched to addresses, and to houses. Friends and acquaintances who had grown up in Canberra showed a keen interest in my project; a number of them were the sons or daughters of clients who had commissioned architect-designed houses.

Once the information regarding client occupations was examined, it became clear that scientists were responsible for commissioning the most highly acclaimed houses in Canberra. These were modern houses whose designs heralded a major shift in the accepted way of thinking about domestic design, and a radical departure from previous examples—most of which were based on historical styles. Of the 11 private houses by Grounds, Romberg and Boyd—considered to be Australia's premier architectural firm during the 1950s and 1960s—that were listed on the Royal Australian Institute of Architects' *2006 Tour Guide*, six were commissioned by scientists, one by an academic, and another by a medical researcher. In addition, at least eight private houses on the institute's *Map of Significant Canberra Architecture* had been built for scientists and their families.[6]

This raised a number of questions. Why, in the post–World War II era, had so many members of Canberra's scientific community commissioned modern houses, whose designs signalled such a radical departure from previous examples? The answer to this question, I suspected, would be located somewhere within a series of related inquiries. Where were the areas of overlap between architecture and science during the period of the study? What were the attitudes of the

---

6   The six scientists' houses on the *Tour Guide* were those for plant physiologist Philip Trudinger at 144 Dryandra Street, O'Connor; population ecologist John Nicholson at 24 Cobby Street, Campbell; geneticist and plant breeder Otto Frankel at 4 Cobby Street, Campbell; environmental physicist John Philip at 42 Vasey Crescent, Campbell; geneticist Bruce Griffing at 44 Vasey Crescent, Campbell; and microbiologist and virologist Frank Fenner at 1 Torres Street (corner of Monaro Crescent), Red Hill. The academic's house was for Manning Clark at 11 Tasmania Circle, Forrest, while the medical researcher's house was for Dr Hilary Roche at 4 Bedford Street, Deakin. Royal Australian Institute of Architects (ACT Chapter), *Tour Guide to Significant Canberra Architecture*, 2006. The scientists' houses on the institute's *Map of Significant Canberra Architecture* included the Fenner, Frankel, Nicholson, Philip and Griffing houses, plus those for research chemist Arthur Birch at 3 Arkana Street, Yarralumla, designed by Noel Potter of Bunning and Madden, for the Director of the Mount Stromlo Observatory, designed by Henry Rolland of the Architects Department, Federal Capital Commission, and for the principal of the Australian Forestry School at Banks Street, Yarralumla (Westridge House), designed by Harold Desbrowe-Annear.

architects who had designed these houses towards science? And, conversely, what were the attitudes of their clients towards architecture? In what ways did the material form of the houses reflect the ideologies of their architects? And how did those same formal aspects reflect the beliefs, or aspirations, of the scientists?

To find the answers, the study was limited to five houses, designed by various architects, for scientists and their families in Canberra between 1950 and 1970. By studying a specific and limited sample of clients—who all shared a common occupation, time and place—it was believed that information could be observed, evaluated and compared in an attempt to isolate and identify the key underlying issues.

The discovery of a series of letters and other correspondence between architects and their scientist clients was another factor that defined the study group. These documents provided intimate insights into the day-to-day concerns of both parties during the briefing, design and construction phases, and, together with material obtained from interviews and secondary sources, revealed the aspirations that drove both architects and clients in their searches for an appropriate house.[7]

The shift in architectural taste towards modernism signposted by these houses was not unique to Australia: numerous processes of modernisation were under way throughout the country, and in overseas locations, during the period of this study. But while the arrival of modernism was not unique to Canberra, the city was, in itself, a special case. This was due to a combination of factors: Canberra's status as a relatively new, planned capital city, the Australian Government's sanctioning of the centring of science in this location, an exceptionally rapid rate of growth in the immediate post–World War II decades, and the massive influx of educated and informed scientists who arrived in the capital city to find a critical lack of existing houses.[8]

The five houses discussed in this book—the Fenner House, the Zwar House, the Philip House, the Gascoigne House and the Frankel House—all emerged from this extraordinarily highly qualified scientific and intellectual community.

---

7 This material was found within the personal papers of the clients at the National Library of Australia, the National Archives of Australia and the Adolph Basser Library at the Australian Academy of Science. The State Library of Victoria's Grounds, Romberg and Boyd collection, and the ACT Heritage Library's Bischoff Collection, provided similar documents from the architects' archives.
8 The nearest equivalent to the Canberra situation, within the international context, would most likely be post–World War II residential communities associated with scientific institutions in North America.

1. Age of the Masters: Establishing a scientific and intellectual community in Canberra, 1946–1968

The Formation of The Australian National University

> Having proven their worth in wartime, scientists in the 1950s were as powerful as they ever had been, confident of their own capacity to change the world, and dismissive of those who stood in their way.
>
> — Stephen Foster and Margaret Varghese[1]

> The architect must be entirely subordinated to the scientific requirements of those who are to inhabit [the building]…I will not be pushed around by an architect for architectural reasons.
>
> — Sir Howard Florey[2]

One evening in April 1946, Australian Prime Minister, Ben Chifley, in London for the first postwar Commonwealth Prime Ministers' Conference, booked a large table for dinner at The Savoy Hotel in The Strand. Also dining with him that night was a thirty-six-year-old economist and planner, Herbert Cole ('Nugget') Coombs,[3] whom he had appointed Director-General of the Commonwealth Department of Post-War Reconstruction, Dr Herbert Vere ('Doc') Evatt, the Minister for External Affairs, and other members of the official party. The Savoy, one of London's most distinguished and elegant hotels, was upgrading its menu now that rationing was over, and under the French maître-chef, dishes from the Normandy region such as *Tripes á la Mode de Caen* and *Canard á la Rouennaise* were available. It is possible that former British Prime Minister Sir Winston Churchill was also there; a frequent patron, he was known to have dined there as often as five times a fortnight.[4] But Chifley was not interested in the guests

---

1   Stephen G. Foster and Margaret M. Varghese, *The Making of The Australian National University 1946–96* (St Leonards, NSW: Allen & Unwin, 1996), 256.
2   Ibid., 72; Howard Florey to Douglas Copland, Vice-Chancellor, ANU, Trevor Williams, *Howard Florey: Penicillin and After* (Oxford: Oxford University Press, 1984), 251–2.
3   For a detailed account of the various explanations for this unusual nickname, see Tim Rowse, *Nugget Coombs: A Reforming Life* (New York: Cambridge University Press, 2002), 1–2.
4   Alison Lech, ed., *The Savoy Food and Drink Book* (London: Pyramid, 1988), 25.

at other tables that evening. He had invited Mark Oliphant,[5] an expatriate Australian nuclear physicist, to join his party, and was transfixed by what he was telling him. Oliphant held the Poynting Chair of Physics at the University of Birmingham, and already had an impressive career: he had worked with Oppenheimer on the Manhattan Project, with MAUD, a secret British committee that investigated the uranium bomb, with the British Admiralty to develop new microwave technology for radar—the one weapon that Hitler conceded had prevented German victory in the Atlantic—and with revered New Zealand-born physicist Ernest Rutherford at the Cavendish Laboratory in Cambridge.[6]

Chifley began by asking Oliphant the question that was on everyone's mind: what was the likely impact of the atomic bomb on the balance of world power? His guest duly obliged, and conveyed a sense of the excitement he had experienced working on the Manhattan Project. He then digressed to his favourite topic: how a new world order would be built around the use of nuclear power for energy purposes. Oliphant was a great communicator; his knowledge and passion soon had his audience captivated. He described his proton synchroton project at Birmingham, and ventured to add that, under the right circumstances, Australia could be a world leader in nuclear physics. As Coombs later recalled, Oliphant 'was absolutely at his spell-binding best, we were all ga ga…the impact on Chifley was tremendous'.[7]

The Prime Ministers' Conference was not the only reason that Chifley and Coombs were in postwar London—they were also headhunting. The cornerstones of Coombs' vision for postwar Australia were the construction, in Canberra, of a new, research-based national university—an 'intellectual powerhouse for the rebuilding of society'[8]—and the reconstruction of the existing Council for Scientific and Industrial Research (CSIR). Coombs, who sometimes referred to himself as an 'economic scientist', was a practical idealist who believed that a combination of careful planning and strategic government intervention would improve Australia's physical and social environment. His vision was essentially utilitarian, based on the premise that improved education in social sciences would result in improved government, and that increased scientific research—particularly in nuclear physics—would allow science to 'serve humanitarian purposes as forcefully as it had served those of mass destruction'.[9] While the origins of his ideologies have been generally credited to Keynesian economic rationalism, Coombs' position was similar to the declarations laid down by a

---

5 Oliphant was named 'Marcus' after Marcus Clarke, the Australian author, whom his parents knew. Most people knew him as 'Marc' until he was knighted in 1959. From then on he changed the spelling to 'Mark'. In spite of the unusual surname they shared, Mark Oliphant was not related to Canberra architect Ken Oliphant.
6 Stewart Cockburn and David Ellyard, *Oliphant: The Life and Times of Sir Mark Oliphant* (Adelaide: Axiom, 1981), 89.
7 Ibid., 145; Foster and Varghese, *The Making of The Australian National University 1946–96*, 21.
8 Ibid., 19.
9 H. C. Coombs, *Trial Balance* (South Melbourne: Macmillan, 1981), 20, 27.

group of prominent modern architects at the Congrès International d'Architecture Moderne (CIAM; the International Congress for Modern Architecture) at La Sarraz and Athens. CIAM envisaged a holistic and integrated approach to planning and building that was 'intimately associated with the evolution and development of human life', in order to satisfy its 'spiritual, intellectual and material needs'.[10]

In the old hospital buildings at Acton, Canberra, where the Department of Post-War Reconstruction was located from early 1943 until its abolition in 1946, Coombs had assembled a group of 'brilliant staff'—including one architect, Grenfell ('Gren') Rudduck—who were credited with providing a significant boost to the intellectual life of the city.[11] One of the plans they hatched there involved luring the cream of Australasian scientists and scholars—all of whom were ensconced in prestigious overseas positions—to Canberra to head up the schools, and to become the 'founding fathers' of the proposed national university. In the first instance, they would be invited to become 'Academic Advisers'. Once they became settled in that role—and once the buildings were established in Canberra—they would be asked to move permanently to Canberra as heads of the various research schools. It was firmly believed that if the top positions could be filled with highly respected names, the rest would follow; as Coombs' colleague Alfred Conlon stated, 'never mind about blueprints, pick the men and the rest will look after itself'.[12] Along with Oliphant, who was to head the Research School of Physical Sciences, the names on Coombs' list were the medical scientist Sir Howard Florey for the Research School of Medical Sciences, the historian William ('Keith') Hancock for the Research School of Social Sciences, and the New Zealand-born anthropologist Raymond Firth for the Research School of Pacific Studies.[13] John Dedman, Minister for Post-War Reconstruction, explained to Parliament the importance of bringing these men back to Australia: 'we must leave no stone unturned to secure their services.'[14]

Oliphant left The Savoy that evening in a buoyant mood, leaving those who remained at the table to ponder how they could possibly lure him back to Australia. 'It's going to cost a hell of a lot of money', said Coombs. Chifley wanted to know if Oliphant would really come. Coombs thought there was a good chance he would. Chifley's response was 'you get Oliphant. I'll persuade Cabinet to face up to it.' As usual, Coombs' hunch was correct: Oliphant was

---

10 John Maynard Keynes' seminal work was *The General Theory of Employment, Interest and Money* (London: Macmillan, 1936). 'Reaffirmation of the Aims of CIAM: CIAM 6, Bridgewater', Joan Ockman, ed., *Architecture Culture 1943–1968* (New York: Rizzoli, 1993), 100–1.
11 Jim Gibbney, *Canberra 1913–1953* (Canberra: Australian Government Publishing Service, 1988), 209–10.
12 Foster and Varghese, *The Making of The Australian National University 1946–96*, 22. Conlon was chair of the Australian Army's Directorate of Research and Civil Affairs.
13 Frank Fenner and David Curtis, *The John Curtin School of Medical Research: The First Fifty Years 1949–1998* (Gundaroo, NSW: Brolga Press, 2001), 9.
14 Foster and Varghese, *The Making of The Australian National University 1946–96*, 22.

beginning to see the limitations of an 'old' country like Britain and was realising that the long-term future of the Commonwealth lay in newer countries like Australia, where 'fresh thinking about academic and technological activities' was possible.[15]

Figure 1.1 Coombs and Chifley in front of Palm House at Kew Gardens, London, 1946

Photograph: National Archives of Australia. NAA: M2153, 22/4

Securing Florey, who was then Professor of Pathology at the University of Oxford, was no less a priority. A team headed by Florey and Ernst Chain had successfully

---

15 Cockburn and Ellyard, *Oliphant: The Life and Times of Sir Mark Oliphant*, 145–8.

converted Alexander Fleming's penicillin from a 'laboratory curiosity'[16] into an antibiotic, becoming 'the most significant medical discovery of the twentieth century', and earning Fleming, Florey and Chain a shared Nobel Prize.[17] But Florey had other attributes. On two significant occasions throughout an illustrious career, he demonstrated a commitment to architecture. As President of the Royal Society in London, he persuaded the organisation to move from a long-established location in Burlington House, off Piccadilly, and to refurbish numbers 6–9 Carlton House Terrace, a group of dilapidated grand mansions designed and built by John Nash. Nash was England's foremost architect of the Picturesque movement and its most successful civic designer. Later in life, Florey became Provost (President) of Queen's College, Oxford, and engaged English architect James Stirling, with whom he worked closely, to design new student residences on a site overlooking the River Cherwell in St Clements. While Florey died before the building was completed, it was named after him as a permanent memorial to his contribution. The Florey Building became one of Stirling's best-known works.[18] While Florey remained in Oxford, and was never 'brought back home' on a permanent basis, his role as Academic Adviser for almost a decade was crucial to the development of The Australian National University. Like Florey, Firth could not be persuaded to move to Canberra, and remained an Academic Adviser only.

With the process of securing the founding fathers under way, attention turned to the design of the university campus. Coombs envisaged a grand design— possibly the result of an architectural competition. But the advisers, particularly Oliphant, favoured a more pragmatic approach, believing that the provision of 'simple buildings' in a short time frame was more important than grand statements. They asked the council to appoint an architect immediately and, following the recommendation of a member, Roy ('Pansy') Wright, engaged Brian Lewis, Professor of Architecture at the University of Melbourne, as consulting architect in late 1947. Wright, who knew Lewis through his position as Professor of Physiology at the University of Melbourne, considered him a 'good fellow', and believed that his robust personality and no-nonsense approach would stand him in good stead for confronting the equally forthright Academic Advisers and Interim Council.[19] Others described the Tasmanian-born architect as 'a pugnacious and learned man, accustomed to having his own way', and 'short, red-haired, blunt, quick in repartee and even more aggressive by nature than Oliphant'.[20]

---

16 Fenner and Curtis, *The John Curtin School of Medical Research: The First Fifty Years 1949–1998*, 3.
17 Walter Isaacson, 'Cover notes', Eric Lax, *The Mould in Dr. Florey's Coat: The Story of the Penicillin Miracle* (New York: Henry Holt, 2004).
18 Florey passed away the same day that work was due to start on site. Williams, *Howard Florey: Penicillin and After*, 357–8.
19 Foster and Varghese, *The Making of The Australian National University 1946–96*, 67–9.
20 Geoffrey Serle, *Robin Boyd: A Life* (Melbourne: Melbourne University Press, 1995), 105; Cockburn and Ellyard, *Oliphant: The Life and Times of Sir Mark Oliphant*, 154.

Lewis immediately prepared a master plan, which a majority of the Interim Council approved, and was sent off to London to meet the advisers. But even though the advisers—who were 'known to be tetchy'[21]—had asked to meet him earlier in the year, they were piqued that Lewis apparently arrived without notice. Oliphant did not help by questioning the architect's credentials for the job: 'We were puzzled', he recalled, 'by the fact that Lewis was able to show us no examples of his work beyond some rather conventional housing and some lavatories for the Great Western Railway'.[22] Believing that he had come to discuss 'their' buildings—physics and medicine—Oliphant and Florey were further dismayed to see a site plan for the whole campus instead. And when they cast their eyes over that, they baulked at an eight-storey structure for administration staff. Believing this was too prominent, they proceeded to give Lewis a lesson in university planning. An administration building, they explained, was lower in the university hierarchy, and should be small and efficient. Furthermore, Florey did not want his medical laboratories to be symmetrical with the other buildings on the campus—possibly because that implied some form of equality to which he did not subscribe. The architect and the council were immediately informed that all plans were to be considered 'absolutely tentative' only. But rather than returning to Australia with his tail between his legs, the irrepressible Lewis was cock-a-hoop. The advisers had all shown off to each other, he told Wright, and were 'a bit bloody silly'. He had handled them well, he said, and had gained their confidence—especially by 'saying what sods the Interim Council were'.[23] It would prove to be a massive misjudgment.

During Easter 1948, the Interim Council and Academic Advisers visited Canberra, and met in the Institute of Anatomy building, next to the university site. Lewis attended the meetings and expected to meet the advisers on site to discuss the proposed campus; however, he found himself snubbed, and complained 'they were too busy on other things'. In fact, the advisers did meet on site, as Figure 1.2 shows—they just did not get around to asking him. On his last night in the capital, Lewis was on his way back to his room at the Hotel Canberra when he came across Oliphant, by chance, in the guests' lounge. Oliphant had recently received the Faraday Medal, and was surrounded by a group of eager journalists. Beckoning the architect over, he called out: 'Oh, Professor Lewis, would you give me a set of your plans—not that I'm interested myself, but my wife would be, she did art when she was at school.' 'Certainly, Professor', Lewis replied. 'And perhaps you could let me have a copy of your physics programme for my own wife. She did physics at school, you know.' Lewis went on to suggest that,

---

21 Foster and Varghese, *The Making of The Australian National University 1946–96*, 33.
22 Cockburn and Ellyard, *Oliphant: The Life and Times of Sir Mark Oliphant*, 154.
23 Foster and Varghese, *The Making of The Australian National University 1946–96*, 70.

in regard to the design of Oliphant's house, it might be a good idea for the scientist to find another architect. Oliphant agreed, adding that he might then get a competent one.[24]

Figure 1.2 Oliphant, Hancock and Florey inspect the university site, Easter 1948. Lewis was not invited

Photograph: Oliphant Papers, Barr Smith Library, University of Adelaide.

At the time, Oliphant and his wife, Rosa, were living on a country estate near Barnt Green, in Worcestershire. Covered with ancient oak trees, the five-acre site contained one of the remaining fragments of Arden Forest—the same forest in which Shakespeare's Orlando was said to have courted Rosalind whilst standing up to his knees in summer flowers.[25] When the Oliphants purchased the property in the late 1930s the main residence was beyond repair, so they built a large, two-and-a-half-storey extension to the original gatekeeper's cottage. Named 'Peto' after a family motto—*Altiora peto*: 'I seek higher things'—the first Oliphant House contained many trademarks of modern British architecture of the interwar period: uncompromising, block-like form, flat wall surfaces, brick construction, regular fenestration, steel-framed windows with small cantilevered hoods, a roof terrace with steel pipe handrails, and a flat roof.

---

24 Cockburn and Ellyard, *Oliphant: The Life and Times of Sir Mark Oliphant*, 154.
25 William Shakespeare, *As You Like It* (1599–1600). The references to the forest of Arden and Shakespeare are cited by Cockburn and Ellyard in *Oliphant: The Life and Times of Sir Mark Oliphant*, 71.

Having ostracised Lewis, Oliphant was left to his own devices regarding architectural advice for his Canberra house. During the Easter 1948 visit, he approached Malcolm Moir, of the husband-and-wife architectural firm Moir and Sutherland. Oliphant, Moir and Charles Daley—who was known unofficially as 'the Mayor of Canberra'—visited several potential sites. Eventually they decided on a large, elevated block that was part of Weetangera sheep station, just outside the surveyed limits of the city (now Dryandra Street, in the suburb of O'Connor).[26] The second Oliphant House was a disappointment to all those involved. A very large, conventional brick house with pitched tile roofs—like an over-inflated, interwar suburban bungalow—it appeared to be the outcome of clients who were obsessed with quantity rather than quality. Like her fictitious namesake, Rosa Oliphant was reluctant to leave the pastoral delights of Worcestershire, and 'demanded solid proof of equal benefit' in Canberra. Mark reminded the university of the sacrifices that he and his wife would be making by coming to Canberra, and insisted that they obtain accommodation equivalent to Peto's 40 squares and six bedrooms.[27] The Oliphant House also suffered from severe budget cuts and design revisions, and protracted, long-distance communications between the clients, who remained in England, and Moir in Canberra.[28] Lewis was not impressed with the final result, noting that the main living-room windows 'faced into a raw cutting driven by a bulldozer' into the hillside, while the spectacular views on the other side were enjoyed by 'the main bedroom, the garage and a second toilet'.[29]

According to the Oliphants' daughter, Vivian, the house was too large for the family, and she felt embarrassed 'by its size and relative grandeur' in comparison with the modest homes of her school friends. Canberra was a small community, and the advantages of being a senior university employee did not go unnoticed. Many residents had their names down on a long waiting list for government housing and resented what appeared to be preferential treatment. Speculation was particularly rife about the Oliphant House—a situation that was not helped when the physicist complained to the local press about the poor

---

26 'When Professor Oliphant decided to return to Australia he asked Mr. Malcolm Moir, of Moir and Sutherland which designed the Oliphant House, to find him a quiet spot out in the bush away from the city and, if possible, with a view.' *Australian Home Beautiful* (March 1955): 47. Daley lived in a central location at 20 Balmain Crescent, Acton, but supported Canberra's expansion into new territory. Locals recalled that during Easter 1948 Daley took Oliphant to 'some rather strange places in the landscape'. Cockburn and Ellyard, *Oliphant: The Life and Times of Sir Mark Oliphant*, 155.

27 Advising the university that Peto was worth about £12 000, he felt that a house worth about £10 000 in Canberra would be appropriate. Cockburn and Ellyard, *Oliphant: The Life and Times of Sir Mark Oliphant*, 155.

28 The lowest tender, from Simmie and Company, came in at almost £16 000—more than 50 per cent over budget. The university offered to build the Oliphants a temporary house on the university site, but Rosa interpreted this as an attempt to avoid their obligations, and insisted that the house go ahead. With significant alterations to the documents to reduce costs, the Oliphant House was eventually built. Papers of Malcolm Moir (1903–1971), Manuscript Collection, National Library of Australia, MS 9169, Box 4, 1/55 O'Connor.

29 Cockburn and Ellyard, *Oliphant: The Life and Times of Sir Mark Oliphant*, 155.

standard of houses in O'Connor that he could see from his upstairs bedroom. Arthur Shakespeare, a member of the Advisory Council, spoke out on behalf of those who were uncomfortable with the disparity between some academic staff and the general population, reporting that the university was 'declaring war on the security of the Canberra community, and, through power and opulence, was able to place itself in a position more advantageous than any other authority'.[30] By 1966, the Oliphants, tired of all the fuss—and most probably of the house as well—moved to a smaller house on the other side of Lake Burley Griffin at 37 Colvin Street, Hughes.[31]

The university attempted to provide accommodation on the campus for staff whose 'irregular hours of work and occasional periods of almost constant attendance, demand accommodation near their jobs', and their families. Lewis was instructed to design a series of houses to be built on university land overlooking the proposed lake—a task for which he enlisted the help of his colleague Grounds, who had replaced him as Professor of Architecture at the University of Melbourne when he took on the university consultancy.[32] A range of houses was developed for different categories of staff: the Vice-Chancellor's would be the largest, followed by a 'Type A' for senior staff, a 'Type D' for the Registrar, a 'Type E' for non-senior staff, right down to the smallest: a single-storey 'Type B' for 'other staff'.[33]

Following protracted discussions and some conflict between Lewis, the university and the National Capital Planning and Development Committee, it was eventually decided that a cluster of five, Lewis-designed 'Type F' staff cottages would be built. These linear, single-storey houses were arranged in two parallel rows that followed the natural contours of the site in order to provide views of the proposed lake.

Lewis also designed a residence for the ANU Vice-Chancellor, Sir Douglas Copland, and his wife, Lady Copland, on a site in Balmain Crescent, accessed via Mills Road. Lewis worked closely with Lady Copland on the design, and in May 1951 asked Canberra-based architect Ken Oliphant to assist with the preparation of specifications and site supervision.[34]

---

30 Gibbney, *Canberra 1913–1953*, 261.
31 Australian Commonwealth Electoral Roll, 1966.
32 *Architecture* (April 1950): 45. The collaboration is also mentioned by Conrad Hamann in Modern Architecture in Melbourne: The Architecture of Grounds, Romberg and Boyd, 1927–1971 (PhD dissertation, Visual Arts Department, Monash University, 1978), 2.1, 43.
33 Lewis to Acting Registrar, ANU, 16 March 1949, ANU Archives, University Records, ANUA 53, Correspondence files, Box 469, 12.1.2.9 (1).
34 In 1950 Lewis designed a large house for the Coplands on a site in McCoy Crescent, opposite the Institute of Anatomy building. Budget considerations, however, forced him to design a smaller residence for an alternative site in Balmain Crescent.

But with Lewis having lost the confidence of Mark Oliphant and Florey—as well as key figures in the university administration—his role in the design of the Research School of Physical Sciences and the Research School of Medical Sciences (by then known as the John Curtin School of Medical Research) was diminished. Florey was adamant from the outset that the John Curtin School was to be designed by himself and his scientist colleagues, with some assistance from an English architect with whom he was acquainted.[35] Lewis, the university's appointed architect, found himself relegated to documenting the external shell and having no real involvement with the design of the exterior or interior. When this situation became known in Canberra, everyone involved—from Lewis to members of the Building and Grounds Committee—was outraged.[36] Florey's steely response, from Oxford, left no doubt as to how he viewed the increasingly isolated architect's position:

> The architect must be entirely subordinated to the scientific requirements of those who are to inhabit [the building]. As Professor Lewis has had no previous experience of constructing laboratories he may not be aware of this point of view. When this initial plan is received I will arrange to have it seen by those in this country with recent experience of building laboratories (scientists not architects!).[37]

Having just appointed the first three medical professors for the John Curtin School, Florey invited them to Oxford to discuss the proposed building. In 1949, Arnold ('Hugh') Ennor, Professor of Biochemistry,[38] Adrien Albert, Professor of Medical Chemistry, and Frank Fenner, Professor of Microbiology, met Florey and his associate, Gordon Sanders, to discuss the layout. Influenced by new laboratories at the British National Institute of Medical Research at Mill Hill, they sketched a 'H'-shaped plan. Inside each parallel wing were south-facing laboratories and service rooms on either side of a central corridor, while the connecting link contained shared facilities such as administration, a library and lecture theatres.[39] Lewis was not invited to the discussions, nor was he consulted; the first he heard about the layout was when Sanders travelled to Melbourne and presented it to him later that year. Lewis wrote to Copland, explaining his concerns that 'no step taken now will hinder it from being a building of world

---

35   By early 1948, Florey decided that he was not happy with the architectural advice he was receiving from Australia, and asked Stephen Welsh, an English architect and Professor of Architecture at Sheffield, to design the medical school in collaboration with the Academic Advisers. This effectively relegated Lewis to the status of documentation architect. Williams, *Howard Florey: Penicillin and After*, 251–2.

36   Lewis was furious, especially when he realised that Welsh's fees were to be deducted from his own. He fired back a hostile response, claiming that Welsh had been 'unethical' and 'impertinent'. He threatened to take the matter to the RIBA and the RAIA, and to resign if the university did not retract. Ibid., 251.

37   Florey to Copland, in ibid., 251–2.

38   While Florey instigated planning of the medical school, it was Ennor, more than any other person, who was responsible for its development into a world-class research centre. He was knighted in 1965.

39   Foster and Varghese, *The Making of The Australian National University 1946–96*, 74; Williams, *Howard Florey: Penicillin and After*, 252–3.

importance', and of the dangers of rushing into an 'ill considered scheme'. He believed that the only way to avoid this was to establish 'personal consultation between the Architect and the Scientists involved'—the very opposite approach to that taken by Florey and his colleagues.[40]

When Sanders visited Lewis's Melbourne office again the following year, he reported back to Florey that 'only one man' was working on the project; this signalled Lewis's denouement.[41] By 1953 his position was untenable, and, 'given a hefty push', he resigned as architect for the John Curtin School of Medical Research building.[42]

In 1957 Hancock requested that a house be built for himself and his family near the existing 'Type F' cottages. The university engaged Max Collard, of Max Collard and Guy Clarke in Sydney—who were architects for the ANU Rock Mechanics Laboratory in Rivett Road—to design it.[43] When Denis Winston—who had replaced Lewis as the university planner—attempted to change the orientation of the house, Hancock, who obviously understood the benefits of a north-facing house, confirmed his preference for the house to run 'due east and west'. His only other concern was for some form of fencing to prevent horses from eating his shrubs.[44] The Hancocks lived in this house for a short time before moving to Campbell.

Lewis battled on designing Oliphant's Research School of Physical Sciences building (later known as 'The Cockroft Building'), despite Oliphant's constant jibing that he was over-designing his laboratories by 'building a palace' when he wanted a shed, and accusations that he was amending drawings without consulting him.[45] Lewis did, however, remain design architect for one university building that neither Oliphant nor Florey had much influence over: University House. An attempt to introduce 'gracious living' to the campus, University House was largely Hancock's idea, but was supported by his fellow advisers because they believed it would make Canberra a more tolerable destination for themselves and their wives. Initially referred to as a 'faculty club', it was based on traditional Oxford and Cambridge colleges. The main functions of University House were to accommodate single university staff members (Albert, a bachelor, lived at University House), researchers and visitors, and to provide

---

40   Lewis to Copland, 21 July 1948, ANUA 53, Correspondence files, Box 469, 12.1.2.9 (1).
41   Fenner and Curtis, *The John Curtin School of Medical Research: The First Fifty Years 1949–1998*, 16; Williams, *Howard Florey: Penicillin and After*, 257.
42   Fenner and Curtis, *The John Curtin School of Medical Research: The First Fifty Years 1949–1998*, 16; Foster and Varghese, *The Making of The Australian National University 1946–96*, 74.
43   The Rock Mechanics Laboratory was completed in 1959. Collard, Clarke and Jackson designed the Research School of Earth Sciences in Mills Road, Acton, in 1959 and 1964, and collaborated with J. Scarborough and Partners on the R. G. Menzies Library building.
44   Extract from minutes of ANU Building and Grounds Committee, 11 September 1957; Hancock to Registrar, 25 September 1957, ANUA 53, Correspondence files, Box 980, 12.1.2.131 (1).
45   Cockburn and Ellyard, *Oliphant: The Life and Times of Sir Mark Oliphant*, 162.

a variety of formal and informal spaces for dining, meeting and study. As the centre of academic social life and the most frequented building on campus, it was to be a showcase of contemporary Australian art and design, demonstrating that while the university maintained Oxbridge traditions, it also supported contemporary Australian culture.[46] Melbourne-based designer Fred Ward—whose furniture design Boyd had praised in *Victorian Modern* in 1947[47]—was commissioned to design furniture and fittings in local timbers, and Australian paintings were hung on the walls. Lewis had recruited Ward to teach interior design in the Architecture Department at the University of Melbourne, and his design approach—a restrained, modernist interpretation of the English Arts and Crafts style, underscored by a sound knowledge of Australian timbers and construction methods—was the perfect match for his own architecture. University House was Lewis's most successful building in Canberra, earning him a Sulman Medal in 1953.

Figure 1.3 University House, The Australian National University, 1954

Photograph: National Archives of Australia. NAA: A1200, L17793

---

46 Foster and Varghese, *The Making of The Australian National University 1946–96*, 71–3.
47 Robin Boyd, 'Frederick Ward and the Raspberry Jam', *Victorian Modern: One Hundred Years of Modern Architecture in Victoria, Australia* (Melbourne: Architectural Students' Society of the Royal Victorian Institute of Architects, July 1947), 20, 45. The handles of a cabinet designed by Ward were made from raspberry jam wood, which smells like raspberry jam when being worked.

Ward moved to Canberra as head of the ANU Design Unit in 1952, and designed some 4000 furniture items, as well as fittings and accessories, for Canberra buildings over the next eight years. His work was incorporated in the John Curtin School of Medical Research, the Australian Academy of Science and the National Library of Australia. Ward's elegant and reductive designs were skilfully interpreted by a generation of European master-craftsmen and cabinet-makers who arrived in Canberra via the Snowy Mountains Hydro-Electric Scheme. Many of them went on to produce refined timber tables and chairs that graced the capital's best modern interiors. One, Oswald Paseka, commissioned an architect to design his hillside O'Connor house.[48]

In the 1950s, Ward's wife, Elinor ('Puss'), wrote a number of articles on architecture and design in Canberra for *Australian Home Beautiful*, becoming an unofficial publicist for the developing national capital. A March 1955 article claimed that Canberra was no longer a 'government town', dominated by politicians and bureaucrats, but that other, 'vital influences' had appeared. The reasons for this shift were due to the CSIRO, which had added a 'large body of scientists and their families', and The Australian National University, which had 'brought in more people of varied and exciting interests'.[49]

All of these new residents needed somewhere to live. While the procurement process for the Oliphant House had been highly unorthodox, the medical professors' houses were a truer reflection of the conditions under which the university appointed senior academics, and the way in which they set up residence in Canberra. At the time, these were circumstances that were not only superior to those enjoyed by other Canberra residents, but were also better than those offered by other Australian universities.[50] To build a university in a country town containing a small number of existing residences, it was essential to offer incentives to prospective employees. For this reason, the Department of the Interior provided professors with a temporary house upon arrival and a block of land upon which to build a house. They had some choice regarding the building site, which was granted at a nominal lease, on the condition that they commenced construction of their house within six months.

---

48   Oswald Paseka built a house at 15 Yapunyah Street, O'Connor, designed by Rudi Krastins. Ann Whitelaw, 'An Open Plan on Sloping Block', *The Canberra Times* (10 February 1970). Other craftsmen who worked with Ward at The Australian National University included Heinz Frank, Kees Westra, Conrad Tobler and Alphonse Stuetz. The architect Derek Wrigley also worked in the Design Unit. Derek Wrigley, 'The ANU Years', in *Fred Ward: A Selection of Furniture and Drawings, Drill Hall Gallery: 2 May – 16 June 1996* (Canberra: Drill Hall Gallery, 1996).
49   These articles in *Australian Home Beautiful* included 'Changing City of Trees and Sunshine' (March 1955): 37–9; 'The House They Wouldn't Alter' (August 1957): 15–19; and 'Look—No Backyards!' (August 1958): 26–9. Canberra had been promoted as the Australian centre of scientific research as far back as 1947. *Australia: The Official Handbook* (Melbourne: Speciality Press, 1947).
50   Fenner and Curtis, *The John Curtin School of Medical Research: The First Fifty Years 1949–1998*, 12.

The fourth medical professor appointed by Florey, John ('Jack') Eccles, Professor of Physiology, insisted that the Department of the Interior provide him with a block of land commensurate with his academic standing and family size. It was to contain a house, 'a square dance lawn, a swimming pool and a tennis court' for his wife, Irene ('Rene'), and their nine children. Eccles described the process by which he acquired a large site at 28 Monaro Crescent, Red Hill:

> One had to select a suitable block of land and then have a house built on it. I had officials of the ANU helping me and eventually on October 9th I selected a very large block of land in a very good site adjacent to the Embassy area. The government owned all the land and one had to make a nominal deposit and then pay a rental of £18 a year which I did on 9th October 1950 for a 99 year lease.

The neurophysiologist did not, however, avail himself of the services of a design architect, preferring to design the house himself and engage Tom Haseler, a Commonwealth Department of Works architect who had supervised University House, to complete the documentation and engage a builder.[51] While Eccles was proud of his efforts as an amateur architect, his daughter Mary thought otherwise: 'He might have been a brilliant scientist, but he was no architect. The house, with its two long dark passages at right angles to each other, was not the best design for living.'[52]

After considering one of Lewis's standard houses for senior staff, Eccles' neighbour Hugh Ennor engaged Robert Warren of Hocking and Warren to design a one-off house at 3 Vancouver Street, Red Hill.[53] Like his client, Warren had just moved from Melbourne, and anticipated great opportunities for architecture and building in the rapidly developing capital city. The Ennor House was built by Austrian immigrant Karl Schreiner. Schreiner had built the Hancock House and both the temporary and the permanent John Curtin School buildings, and his furniture had been featured in the Wards' article on local design.[54] The Wards described the Ennor House as typifying a 'new kind of architecture' that was appearing in Canberra in the 1950s—one that formed a complete break from previous styles.[55]

---

51   John Eccles, Papers of John Eccles (1911–1997) (manuscript), National Library of Australia, MS 9330, Folder 1, 164. The Eccles House was demolished for Enrico Taglietti's 1976 Apostolic Nunciature.
52   Mary Mennis, *The Book of Eccles: A Portrait of Sir John Eccles, Australian Nobel Laureate and Scientist, 1903–1997* (Queensland: Lalong, 2003), 150.
53   Lewis to Robert ('Bob') Osborne, ANU Registrar, 8 November 1948, ANUA 53, Correspondence files, Box 469, 12.1.2.9 (1).
54   Schreiner arrived in Canberra in 1949 and built up a successful construction business based in Lonsdale Street, Braddon, with a factory in Cotter Road. He later returned to his native Austria. Gibbney, *Canberra 1913–1953*, 240.
55   *Australian Home Beautiful* (March 1955): 55–9.

1. Age of the Masters: Establishing a scientific and intellectual community in Canberra, 1946–1968

Figure 1.4 The four medical professors—Eccles, Albert, Fenner and Ennor—study plans for the John Curtin School of Medical Research, Canberra, August 1950

Photograph: Australian News and Information Bureau, The Australian National University Collection

Another close neighbour was Fenner. When it came to choosing an architect, his decision was a direct result of the feud between Lewis and Oliphant. After looking at existing houses in Canberra and seeing nothing to his liking, Fenner asked Lewis if he could recommend an architect. With an oblique reference to the Oliphant House, which he obviously regarded as a failure, Lewis's blunt response was that there were 'two excellent architects in Melbourne—Roy Grounds and Robin Boyd—and none in Canberra'.[56] He distinguished between Grounds and Boyd by saying that 'if you choose Roy Grounds, he'll build you a nice house, but you'll live in the house that he designed. If you choose Robin Boyd he'll build you a nice house, but you'll live in the house that he designed *for you*. He will follow your wishes.' Based on this advice, Fenner contacted Boyd.[57]

On 29 September 1949, another future Boyd client left the comforts of Melbourne to begin a new life in the national capital. Although this event was not particularly significant in itself, the repercussions would have a major

---
56 Serle, *Robin Boyd: A Life*, 133.
57 Frank Fenner, Interview by the author, 18 October 2007. Serle's account of Fenner's recollection is essentially the same: 'the client would have to live in whatever house Grounds built, whereas Boyd would build a house that incorporated the wishes of the client.' Serle, *Robin Boyd: A Life*, 133.

impact on Australian historiography. When Australian historian Manning Clark left coastal Melbourne for the inland high country of the national capital to become foundation Professor of History at Canberra University College (later incorporated into The Australian National University), he was seen to be leaving behind outmoded ideals and practices and making a fresh start.

Manning and his wife, Dymphna, initially bought a large site at the foot of Red Hill, intending to build a house 'facing the blue hills behind Canberra'. But Manning became concerned that it was completely 'naked', stranded on the 'outskirts' of the city, and near an 'ugly rash of suburbia'. Fortunately, when Eccles arrived, a department official asked the Clarks if they wanted to exchange this large site, which would suit Eccles perfectly, for a smaller one, closer in. Manning and Dymphna inspected a site at 11 Tasmania Circle, Forrest, and immediately accepted the offer.

In 1952, Dymphna—to 'cheer' her husband up as he recovered from rheumatic fever—suggested to Manning that they engage Boyd to design a house for their new site. Boyd, whom they both knew from Melbourne, was reflecting on the nation's history of domestic architecture for *Australia's Home*,[58] and he travelled to Canberra to meet his clients. Discussing details of the interiors with Dymphna, Boyd proposed a 'dark soft red' for the living-room ceiling and as much natural light as possible. His client, however, opted for 'galah pink', and expressed concerns about large expanses of glass. Afterwards, as Boyd was rushing to catch his plane back to Melbourne, Manning called out to him: 'Is the house going to be single storey with my study in the basement?' Boyd paused, and shouted back: 'Single storey with the study upstairs.'[59] And so what began as an afterthought became Clark's celebrated rooftop study, accessible only by ladder, perched like a tree-house over the central link in the binuclear plan. In the week that the builders were finishing the house, Australian poet Alec Hope stood with Manning in the study, looked out of the windows towards Mount Ainslie and Black Mountain, and said 'I see books being written here'.[60] And he was right. It was there, as the suburb of Forrest was built around him, that Clark wrote his six consecutive volumes of *A History of Australia*.[61] The impact of this work on the national consciousness was so profound that, for a significant time

---

58 Robin Boyd, *Australia's Home: Its Origins, Builders and Occupiers* (Melbourne: Melbourne University Press, 1952).
59 Papers of Manning Clark (1907–1992), Manuscript Collection, National Library of Australia, MS 7550, Box 27, Folder 223, 'Houses 1949–53', Robin Boyd to Dymphna Clark, 19 April 1952 and 2 July 1953, and Dymphna interviewed in *Australian Home Journal* (September 1973). My thanks to Mark McKenna for these sources. Similar descriptions of the conversation between Boyd and Clark were described by Serle in *Robin Boyd: A Life*, 132, and by Peter Freeman in 'Manning Clark House: An Architect's View', in Trevor Creighton, Peter Freeman and Roslyn Russell, *Manning Clark House Reflections* (Canberra: Manning Clark House, 2002), 36.
60 Creighton, Freeman and Russell, *Manning Clark House Reflections*, 37.
61 C. M. H. Clark, *A History of Australia* (Carlton, Vic.: Melbourne University Press, 1962).

afterwards, it was as if no previous Australian history existed.[62] Manning Clark House is now administered under a family trust for the purposes of scholarly and cultural pursuits.

The last of the ANU founding professors was known as 'the father of the contraceptive pill'. While researching hormones for fighter pilots during World War II, Arthur Birch, Professor of Organic Chemistry at the University of Sydney, experimented with the manufacture of male hormones through a synthetic process, and by 1950 was able to prepare analogues of natural steroid hormones. The process he invented, but never patented—'Birch Reduction'—became universal practice in modern synthetic organic chemistry, and paved the way for others to manufacture oral contraceptives in the 1960s.[63] In the late 1950s, when the idea of a research school of chemistry was raised, Ennor made it his priority to recruit Birch. But his quarry, by then established in Manchester, had reservations about moving to Canberra, and was hesitant to commit. After a lengthy period of negotiation, Birch issued an ultimatum to the university: he would come if he was paid a certain amount, was made head of school and could obtain a 'decent house'. Sydney-based architects Bunning and Madden, who were then working on the Haydon-Allen Building for the Faculty of Arts and the National Library of Australia, were engaged to design the Birch House. Sydney University-trained Noel Potter, who had moved to Canberra with Bunning and Madden in 1962 to oversee the library, was appointed design architect.[64]

Arthur and his wife, Jessie, travelled to Canberra to meet Potter and to inspect five alternative sites offered by the commission (all of which had been set aside for diplomatic purposes). The site that was agreed upon—a private battleaxe block on the crest of a low rise at 3 Arkana Street, Yarralumla—was chosen because of the magnificent views it provided of the Brindabella Ranges. Arthur was so impressed that he shot an 8 mm film of the site to show his children when he arrived back in England. He and Jessie discussed the design with Potter. Arthur liked the concept of an 'Australian house with verandahs all around'. Jessie suggested that the verandahs might face inwards, similar to the 'flat-roofed, white-painted, Spanish-style haciendas' they had admired in California and Mexico. Based on these discussions, Potter designed a rectangular, single-level house enclosing a central courtyard with swimming pool. With large expanses of glazing, the house was very open in character: panoramic views of the Brindabellas were obtained from the entire living areas, most rooms looked

---

62 This view was identified, and then questioned, by Stuart Macintyre in his Trevor Reese Memorial Lecture of 28 April 1992 titled 'History, the University and the Nation', Sir Robert Menzies Centre for Australian Studies, Institute of Commonwealth Studies, University of London. The belief that no previous Australian history existed would not have been shared by Hancock, who wrote *Australia* (London: Ernest Benn, 1930).
63 'Chemist Had a Thirst for Research', [Arthur Birch obituary], *The Australian* (19 December 1995); 'A Medal for the Birch Reduction', *The Canberra Times* (21 December 1972).
64 Noel Potter, Interview by Margaret Park, National Library of Australia, 16 August 2004.

into the internal courtyard, and a clear sightline was maintained from the front door right through the centre of the building to the landscape beyond.[65] When the family relocated to Canberra, Jessie was a frequent visitor to the building site and was involved in the selection of finishes, fittings and furniture.

Figure 1.5 Birch House, central courtyard with swimming pool

Photograph: Max Dupain, 1968. Max Dupain & Associates Archives

Arthur Birch was also involved with planning the new building for the Research School of Chemistry, which was designed by Victorian architects Eggleston, Macdonald and Secomb. Birch proudly described it as a 'beautiful, simple, scientific building'—one that was 'technically and aesthetically the best in the University'.[66] With his laboratories and house finalised, he was installed as foundation Dean of the University's fifth research school, the Research School of Chemistry, in 1967.[67] The Birch House was awarded the C. S. Daley Award

---

65 Potter claimed that the openness of the design was influenced by an earlier house he had designed in Lightning Ridge, NSW, for Patricia Waterford. He described this precursor as 'a slab on the ground, every room opened out, little courtyards. Every room you either had a courtyard or a garden you just walk through. Open plan and tiles all throughout.' Ibid.
66 'A Medal for the Birch Reduction', *The Canberra Times*.
67 Foster and Varghese, *The Making of The Australian National University 1946–96*, 120, 229–31.

(named after Charles Daley) for domestic architecture in Canberra by the Royal Australian Institute of Architects in 1968, was featured in *The Australian Women's Weekly* and *Australian House and Garden* in 1969,[68] and became a well-known venue for social functions in the capital city. When the Birch children had grown up and left home, the house was sold to the architect Romaldo ('Aldo') Giurgola, the designer of Australia's Parliament House. Potter was delighted when Giurgola phoned him to say 'it was the best house he ever lived in'.[69]

The Reformation of the Council for Scientific and Industrial Research

[T]he great surge in the popularity of scientific education in the post-war era was…propelled…by the hope that scientific rationality would be able to fashion a new world order.

— Boris Schedvin[70]

At the second Annual General Meeting of the Australian Academy of Science, held in temporary premises at The Australian National University from 26 to 28 April 1956, the Treasurer, Hedley Marston, placed an architectural sketch on the table. Marston wanted the academy to build a national headquarters in Canberra, and had, along with Eccles, been given the task of finding a suitable architect. The sketch he presented to the other fellows had been prepared by an architect friend in Adelaide, and depicted a classical-styled structure with columns. Also attending the meeting were Oliphant, President of the Academy, Otto Frankel, Vice-President and Head of the Division of Plant Industry at the CSIRO, and John Nicholson, Secretary for Biological Sciences.

Frankel was the first to react. He was appalled by the proposal, believing it to be 'the kind of building that an Academy might have selected some 50 years ago'. Concerned that such a regressive style of architecture might become accepted as a 'pattern for the building', he vetoed it and initiated the appointment of a design committee.[71] Unbeknownst to the others, Frankel had already approached Oscar Bayne, a Melbourne architect who later worked for Grounds, to ask his opinion

---

68 Ron Berg, 'Canberra House Wins Design Award', *The Australian Women's Weekly* (23 April 1969): 70–2; 'Contemporary Canberra, A Winner all the Way', *Australian House and Garden* (August 1969): 36–7, 78–9.
69 Noel Potter, Interview by Margaret Park.
70 Boris Schedvin, *Shaping Science and Industry: A History of Australia's Council for Scientific and Industrial Research, 1926–49* (North Sydney: Allen & Unwin, 1987), 287.
71 Otto Frankel, 'A Personal Memoir on the History of the Design of the Australian Academy of Science Building', 16 September 1970, Frankel, Sir O. H., FAA (1900–2007), Manuscript Collection, Adolph Basser Library, Australian Academy of Science, MS 106, Box 13, Item C, 2.

about a suitable architect for the academy building. Bayne had accompanied Grounds and Geoffrey Mewton on an overseas trip between 1928 and 1933, and was well connected in Melbourne circles.[72]

Frankel had explained to Bayne that it was important to avoid 'the safe and conventional' route, and how he wanted to engage an architect who was 'modern in outlook', but whose competence could not be questioned. He wondered if Walter Gropius, founder of the Bauhaus School, would be suitable. Bayne replied that it was essential to employ an Australian architect—'it is Australia's job to do its best and let it stand or fall on that'—and provided Frankel with a list of prospective firms.[73] It was decided to hold a limited design competition and to invite those on Bayne's list to submit a proposal. When news of this came out, Frankel was confronted by Race Godfrey, President of the Royal Australian Institute of Architects, who claimed that the terms of the competition had to be in accordance with the institute's rules. But Frankel would not have a bar of it: he wanted scientists to be in control and was not about to be dictated to by architects. If the Institute of Architects took over, decision making would be removed from the scientists and placed in the hands of an external assessor. Frankel discussed with Oliphant the idea of having one architect sit alongside the scientists on the committee in an advisory capacity, as a form of adjudicator in case they got stuck on some technical matter. Fearful of receiving conservative advice from an unknown quantity—such as Godfrey—they asked Bayne if he would fulfil that role.[74]

For a fee of £50 to appease the institute, Bayne attended the one and only meeting of the Building Design Committee, held in Marston's library in Adelaide on 1 December 1956. By this time another entry had appeared on the scene: Warren, having heard that no Canberra architect had been invited, had complained to the academy and been given permission to submit a proposal.[75] Oliphant—who deferred to Frankel's better judgment when it came to matters of architectural aesthetics—asked Frankel to take the chair, and six design proposals were

---

72 Phillip Goad, The Modern House in Melbourne 1945–1975 (PhD dissertation, University of Melbourne, 1992), part 1, 30.
73 Bayne to Frankel, 17 May 1956, Frankel, Sir O. H., FAA (1900–2007), 13/C. Gropius had also been mentioned by Moir as a possible architect for University House. See Jill Waterhouse, *University House As They Experienced It: A History 1954–2004* (Canberra: The Australian National University, 2004), 26.
74 Bayne was a highly influential figure. Some time later, he was asked to advise on a list of suitable architects for the Victorian Arts Centre, for which Grounds was eventually selected. Vicki Fairfax, *A Place Across the River: They Aspired to Create the Victorian Arts Centre* (Victoria: Macmillan, 2000), 63.
75 Warren's design was a rectangular building with various elements cut in, or added, to the overall form: a fan-shaped entry on the Gordon Street side, an auditorium perched like a landed spacecraft on the roof, and a raised volume at the western end for accommodating visiting scientists. AAS Collection, Basser Library, MC 4, Items 10, 11, 12.

considered. Of these, the committee voted unanimously in favour of the dome-shaped proposal by Grounds, Romberg and Boyd, who were selected as architects for the Australian Academy of Science building.[76]

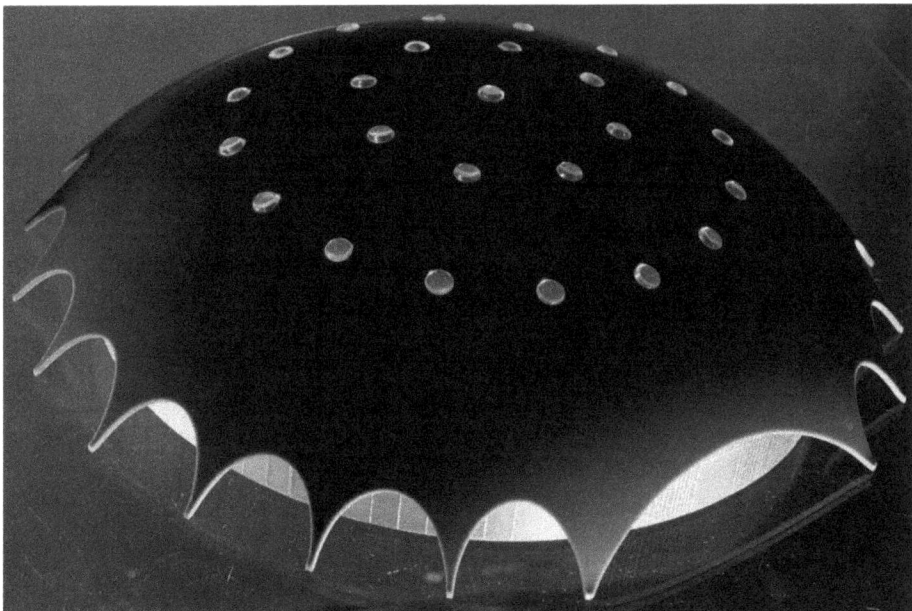

Figure 1.6 Model of the Australian Academy of Science, Canberra

Photograph: Wolfgang Sievers, 1963. National Library of Australia. nla.pic-vn4474852

Frankel looked back upon this process as 'an adventure'. The committee, he recalled, was an 'active and highly argumentative body' whose members all contributed ideas and criticisms. He believed that the success of the completed building was due to a combination of Oliphant's obsession with quality of material and services and his own concern with architectural design. Grounds' contribution was an amalgam of 'imaginative initiative, resilience, and, at times, tolerance', and he believed that all those involved, including the architect, were 'richer for the experience'.[77] The academy building, for which the architects won a Sulman Medal in 1959, was an unqualified success. Frankel described how it 'helped to generate a corporate consciousness and, thanks to its architectural distinction, it enhanced a growing pride in the Academy. For the

---

76 The submissions were by Borland, McIntyre & Murphy, Powell, Mansfield and Maclurcan, Grounds, Romberg & Boyd, Hassell and McConnell, Mockridge, Stahl & Mitchell, and Robert G. Warren. 'The Academy Building', Frankel, Sir O. H., FAA (1900–2007), Box 13, Item D, 3. For an account of the design submissions, see Philip Goad, 'Shells, Spires and a Dome, Science and Spirit in the Space Age', in Ann Stephen, Philip Goad and Andrew McNamara, *Modern Times: The Untold Story of Modernism in Australia* (Melbourne: Miegunyah Press, 2008), 134–41.
77 Otto Frankel, 'A Personal Memoir on the History of the Design of the Australian Academy of Science Building', 16 September 1970, Frankel, Sir O. H., FAA (1900–2007), Box 13, Item C, 5–6.

public it became a symbol of Australian science.' Philip Goad described it as 'Canberra's, and Australia's, first public building of national significance since World War II', and ventured to add that it signified a turning point beyond which modernist ideals began to gain acceptance.[78]

Given Frankel's background, it is no surprise that he played such a key role in the Academy of Science building. A charismatic, idealistic, but sometimes brusque man, he held strong convictions about a range of issues. One colleague described him as a 'geneticist by training, plant breeder by occupation, cytologist by inclination, and genetic conservationist by acclaim'.[79] What he failed to mention was the scientist's extraordinary contribution to the promotion and cultivation of modern architecture: it was Frankel, more than any other individual, who was responsible for creating what will be demonstrated to be an 'architectural culture' within the CSIRO during the 1950s and 1960s.

So where did Frankel's passion for architecture come from? Born into a well-off family in Vienna in 1900, he studied at universities in Munich, Vienna and Giessen. An idealistic trait was evident from an early stage: Frankel withdrew from chemistry and enrolled in agriculture because he saw that as a better way to fight world hunger. Sometimes his strong convictions led to trouble: as a student in Vienna after World War I, he was a committed communist, and on one occasion was arrested for addressing a street gathering. This readiness to stand up for what he believed in remained with him throughout his career: at the age of eighty-nine, he was photographed at a Canberra rally protesting against government cutbacks to science budgets.[80]

In Berlin, Frankel gained a doctorate for a study of genetic linkage and married a German woman, Mathilde ('Tilli') Donsbach. He worked as a plant breeder on a private estate near Vienna and gained work experience in Palestine and England, before accepting a position as a geneticist in Christchurch, New Zealand, with the Wheat Research Institute. Frankel immersed himself in his work and in the many outdoor activities offered by New Zealand's South Island—including tramping, camping and fly-fishing. A pioneer skier in Canterbury, he helped to establish the Christchurch Ski Club and facilities at Arthur's Pass, and regularly competed in events throughout the South Island. But he always felt like a foreigner in Christchurch, stating that he was only really accepted in the ski huts.

---

78   Otto Frankel, quoted by Lloyd Evans, 'Otto Herzberg Frankel 4 November 1900—Elected FRS 1953', Frankel, Sir O. H., FAA (1900–2007), MS 106, Box 12, Item A, 54; Philip Goad, in Ann Stephen, Andrew McNamara, Philip Goad, *Modernism & Australia: Documents on Art, Design and Architecture 1917–1967* (Melbourne: Miegunyah Press, 2006), 899–901.
79   Lloyd Evans, quoted in Brad Collis, *Fields of Discovery: Australia's CSIRO* (Crows Nest, NSW: Allen & Unwin, 2002), 205–6.
80   Ibid., 205–6.

1. Age of the Masters: Establishing a scientific and intellectual community in Canberra, 1946–1968

Figure 1.7 'Margaret and Otto Honeymoon, 1940, Lake Wanaka, New Zealand'

Photograph: Manuscript Collection, Adolph Basser Library, Australian Academy of Science. Frankel, Sir O. H., FAA (1900–2007), MS 106, Box 13

In 1937 Frankel divorced Tilli, and two years later married Margaret Anderson, a Christchurch artist and art teacher with whom he had conducted a secret affair for eight years—a very unusual practice in conservative, 1930s New Zealand.[81] A painter and potter, Margaret had studied art in New Zealand and had lived in Paris. With a group of artists and writers including Cora Wilding,

---

81 Margaret Evans, Speech given on the occasion of Margaret Frankel's eightieth birthday, 8 October 1982, Frankel, Sir O. H., FAA (1900–2007), Box 12, Item B. Otto met Margaret when she and some friends asked Tilli about German lessons. Even though she and Otto were living apart, Tilli would not agree to a divorce, so Otto and Margaret virtually lived together for nine years. In 'discrete, NZ—Ch-Ch style'; however, during this time Margaret always returned home for breakfast. Lloyd Evans, Handwritten notes, 'Otto', Frankel, Sir O. H., FAA (1900–2007), Box 15, Item F, 202.

Dame Ngaio Marsh, Edith Wall, Evelyn ('Eve') Page and Viola McMillan Brown, she formed The Group, a breakaway from the conservative local arts society. Margaret and Page painted each other naked in the Port Hills, and arranged their own exhibitions.[82] The Frankels were regular visitors to Waitahuna, the Pages' homestead at Governor's Bay, which became a mecca for many of New Zealand's most prominent creative minds. Guests, who included the painter Toss Woollaston and the poet Denis Glover, were served culinary delights such as beef cooked according to a Virginia Woolf recipe. The Frankels became key figures in the Christchurch artistic and cultural world, associating with other progressive thinkers such as university academics, musicians, skiers and artists.[83] With Margaret's parents, they established the Risingholme Community Centre on the Anderson family estate (later known as Risingholme Park) in Opawa.

Figure 1.8 'Otto's two wives Margaret Anderson and Tillie Donsbach in the Port Hills'

Photograph: Manuscript Collection, Adolph Basser Library, Australian Academy of Science. Frankel, Sir O. H., FAA (1900–2007), MS 106, Box 13

---

82 Margaret Evans, Speech given at Margaret Frankel's funeral, 11 December 1997, Frankel, Sir O. H., FAA (1900–2007), Box 12, Item B. 'When Margaret F. described how she & Eve Page painted one another nude in a valley near Ch.Ch., Otto boasted "I soon cured her of her lesbian tendencies."' Lloyd Evans, 'Otto 31.10.84', Handwritten note, Frankel, Sir O. H., FAA (1900–2007), Box 15, Item E, 167.
83 Lloyd Evans, 'Otto Herzberg Frankel 4 November 1900—Elected FRS 1953'. The painter Toss (later Sir) Woollaston was among their Christchurch friends from that period. In later years, Otto and Margaret gifted two of his paintings to the National Gallery of Australia. Glover and the Virginia Woolf recipe are mentioned by Glenys Bowman in 'A Page of NZ Artistic History', *New Zealand Woman's Weekly* (23 February 1987): 35.

In the same year that he married Margaret, Otto made another commitment—one that would alter the trajectory of twentieth-century New Zealand architecture. From 1937 to 1939, he was secretary of a committee that assisted Jewish refugees to immigrate to New Zealand. Frankel and the chair of the committee, Karl Popper (who had attended the same school as Frankel in Vienna, in a class with his younger brother, Paul), favoured the importation of intellectuals. The New Zealand Government, however, believed there were already enough of those types in the country, and preferred migrants with more practical skills. After managing to bring in a number of Jewish intellectuals 'under the guise of cabinetmakers and pastrycooks', Frankel must have thought that Ernst Plischke, the young Viennese modernist architect whose immigration he sponsored in May 1939, offered the best of both worlds.[84] Frankel's connection to Plischke had been established through his brother, Theo, who had commissioned the architect to design his house in Vienna.[85] Plischke had all the right credentials: he had studied in Peter Behrens' Master School at the Vienna Academy—where his final project in 1926 had been an academy of science building—had worked in Behrens' office, and was regarded as a leader of the European modern movement.[86] In New Zealand, he settled in Wellington, where he worked for the Housing Department from 1939 to 1947. He then went into private practice with Cedric Firth—who, coincidentally, was the brother of Raymond, the ANU Academic Adviser for the Research School of Pacific Studies.[87] Over the next two decades, Plischke became the architect of choice for Wellington's intellectual and artistic elite, and one of New Zealand's most important practitioners.

Frankel's contribution to Plischke's antipodean career was significant: he not only assisted the architect's passage to New Zealand, he also provided him with his first house commission—the Frankel House, at 9 Ford Road, on part of the Anderson family's Risingholme estate.

A single-storey, 'L'-shaped timber house, the Frankel house was designed to maximise afternoon sun while providing privacy from both road and neighbours. With a functional plan that abandoned internal circulation in favour of a very optimistic 'sunporch', a flat roof, large sliding doors and austere, crisp forms, it was a radical concept for New Zealand in the late 1930s—particularly for the

---

84   Evans, 'Otto Herzberg Frankel 4 November 1900—Elected FRS 1953'; Evans, Handwritten notes, 'Otto 25/5/87, notes from dinner', Frankel, Sir O. H., FAA (1900–2007), Box 15, Item E, p. 155, Note 3.
85   Evans, 'Otto Herzberg Frankel 4 November 1900—Elected FRS 1953'. Another connection was through the modernist Viennese potter Lucie Rie and her husband, Hans, whom Theo Frankel met skiing at St Anton. The Ries had provided Plischke with one of his first commissions: the interior of their apartment at 24 Wollzeile in Vienna. In 1938, Theo assisted the Ries to move to England. Tony Birks, *Lucie Rye* (Somerset: Marston House, 1987), 28–9, 33.
86   Ernst Plischke, *On the Human Aspect in Modern Architecture* (Vienna: 1969), 18; D. G. Porter, 'An Immigrant Brought Live Vision to New Zealand', *The Dominion* (6 April 1963).
87   'His brother, Raymond Firth, had become an internationally acclaimed anthropologist.' Greg Bowron, 'Firth, Cedric Harold 1908–1994, Builder, Architect, Writer', *Dictionary of New Zealand Biography*, <http://www.dnzb.govt.nz>

Dominion's most English city, where it generated 'as much notoriety as Frank Lloyd Wright's Taliesin House in Arizona'.[88] Frankel proudly claimed his house to be 'the first modern house in Christchurch'.[89] But the Frankels' assistance to Plischke's architectural career did not end with their own house; he went on to design a number of others for members of their social and artistic milieu.[90]

Figure 1.9 Frankel House, Opawa, Christchurch, c. 1940

Photograph: Manuscript Collection, Adolph Basser Library, Australian Academy of Science. Frankel, Sir O. H., FAA (1900–2007), MS 106, Box 13

In Christchurch, the Frankels established a number of living and working patterns that would stay with them for the remainder of their lives. By building a house that, for its time and place, was radically modern, they demonstrated a commitment to contemporary design. They developed gardens around their home that were described as 'a tribute' to their 'imaginative and energetic work', while at the Wheat Research Institute—where he became Chief Executive Officer in 1942—Otto embarked on a major construction program of new research facilities.[91]

---

88 Evans, Handwritten note quoting Nancy Sawyer, Basser, Frankel, Sir O. H., FAA (1900–2007), Box 15, Item D, 74.
89 Evans, 'Otto Herzberg Frankel 4 November 1900—Elected FRS 1953'. See also Douglas Lloyd Jenkins, *At Home: A Century of New Zealand Design* (Auckland: Godwit, 2004), 82.
90 For instance, Evelyn Page and her husband, Frederick, commissioned a Plischke house at Waikanae, near Wellington, in 1951. This is mentioned in a letter that Frankel's first wife, Tilli, wrote to him about mutual friends 'Eve and Fred', and their dealings with Plischke. Tilli Aldrich to Otto Frankel, Takapau, Hawke's Bay, 30 October 1967, 3 November 1967, 4 November 1967 [same letter]. AAS Adolph Basser Library, Frankel, O. H., MS 106, Box 13, Item B.
91 'New Post in Australia. Leading Plant Geneticist. Christchurch Pair Will Be Missed', *New Zealand Herald Free Lance* (19 September 1951): 22.

1. Age of the Masters: Establishing a scientific and intellectual community in Canberra, 1946–1968

In 1949, the Australian Council for Scientific and Industrial Research acquired a new name—the Commonwealth Scientific and Industrial Research Organisation (CSIRO)—and appointed a new chairman, the agricultural scientist Ian Clunies-Ross. This was an important period for the organisation, which was benefiting from unprecedented confidence in Australian science and a dramatic increase in research funding.[92] But Clunies-Ross could see problems in the Division of Plant Industry, which was suffering from low morale and a lack of direction.[93] There was also the need to implement Coombs' vision, whereby the organisation would not only be capable of reacting to immediate problems, it would also be able to anticipate future tasks and act as a public advocate for scientific research.[94] One of the Chairman's first responsibilities was to appoint a scientist capable of heading the division and of addressing these issues. Frankel, still living in New Zealand, was somewhat surprised when he was offered the job, given his already formidable reputation as a critic and 'stormy petrel'.[95] But it was partly those qualities that attracted Clunies-Ross to him. A feeling of intellectual isolation in New Zealand, combined with a lack of 'old stones and modern art', led to Frankel's decision to accept the position in Canberra. Although he felt even less at home in the Australian landscape, and was no closer to the European culture that he longed for, Frankel claimed he was 'never made to feel a foreigner' in Australia.[96]

When Frankel arrived in Canberra, he noted that the division was 'getting older', and immediately set out to attract 'very good young people in scientific fields' whose expertise was directly related to the environmental problems facing Australia.[97] The atmosphere of scientific autonomy that pervaded the CSIRO, combined with the postwar impetus, provided a context in which he was able to recruit highly qualified scientists.[98] In the first two decades after

---

92 'In scale, range and self-confidence, the organization was unrecognisable in 1945 compared with the small and somewhat defensive entity of the late 1930s. The most obvious change was the four-fold increase in size…CSIR was in an exceptionally favourable position at the end of the war to achieve its scientific ideals. It received much of the credit for the rapid wartime technological progress, and had established itself as the premier scientific institution in the country.' Schedvin, *Shaping Science and Industry: A History of Australia's Council for Scientific and Industrial Research, 1926–49*, 309, 318. While biological and environmental scientists enjoyed the spoils of wartime success, the same could not be said for physicists. There was much unease about nuclear physics since atomic bombs had been dropped on Japanese cities, and 'Cold War paranoia' affected many scientists working in that field. Ibid., 318.
93 Collis, *Fields of Discovery: Australia's CSIRO*, 206.
94 The Minister, John Dedman, stated that a postwar council needed to do more than solve technical problems. In March 1944, he began to urge the council to plan ahead, so that in a postwar environment it was ready to take on a broader role as public advocate of the benefits of scientific research: 'CSIR must be more than a great scientific organisation—it must…play an important part in public education, in foreseeing the problems which will cry out for solution in ten years' time.' Schedvin, *Shaping Science and Industry: A History of Australia's Council for Scientific and Industrial Research, 1926–49*, 325.
95 Bruce Juddery, *The Canberra Times* (29 May 1968).
96 Evans, 'Otto Herzberg Frankel 4 November 1900—Elected FRS 1953'.
97 Bruce Juddery, *The Canberra Times* (29 May 1968).
98 One of the founding principles of the organisation was that it would be managed by scientists rather than by bureaucrats, so that research priorities would be, as far as possible, insulated from potentially conflicting

World War II, 'some of the world's most brilliant minds' arrived in Canberra to work in the rapidly expanding CSIRO. As Brad Collis explained, 'the benefits to a young, developing country were incalculable'.[99]

At the same time, Frankel became convinced that he needed a 'big science' project to 'put the division on the world map', and to lift the CSIRO's profile and morale. For Frankel, there was no better way to encapsulate the spirit of this venture than through architecture. The project soon evolved into the idea of a building, whose form would be a physical manifestation of the expertise, energy and goodwill that science was attracting. But the building could not be a mere symbol of Australian science's improving fortunes; it required a function. The rationale for the building became more apparent as Frankel considered the myriad diverse climates and environments across the Australian continent, and the logistical problems associated with carrying out research in isolated locations. If a large building, capable of simulating various climates, could be constructed in Canberra, it would centralise plant research across Australia, eliminate weather hazards encountered in remote field stations and provide the CSIRO with major reductions in running costs. The only similar building in the world at the time—although it was closed shortly afterwards—was at the California Institute of Technology ('Caltech') in Pasadena.[100] Frankel and his colleagues developed a sophisticated concept that improved on the Caltech prototype. To reduce the amount of time and energy that was consumed transporting plants into different rooms, it was decided to reverse this process in Canberra so that the climates—controlled by the latest airconditioning and remote-control techniques—would be taken to the plants.[101] The 'Phytotron', as it became known, was designed by Grounds, with whom Frankel had nurtured a friendship through the Academy of Science building. It was subdivided into a series of individual chambers, each of which simulated a different climate, to enable scientists to research the responses of plants to varying climatic conditions.

---

political agendas.
99 Collis, *Fields of Discovery: Australia's CSIRO*, xii, vii, xiii.
100 The Caltech Phytotron at Pasadena existed largely due to Frits Went, a Dutch biologist who moved to Caltech in 1933. In 1949, with the support of a generous benefactor, Harry Earhart, Went constructed the Earhart Plant Research Laboratory, which his Caltech colleagues nicknamed the 'Phytotron'. This building became the prototype for the Canberra installation and for others around the world. The Caltech Phytotron was demolished after a few years, when it became apparent that its enormous operating costs far exceeded the institute's budget. *Biographical Memoirs, National Academy of Sciences (US)* (Washington, DC: National Academy Press), vol. 74, 351–2.
101 *Architecture in Australia* (December 1964): 108–9.

1. Age of the Masters: Establishing a scientific and intellectual community in Canberra, 1946–1968

Figure 1.10 Phytotron hothouse, Commonwealth Scientific and Industrial Research Organisation, Canberra, 1962

Photograph: National Archives of Australia. NAA: A1200, L42101

Legacy

Talents as well as bacteria need a nourishing medium in order to thrive.

— Siegfried Giedion[102]

The absolute power that the Academic Advisers—particularly Oliphant and Florey—exerted during their reign had profound consequences for the architecture of the ANU campus. At the core of their being was an unwavering belief that scientific rationality would build a better world, and that no-one—not even a highly regarded architect—was going to prevent them from achieving their goal. The control that Florey and the founding medical professors imposed over the design of the John Curtin School was based on function: they had clear

---

102   Giedion stated that the architect Richard Neutra would not have enjoyed the success that he did if he had not left Austria early in his career. Siegfried Giedion, 'R. J. Neutra, European and American', in *Richard Neutra 1923–50: Buildings and Projects* (London: Thames and Hudson, 1964), 8.

ideas about the overall form of the building (based on the success of a previous model) and about the internal requirements of the laboratories, with their specialised equipment. The medical professors, in their relentless pursuit of functionality, were prepared to relinquish control of only one part of the building: the external cladding; an aesthetic matter, it was of little concern to them. As Florey stated so unequivocally: 'The architect must be entirely subordinated to the scientific requirements of those who are to inhabit [the building].'[103] Sometimes the architectural results of this rigid, authoritarian approach—fed by their considerable personal successes—were unsuccessful: the first Oliphant house in Canberra was one example. But generally, the Academic Advisers were not driven by arrogance or hubris as much as they were motivated by the desire to implement Coombs' primary vision—that science should serve humanitarian purposes in an attempt to improve Australia's physical and social environment.

The Academic Advisers' parallel building project—constructing the personnel component of the university—brought to the national capital a group of young, highly qualified and highly specialised scientists and academics, many of whom were world leaders in their fields. In accordance with the spirit of postwar rejuvenation, all of the scientists who accepted chairs at the university were in their thirties or forties when appointed.[104] Most were well travelled; many had served overseas during World War II, or had completed postgraduate studies or work experience in Europe or North America. In this way, they had been directly exposed to new developments in modern architecture within university campuses, scientific institutions and private residences. Confident, forward thinking and optimistic about the modern world, they brought fresh impetus to the city. Furthermore, their involvement in building a new research university that was not restricted by the need to maintain established traditions or ideologies placed them in a professional context that actively encouraged new ways of thinking.

Through a network of contacts and recommendations, many of these new arrivals commissioned architects to design their houses. Fenner recommended Boyd to Dr Clark from the CSIRO, and to Dr Hilary Roche, a physician from the Department of Health.[105] One of Fenner's first appointments, the microbiologist Ian Marshall, and his wife, Kathleen, commissioned Theo Bischoff—who had moved from Melbourne to work on the John Curtin School—to design their

---

103   Florey to Copland, in Williams, *Howard Florey: Penicillin and After*, 251–2.
104   Fenner, Professor of Microbiology, was aged thirty-four; Ennor, Professor of Biochemistry, was thirty-five; Titterton, Professor of Nuclear Physics, was also in his mid-thirties; Albert, Professor of Chemistry, was forty-one; Eccles, Professor of Physiology, was aged forty-seven; while Birch, appointed Dean of Chemistry some years later, was in his mid-forties. The Academic Advisors were all under fifty years of age: Oliphant was forty-five; Florey—already a co-recipient of the Nobel Prize for the development of penicillin—and Hancock were both forty-eight.
105   Of these, only the Roche House, at 4 Bedford Street, Deakin, which Boyd designed in 1955, went ahead.

house in Curtin.[106] Vladimir ('Val') Paral, official photographer for the John Curtin School, and his wife, Heather, commissioned Derek Wrigley to design their house in Narrabundah.[107] Gordon Ada, who replaced Fenner as Professor of Microbiology in 1968 when he became Director of the John Curtin School, lived in a house in Pearce designed by Kevin Curtin.[108] Gutta Schoefl from the John Curtin School and her mathematician partner commissioned Roger Pegrum to design their Wamboin house. Ernest Titterton, appointed Professor of Nuclear Physics by Oliphant, and his wife, Peggy, built a modern house in Forrest; the geologist John Lovering and his wife, Kerry, engaged Sydney architects Ancher, Mortlock and Woolley for their house in Deakin; while geophysicist Mervyn Paterson and his wife, Katalin, commissioned Canberra-based architect Enrico Taglietti for their Aranda house.[109]

Many of these clients had firm ideas regarding the type of house they wanted to live in. Paola Favaro claimed that it was largely because of the Patersons' input that Taglietti—who had previously demonstrated a limited affinity with the Australian landscape—showed, in their house, a closer connection to the colours and textures of the surrounding environment.[110] Ken Charlton described how the fortress-like appearance of the Paterson House was the result of the clients' request for a private house that withdrew from its suburban neighbours. He also noted that Taglietti amended his design for the living-room fireplace so that the occupants could gather around the hearth, as was the practice in Katalin Paterson's native Hungary.[111]

University administrators, and academic staff from the general studies, social sciences and Pacific studies faculties, extended the network of house commissions. University Registrar, Ross Hohnen, and his wife, Phyllis, commissioned

---

106   Ian Marshall and Kathleen Sutton, a laboratory technician, moved to Canberra, from Melbourne, at the same time. But, as their former employer Fenner explained, they 'made the mistake of not getting married before they came up, so they were separately located in boarding houses. And they got married, and they had a hell of a job in trying to get a house built for themselves.' Frank Fenner, Interview by the author, 18 October 2007. The Marshall House, at 86 Morgan Crescent, Curtin, was designed by Bischoff in 1966. An upstairs extension has since been added. Ann Whitelaw, 'Children Have Their Own Living Area', *The Canberra Times* (9 July 1968).
107   The Paral House was at 22 Brockman Street, Narrabundah. In 1965 it received a Commendation from the Royal Australian Institute of Architects (ACT Chapter).
108   Whitelaw wrote that the Ada House, at 71 Parkhill Street, Pearce, was designed by Kevin Curtin and was being built for Mr H. Constable when the Adas bought it. 'Character in a House', [Homes and Building], *The Canberra Times* (30 June 1970).
109   The Schoefl–Miles House was at 1 Sutton Road, Wamboin, NSW; the now-demolished Titterton House was at 8 Somers Crescent, Forrest; the Lovering House of 1967 was at 38 Beauchamp Street, Deakin; and the Paterson House was at 7 Juad Place, Aranda. For the Lovering house, see Whitelaw, 'Reaching for the Stars at Deakin', [Homes and Building], *The Canberra Times* (12 November 1968).
110   Paola Favaro, Drawn to Canberra: The Architectural Language of Enrico Taglietti (PhD dissertation, Faculty of the Built Environment, University of New South Wales, 2009), 287–8, 292.
111   Ken Charlton, Bronwen Jones and Paola Favaro, *The Contribution of Enrico Taglietti to Canberra's Architecture* (Canberra: RAIA, ACT Chapter, Register of Significant Twentieth Century Architecture Committee, 2007), 6, 51.

John Scollay—who had worked with Lewis on University House—to design a house in Deakin.[112] Economic historian Alan Barnard appointed Anthony Pegrum for his house in Campbell,[113] while Bischoff was engaged by Professor Douglas Pike—a historian whom Hancock had appointed founding Editor of the *Australian Dictionary of Biography*—to design a house for himself and his wife, Louisa, in Campbell.[114] Historians Deryck Scarr and Margaret Steven commissioned Hancock, Courtney and Renfree to design their houses in Curtin and Garran respectively, while anthropologist Derek Freeman and wife, Monica, engaged Wrigley for their Deakin house. Another who commissioned Wrigley was statistician Ted Hannan and his wife, Irene, whose house was in Red Hill.[115]

Oxford-trained philosopher Bruce Benjamin from the School of General Studies and his wife, Audrey, commissioned Melbourne architect Alex Jelinek to design their house at 10 Gawler Crescent, Deakin. In 1957, the Benjamin House overcame stiff opposition from such luminaries as Seidler, Boyd, Ancher, Mortlock and Murray, John Dalton and Peter Muller to be awarded House of the Year by the editors of *Architecture and Arts*.[116] Commonly known in Canberra as the 'round house', the Benjamin House was in fact based on a Pythagorean spiral. Due to its striking appearance and prominent corner location, it is probably the most well-known modern house in the capital city.

Through his overall influence on the CSIRO, and his personal involvement in a number of significant architectural commissions, Frankel's contribution to the architecture of postwar Canberra was significant. In addition to his central roles in the Academy of Science building and the Phytotron, he built two modern houses for himself and Margaret in the capital (see Chapter 6). Frankel possessed as much confidence in his beliefs as his ANU equivalents, and at least as much commitment to carrying them out. Like them, he was single-minded, determined and dismissive of those whose opinions he did not respect. But he had additional qualities. When it came to architectural patronage, Frankel arrived in Canberra with considerable form, having worked with Plischke on his own house and having supervised the construction of new scientific facilities at the Wheat Research Institute. Frankel was a discerning aesthete with confidence in his

---

112   The Hohnen House, c. 1956, was located on the corner of Empire Circuit and Grey Street, Deakin.
113   The Barnard House, c. 1963, was at 18 Godfrey Street, Campbell. Patricia Clarke, 'Couple Build Solar House for £7,500', [Homemakers], *The Canberra Times* (17 July 1964).
114   The Pike House, designed by Bischoff in 1965, was at 2 Garsia Street, Campbell. See Whitleaw, 'Courtyard and Fountain Provides Bright Focal Point', *The Canberra Times* (4 June 1968).
115   The Scarr House, designed in 1966, was at 38 Munro Street and the corner of Munro Place, Curtin. Whitelaw, 'House Which Seems Bigger than it Really Is', [Homes and Building], *The Canberra Times* (30 August 1968). The Steven House of the same year, at 3 Bonwick Place, Garran, was not designed specifically for Steven; it was already under construction when she arranged to purchase it. Margaret Steven, In discussion with the author, 2007. The Freeman House was at 5 Daly Street, Deakin, while the Hannan House, c. 1962, was at 8 Penrhyn Street, Red Hill.
116   *Architecture and Arts* (March 1958 and June–July 1958). The Benjamin House, at 10 Gawler Crescent, Deakin, was designed by Jelinek in 1956. Bruce and Audrey's son, Roger, is writing a book on the Benjamin House.

own aesthetic judgment, and he would not hesitate to back his own opinion when it came to questions of architectural language and form. These qualities were what led to the mutual respect, and close friendship, that he developed with Grounds—a working relationship that underscored (and survived) their collaboration on a number of houses and buildings.

Figure 1.11 Benjamin House, view from north-west

Photograph: Wolfgang Sievers, 1958. National Library of Australia. nla.pic-vn4503045

Grounds' continuing success in Canberra owed much to Frankel. In addition to the above buildings, he designed the School of Botany for The Australian National University. A number of Grounds' subsequent residential commissions for scientists were a direct result of these larger projects. In addition to the Frankel House, there were the Campbell houses for John Nicholson and his wife, Phyllis, John and Frances ('Fay') Philip and Bruce and Penny Griffing, the Philip and Moira Trudinger House in O'Connor, and an unbuilt proposal for Sir Rutherford ('Bob') Robertson.[117] Some of Grounds' commissions extended

---

117 The Nicholson House, designed in 1965, was at 24 Cobby Street, Campbell; the Philip and Griffing houses, completed in 1961, were at 42 and 44 Vasey Crescent, Campbell; and the Trudinger House of 1965 was at 144 Dryandra Street, O'Connor. The Robertson House was not built. It was listed as a project of c. 1966 in Hamann, Modern Architecture in Melbourne: The Architecture of Grounds, Romberg and Boyd, 1927–1971, vol. 2, 66.

outside the boundaries of the Australian Capital Territory: in 1958, he designed a clubhouse building in Guthega for the 'Blue Cow' Ski Club, of which Frankel was a founding member.

But Grounds was not the only architect employed by scientists from the CSIRO. The entomologist Doug Waterhouse and his wife, Dawn, engaged Moir and Sutherland for their house at 58 National Circuit (corner of Melbourne Avenue), Deakin. A modern interpretation of the Georgian style, the Waterhouse House was reminiscent of Doug's family home, Eryldene, in Gordon, NSW, which was designed in 1913 by William Hardy Wilson for his parents.

The network of commissions extended to newer architectural firms in the capital city. George Stewart engaged Latvian immigrant architect Rudi Krastins, whom his wife, Valeska, had met through the local Latvian community, to design their house in O'Connor. Stewart's colleague Ralph Slatyer and wife, June, engaged Krastins for their house on an adjacent site. Keith and Mary Boardman hired Scollay to design a house in Forrest. When Aranda—to the north-west of the CSIRO's Black Mountain location—was developed, John and Enid Falk, and Colin and Pam Macdonald, employed Roger Pegrum to design their houses in that suburb.[118]

Underlying the way in which these scientist-clients approached the problem of building a house was an acute awareness of climate and environment—a situation that was not altogether unexpected, given the nature of their day jobs. When asked why they commissioned architects to design their houses, they invariably responded that it was due to a lack of appropriate housing at the time. Their criticisms of existing models were based on two major concerns: inappropriate style and lack of sensible, environmentally aware design. All considered the popular way of building in historical styles, such as 'Tudor' or 'Spanish', as totally inappropriate solutions to the problem of building a house in Australia. June Slatyer explained how she and Ralph wanted 'something that was more in tune with the land, more environmentally aware', and were impressed by the understated, well-orientated solution that Krastins had provided for the Stewarts. As a result, the Slatyers commissioned the same architect to design their house on an adjacent site. The Slatyer House was, June believed, 'one of the first solar passive houses, orientated for north sun', in Canberra.[119]

---

118   The Stewart and Slatyer houses were at 6 and 8 Hobbs Street, O'Connor. For the Stewart House, see Whitelaw, 'The House with a Swinging Wall', [Homes and Building], *The Canberra Times* (25 November 1969). The Boardman House was at 6 Somers Crescent, Forrest; the Falk House was at 18 Araba Place, Aranda; and the Macdonald House was at 46 Mirning Crescent, Aranda.

119   Like Krastins, Stewart's wife was Latvian. June Slatyer believed this was the connection that linked the Stewarts to Krastins. Interestingly, the Slatyer House contained an oval-shaped kitchen that June Slatyer described as being 'very Freudian—an egg shape for the lady of the house'. Whether or not her husband,

John Zwar, a plant physiologist who was one of Frankel's earliest recruits to the Division of Plant Industry in 1952, went further afield by commissioning Sydney-based Seidler to design his house in O'Connor. Zwar believed that existing Canberra houses were 'pretty dreadful'. Describing the brick-and-tile houses that were constructed en masse in suburbs such as Turner in the immediate postwar years, he noted that they were 'very well built houses, brick houses...but there's no light in them at all!' Zwar considered that 'building houses in imitation of something in the past...was just the most stupid thing you could do'.[120] John and Frances Philip admired the way in which some early Australian buildings dealt with the harsh climate, but had specific ideas about how their own house should deal with issues of sun control and heating—both of which John was able to quantify to Grounds through mathematical calculations.[121]

The idea of an architecture based on rational, environmental principles was nurtured and propagated throughout the corridors and tearooms of the Acton campus and Black Mountain laboratories during the 1950s and 1960s, where scientists regularly discussed houses, and architecture in general, with their colleagues. Often the results of these encounters were profound: it was through discussions with his colleagues that Zwar ended up asking Seidler to design his house, while discussions between Frankel and Philip resulted in the complete replanning of Frankel's second Canberra house.[122] Many scientists and their partners demonstrated a wider concern for their adopted environment by becoming involved in environmental organisations and lobby groups. Five—Hancock, Slatyer, Fenner, Frankel and Audrey Benjamin—formed a residents' group with architect Wrigley and sought a legal injunction to stop construction of a telecommunication tower (now known as 'Telstra Tower') on Black Mountain.[123] That so many of those involved in building this scientific and intellectual community in the national capital were honoured with knighthoods for their work—Florey, Oliphant, Ennor, Copland, Clunies-Ross, Frankel, Hancock, Grounds, Titterton and Eccles (Eccles was also a recipient of the Nobel Prize and was Australian of the Year in 1963, while Coombs resisted the offer of a knighthood on several occasions)—is a measure of the enormity of their contributions. It was the legacy left by this extraordinary and unprecedented

---

Ralph, spent a lot of time in that room is not particularly relevant, yet it seems that the ovoid space might have contained equal significance for a biological scientist. June Slatyer, In discussion with the author, 28 October 2008.
120   John Zwar, Interview by the author, 26 September 2008.
121   See Chapter 4.
122   Frankel to Grounds, 6 November 1969, Frankel, Sir O. H., FAA (1900–2007), Box 13, Item C.
123   Their attempt, in 1973, was unsuccessful. NLA Manuscripts Collection, MS5350; National Archives of Australia, NAA: 8869243, A10273.

colony of national capital inhabitants, fired by the uncompromising ideals, energies and enthusiasms of the Academic Advisers amongst them, which led to the building of the houses discussed in the following chapters.

> May you live for as long as man will bend the knee, or doff the lid, to imagination, truth and integrity.
>
> — Grounds' tribute to Otto Frankel upon his knighthood[124]

---

124   Grounds to Frankel, 14 January 1966, Frankel, Sir O. H., FAA (1900–2007), Box 13, Item A.

2. Paradigm Shift: Boyd and the Fenner House

Designed for the ANU Professor of Microbiology, Frank Fenner—'the most highly decorated and awarded Australian scientist of the 20th and 21st century'[1]—his wife, Bobbie, and their two children, the 'binuclear'-planned Fenner House was Boyd's first commission in Canberra, and the second house that he designed for these clients.[2] The first design was for a site in Hotham Crescent, Deakin, but it proved to be too expensive and was abandoned. The second design—for a much larger site that the Fenners acquired on the corner of Monaro Crescent and Torres Street, Red Hill—was built during 1953 and 1954 by Karl Schreiner for the contract sum of £8500.[3]

Figure 2.1 Fenner House, view from north-east

Photograph: from 'House at Red Hill, Canberra', *Architecture and Arts* 13 (August 1954)

---

1   Ann Moyal, 'Preface', in Frank Fenner, *Nature, Nurture and Chance: The Lives of Frank and Charles Fenner* (Canberra: ANU E Press, 2006), vii.
2   Fenner initially engaged Boyd in 1950 to design a house for the Hotham Crescent site. In 1952–53, Boyd modified the design to suit his client's new site in Torres Street, Red Hill. Boyd's other early Canberra house, for Manning and Dymphna Clark, was designed in 1952 and completed in late 1953.
3   Regarding the first design, Fenner recalled: 'The builders in Canberra had never seen anything like [it] and did not want to build it so they tendered quotes that were far beyond our reach.' Only one tender was received, for £25 000. 'At the time, I was a young professor, it was just out of my [price range] altogether.' Geoffrey Serle, *Robin Boyd: A Life* (Melbourne: Melbourne University Press, 1995), 133. Frank Fenner, Interview by the author, 18 October 2007. The final figure of £8500 excluded heating.

Everything about this house was different. While most houses in Canberra faced the street, the Fenner House straddled the large corner site diagonally in two completely separate blocks, connected only by a barely visible glass link containing an entrance hall. It was hard enough to distinguish where the 'front' was, let alone the entry. Unfamiliar from every angle, and deliberately eschewing any gesture to known symbols or established reference points of what houses were supposed to contain—front and back, prominent entrance, verandah, street elevation, facade, symmetry, dominant roof-form—the Fenner House, to many, hardly qualified as a house at all. It attracted a lot of attention from neighbours—and some interesting comments. As Fenner recalled, some of them thought that it was 'a farming shed or something like that'.[4]

Those who ventured inside might have been further surprised by the fact that the professor's house was so fundamentally grounded in functionality and rational thought that it was laid out according to what time of day it was. To the right of the entrance hall, a north-facing 'diurnal' block catered for daytime activities: living room, dining room, kitchen and laundry. To the left of the entrance, the south-facing 'nocturnal' block contained a garage, playroom, bedrooms, bathroom and study.

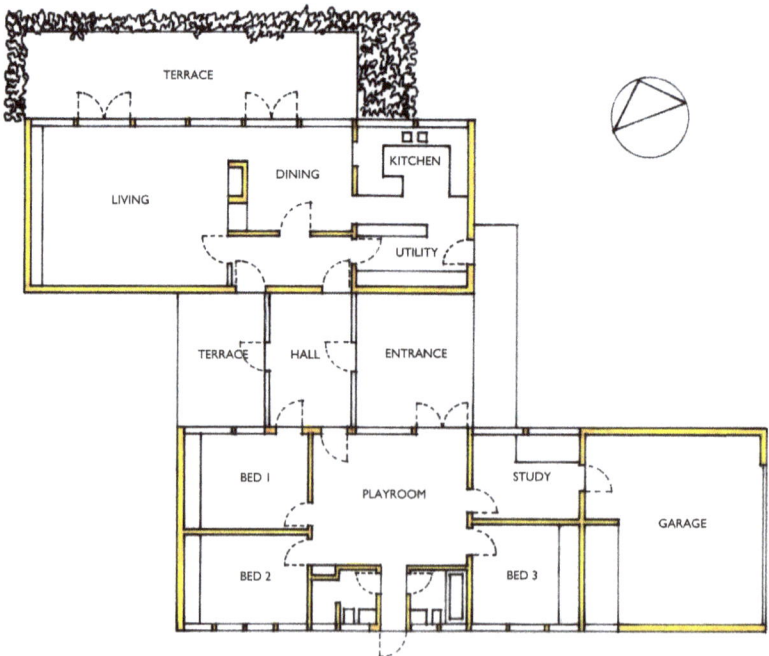

Figure 2.2 Fenner House, floor plan

Image: redrawn by the author from Robin Boyd. Courtesy of the Robin Boyd Foundation

---

4   Frank Fenner, Interview by the author, 18 October 2007.

2. Paradigm Shift: Boyd and the Fenner House

Figure 2.3 Fenner House, view from west. The diurnal block is on the left; the nocturnal block on the right

Photograph: from 'House at Red Hill, Canberra', *Architecture and Arts* 13 (August 1954)

Figure 2.4 Fenner House, view from west

Photograph: from 'House at Red Hill, Canberra', *Architecture and Arts* 13 (August 1954)

In spite of any reservations that the neighbours might have had, the Fenner House was highly regarded by the architectural fraternity. Reported to have 'contributed much to architectural thinking and contemporary design', it was awarded the inaugural ACT Chapter Medallion from the Royal Australian Institute of Architects in 1956.[5]

Figure 2.5 Viewing Canberra Medallion on wall of Fenner House, 1956. From left: Karl Schreiner (holding screwdriver), Vicki Fenner, Mrs Schreiner, John Scollay (ACT Chapter, RAIA), Frank Fenner, Marilyn Fenner and Bobbie Fenner. Boyd was in the United States at the time

Photograph: Manuscript Collection, Adolph Basser Library, Australian Academy of Science. Fenner, F. J., FAA (1914–2010), MS 143, Box 3

The story of the Fenner House is chronologically and conceptually linked to Boyd's seminal 1952 publication, *Australia's Home*, an analysis of Australian houses in which he was particularly critical of those in Canberra. It is highly likely that, in 1950, when Boyd stood in 'the lonely valley' and lamented the 'kaleidoscope' of historical styles—'jazz, Californian bungalow, Spanish Mission and Elizabethan', all borrowed from Sydney and Melbourne, and the 'curving avenues of florid, pretentious façades'—he had travelled to Canberra to meet the Fenners and was standing on their house site.[6] The Fenner House

---

5   *The Canberra Times*, November 1956.
6   Robin Boyd, *Australia's Home: Its Origins, Builders and Occupiers* (Melbourne: Melbourne University Press, 1952), 206. Boyd began writing *Australia's Home* before he and Patricia departed for their overseas study tour in the second half of 1950, completed it after his return to Australia, and published it in 1952. Boyd's critique of Canberra in *Australia's Home* is dated 1950, the same year he was first commissioned by Fenner: 'By 1950 the lonely valley had grown into a city.'

was Boyd's reaction to all that had come before. A riposte to Canberra's existing domestic architecture, it signalled the arrival in the national capital of a new way of thinking about architecture, and a new aesthetic.

Figure 2.6 Fenner House, view from north-west

Photograph: Ben Wrigley, 2012

Members of the Fenner family still live in the house, more than half a century after it was built.[7] While the interior is virtually the same as it was in the 1950s,[8] the exterior is now largely screened by trees, providing a vivid contrast with the early photos depicting a white house of simple, bold forms with splashes of primary colours, sitting in an open landscape. The colours have mellowed, trees and bushes have grown, and all that is visible is the garage to Monaro Crescent, an addition to the Torres Street side—which replicates the forms and detailing of the original house—and part of the glazed gable wall above the rampant *Juniperus sabina*. But the house remains incongruous with its neighbours— perhaps more than ever. Many of the original houses in the suburb have been demolished and replaced with large Palladian, Tuscan and Balinese-style, airconditioned mansions with swimming pools, high steel fences, automatic

---

7   Frank Fenner passed away in 2010. Marilyn Fenner, who grew up in the original house, now lives there with her family.
8   In 2007 the interior of the house was virtually unchanged from when it was first built—right down to the blue Grant Featherstone Contour chair. Fenner seemed proud of the original state of the house, confirming that the only changes were the addition of a microwave oven and compact disc player.

gates and imported chandeliers—the last alone, in some cases, reputedly costing as much as the original Fenner House.[9] These are a far cry from this genuine attempt by Boyd and the Fenners to find an appropriate postwar house.

A New Type

> The simplicity of this work was akin to the simplicity of the farm-building and out-house.
>
> — Robin Boyd, *Australia's Home*[10]

As eminent practitioners and writers within their professions, Fenner and Boyd were both conversant with systems of typological classification. Fenner's introduction to typology began while he was a boy at secondary school. His father, Charles—also a scientist—took him to see the rocks at Hallets Cove, where Frank accumulated 'quite a good collection of fossils'. By trading with other collectors, he eventually acquired a Triassic fossil of ginkgo leaves, and claimed to have the best ginkgo tree in Canberra in his garden at Torres Street. Fenner believed that these early interests in the order of the natural world played a large part in the direction of his career.[11]

The concept of type as a classificatory system is not unique to architecture or to science, but is a device that both have employed, in various manifestations, since the eighteenth century. The introduction of type within architectural discourse can be traced back to scientific classificatory systems, particularly to Georges Buffon's *Histoire Naturelle* of 1749, to Carl Linnaeus's *Species Plantarum* of 1753, and to Jacques Francois Blondel's 1777 *Cours d'Architecture*. All of these were ambitious attempts at global classification of biological phenomena.[12]

---

9   Mike Power, resident of Vancouver Street, Red Hill, In discussion with the author, 2007.
10 Boyd, *Australia's Home: Its Origins, Builders and Occupiers*, 119. Boyd was referring to the austerity of postwar Australian houses.
11 Frank Fenner, *Nature, Nurture and Chance: The Lives of Frank and Charles Fenner*, 9–10. Frank Fenner, Interview by Ann Moyal, 8 March 2001, 4 April 2001, Canberra, National Library of Australia, Oral History Section.
12 For Buffon, see George Louis Le Clerc, Count of Buffon, *Natural History of Birds, Fish, Insects and Reptiles*, 6 vols (London: H. D. Symonds, 1808), or *A Natural History of the Globe, and of Man; Beasts, Birds, Fishes, Reptiles and Insects, from the writings of Buffon, Cuvier, Lacepede, and other eminent naturalists. To which are added, Elements of Botany*, Corrected and enlarged by John Wright, 4 vols (London: F. Z. S., T. T. and J. Tegg, 1833). For Linnaeus, see *Species Plantarum*, Facsimile of the first edition, 1753 (London: Ray Society, 1959). For Blondel, see Jacques Francois Blondel, *Cours d'Architecture, Desaint* (Paris, 1777). Blondel's *Cours d'Architecture* is frequently cited as the origin of the modern architectural system of typological classification, but that system was essentially based on genres and appropriate character rather than on morphology. Other important contributions were made by the poet-scientist Goethe, who invented the word 'morphology'—the science of form—and Georges Cuvier. Nineteenth-century German architect and writer Gottfried Semper based his theory of architectural type on animal and plant morphology. His 'prototypical forms'—*Urformen, Normalformen, Urkeim* and *Urmotiven*—were all taken from Goethe's theories of plant and animal form. Gottfried Semper, *Style in the Technical and Tectonic Arts; or, Practical Aesthetics*, Translated by Harry Francis

More recent examples of architectural classification were contained in Boyd's *Victorian Modern* of 1947, and in *Australia's Home*. In *Victorian Modern*, Boyd teased out and wove together selected strands of twentieth-century domestic architecture that he believed were most appropriate for the Victorian context to form a specific, ideal type. He termed this the 'Victorian Type'. Boyd believed that, subject to local climatic variations, the basic principles underlying the Victorian Type were relevant to all of Australia. Although the existence of such a type has since been questioned, it is useful in understanding Boyd's architectural criticism and practice to examine his intent.[13] The Victorian Type was essentially a 'long, low, light house [that] spreads over the lot…made up of wings of single room width…One long simple stretch of low roofed house'.[14]

In *Australia's Home*, Boyd attempted to classify twentieth-century houses on a national basis, condensing what initially appeared to be 'at least seven hundred varieties' down to five principal house types. These were 'The Primitive Cottage', 'The Bungalow', 'The Asymmetrical Front', 'The L-shape' and 'The Triple-front'.[15] Notably, his Fenner House did not fit any of these categories. It will be established that this house—designed at the same time that Boyd was formulating his typology of Australian domestic architecture—was heavily influenced by his reaction to that research.

Another Australian architect whose houses departed from Boyd's classification was Seidler. Seidler had previously worked for Marcel Breuer in New York, where he had drawn the plans for the Geller House, Breuer's first realised binuclear house. Boyd described Seidler's houses, which were heavily influenced by Breuer, as 'sure, mechanically precise things…square, straight, white and challenging'.[16] The 1948 Rose Seidler House, designed for the architect's mother in Turramurra (then on the northern fringes of Sydney), was essentially a solid, white object raised above the landscape and 'hollowed out' to accommodate an outdoor deck. The Rose Seidler House owed everything to International Style modernism, and nothing to existing Australian house typology. Seidler's houses demonstrated to Boyd that regionalism, as exemplified by the Victorian Type, was not the only solution for the postwar house in Australia.[17]

Mallgrave and Michael Robinson (Los Angeles: Getty Publications, 2004). In a further link to biological classification, Adrian Forty even suggested that the number of types recognised by Semper—four—was influenced by Cuvier's identification of that same number of types within the animal world. Adrian Forty, *Words and Buildings: A Vocabulary of Modern Architecture* (London: Thames and Hudson, 2000), 304–6.
13   Philip Goad, 'Eclectic Synthesis and the Emergence of the So-Called Victorian Type', in The Modern House in Melbourne 1945–1975 (PhD dissertation, University of Melbourne, 1992), 37.
14   Robin Boyd, *Victorian Modern* (Melbourne: Architectural Students' Society of the Royal Victorian Institute of Architects, 1947), 60, 63, 67.
15   Boyd, *Australia's Home: Its Origins, Builders and Occupiers*, 7–11.
16   Ibid., 181.
17   For a discussion of Seidler's influence on Victorian architects, see Philip Goad, 'Melbourne, Harry Seidler and the East Coast International Style', in The Modern House in Melbourne 1945–1975, 5/66–5/81.

In addition to the morphological system, the other common method of classification within architecture is by function—for instance, 'house', 'school', 'farming shed', 'factory' or 'laboratory'. Much of the discourse around typology has focused on the nexus between the two systems—that is, the extent of correlation between formal types and functional types. It is within that lacuna between morphological classification and functional classification that this analysis of the Fenner House is located.

It is important to note the formal similarities between the Fenner House and its client's temporary and permanent laboratories at the John Curtin School of Medical Research. All three buildings were essentially 'H'-shaped, binuclear plans comprising two separate blocks and a connecting link. Fenner described how the temporary John Curtin School facilities 'were built by juxtaposing two prefabricated wooden buildings and constructing a passage where the adjoining roofs touch'.[18]

It appears that houses and laboratories, as quite distinct functional typologies within architectural classification, were in fact never far from each other in Fenner's mind. When visiting virology laboratories across the United States in 1953, he simultaneously visited many private houses of his colleagues, and made comments in his travel diary about each. In Baltimore, he visited Dave Bodian, whose house was 'a converted barn, amid trees in the country, but only 8 miles from his labs'. Back in New York, he engaged in a 'long talk with Rene and Jean about the plans of our lab as well as the house'.[19]

Boyd's colleague in the Small Homes Service in Melbourne, Neil Clerehan—who had assisted Boyd with research for *Victorian Modern*—experimented with a range of plan types in the early years of the service, and designed two modest binuclear houses: the T226 in 1948 and the T280 in 1950. Both of these were published in *The Age*. Another binuclear plan was Seidler's Hutter House of 1952 in Turramurra, completed in the same year that Boyd designed the second version of the Fenner House. For Seidler, the binuclear plan had two advantages over a standard plan. First, it was a way of keeping children away from the 'more delicately furnished adult living quarters', and second, the disjunction of blocks permitted a more economical bedroom wing, as 'comparatively little time is spent there'.[20] Given Boyd's interest in Seidler's houses, the Hutter House would have undoubtedly been a significant influence—an opinion that was shared by Conrad Hamann.[21]

---

18 Frank Fenner and David Curtis, *The John Curtin School of Medical Research: The First Fifty Years, 1948–2008* (Gundaroo, NSW: Brolga Press, 2001), 22.
19 Frank Fenner, 'Collins Trip Book', 1953, entries for 22 July 1953, 21 August 1953, Fenner, F. J., FAA (1914–2010), MS 143/8, Box 22. This was a reference to Rene and Jean Dubos.
20 Harry Seidler, *Houses, Interiors and Projects* (Sydney: Associated General Publications, 1954), xvi.
21 'Seidler's work…encouraged Boyd immensely, and he gave Seidler considerable prominence in *Australia's Home*, and directly incorporated the forms of Seidler and his mentor, Marcel Breuer, in some of his own

In terms of architectural typology, the Fenner House is a direct descendant, via the Hutter House, of Breuer's first built version of the binuclear house, the Geller House I in Long Island, New York, of 1944–46. The plans are quite similar: from the two separate blocks for daytime and night-time activities to the open-plan living areas and central play area within the bedroom wing. In final architectural resolution, the Fenner House departed from the Geller House, and reflected Boyd's evolving position within the architectural zeitgeist of the early 1950s, which he described as somewhere between 'the white cubes of the Functionalists and the woody intricacy of Organicism'.[22] With its merging of International Style binuclear plan type with less austere, Victorian Type low-pitched roofs, the Fenner House consolidated Boyd's position between those two poles.

But why did Boyd choose the binuclear configuration? Was it more than a coincidence that the Fenner House layout resembled that of the John Curtin School laboratories? It is possible, but highly unlikely, that the plan was an interpretation of Fenner's work environment—the reference is perhaps too obvious for Fenner not to have mentioned it. It is also important to remember that the binuclear plan type was not Boyd's first choice for the Fenner House— the small area of the original Hotham Crescent site precluded that type. For Hotham Crescent, Boyd designed a compact, linear house, sited across the contours to provide two levels of accommodation at one end. When that design proved to be too expensive, and the larger site was acquired, Fenner described Boyd's transition from the first proposal to the binuclear plan as a form of natural evolution:

> [W]hat Robin then did was just to shift them like that [places hands on top of one another, and then slides one hand across until they are separate and parallel]. So that instead of the bedroom part, which is the rear block of that house, being the upper level, it just went down.[23]

While this was a logical process, it was not an inevitable outcome. A number of permutations were possible by rearranging the building blocks on the new site, and the binuclear arrangement represented only one of those. For Boyd, this was merely one of a number of plan types to try out. In the early 1950s, he was enmeshed in an intensely creative period, referred to as his 'experimental' or 'style-forming' phase. During that time he designed a range of small, low-

---

architecture.' Conrad Hamann, Modern Architecture in Melbourne: The Architecture of Grounds, Romberg and Boyd, 1927–1971 (PhD dissertation, Visual Arts Department, Monash University, 1978), 159. See also Robin Boyd, 'A New Eclecticism', *Architectural Review* CX, no. 657 (September 1951): 151–3.
22 Boyd, *Australia's Home: Its Origins, Builders and Occupiers*, 183.
23 Frank Fenner, Interview by the author, 18 October 2007.

budget houses of varying plan form. Breuer's Geller House I—still only some six years old—and Seidler's more recent Hutter House would both have been on his mind.

Given that Boyd's other house in Canberra, designed about the same time for Manning and Dymphna Clark, was another interpretation of the binuclear model, it would appear that there was more to it than random experimentation. Perhaps there was something about these particular academic clients—or about Canberra—that led Boyd to this plan type. In relation to the clients, the Fenners and the Clarks were both fairly typical postwar 'nuclear' families: two parents with between two and four children.[24] Boyd held similar views to Seidler regarding children in the house, believing that the postwar 'elevation of the rights of children' had given them free reign over the house, and that as a result the suitability of the open plan was brought into question. One solution suggested by Boyd was separate zoning of different activities or age groups.[25] But most of Boyd's clients were from a similar demographic, and while he often provided separate zones within his houses, he did not design binuclear houses for all of them.

It does not appear that privacy was the key determinant of plan form. Fenner carried out most of his work in the John Curtin School, and had no specific requirement for a completely private study at home (although there was a study in the house). Clark wrote from home and did require a quiet space; however, Boyd provided that by placing the study on a higher level rather than relying on the horizontal segregation provided by the binuclear plan.

The fact that Boyd, after these two commissions, designed no further binuclear houses in Canberra to some extent reinforces the notion that it was simply an experiment that followed Breuer and Seidler houses of the same period. But when all aspects of Boyd's domestic architecture in Canberra are considered, a compelling argument for the use of the binuclear type relates to the influence of Canberra itself. In the early 1950s there was not a lot there. Hindered by postwar restrictions and shortages in regard to building approvals, materials and labour, Canberra was in the doldrums. It consisted of not much more than the meandering Molonglo River, a network of unformed roads and scatterings of houses in a few inner suburbs. Between all of this was a lot of open space crisscrossed with walking tracks. No significant facilities had been completed on the ANU campus, whose new academic arrivals were often met at the airport or the train station by the Registrar, Ross Hohnen. Tall and bespectacled, he would proudly take them on a tour of the new university site, pointing out the location

---

24   The Fenners had two children, Marilyn and Vicki. When the Clarks moved to Canberra, they brought four of their children to live with them: Sebastian, Katerina, Axel and Andrew.
25   Boyd, *Australia's Home: Its Origins, Builders and Occupiers*, 149–52.

of proposed future buildings. But many were not impressed; as Stephen Foster and Margaret Varghese wrote, 'it took a fair stretch of the imagination to accept Hohnen's vision of a university in a paddock'.[26] In the open landscape of 1950s Canberra there was no density, no sense of urbaneness and little sense of place. In this way it was a totally different environment to both Melbourne—where Boyd and many of the new academic arrivals had been living—and Sydney.

Figure 2.7 Manning Clark House, entrance hall showing ladder to study

Photograph: the author, 2010

Within this open, semi-rural landscape, lacking clear definition and any sense of urban structure, it is possible that Boyd saw the need to place a strong figure—a plan form with clear definition and a strong sense of place. It can also be hypothesised that this distinct plan form was a reaction against what Boyd saw as the mediocrity and sameness of the few predominant house types that existed in Canberra. By importing what was, to Canberra, a 'new' paradigm in terms of house type, he was deliberately proposing an alternative approach

---

26 Stephen Foster and Margaret Varghese, *The Making of The Australian National University 1946–96* (St Leonards, NSW: Allen & Unwin, 1996), 67, 237, 241.

to residential design for this location, and one that did not—in accordance with his vehement rejection of the superficiality of Canberra's 'kaleidoscope' of historical styles—resort to stylistic borrowing.

Lindsay Pryor's landscape design reinforced Boyd's siting. Pryor, a schoolboy friend of Fenner from Adelaide, was Keeper of Parks and Gardens for the Australian Capital Territory, and a graduate of the Australian Forestry School. The Fenner House landscaping represented a clean break from the traditional Canberra garden typology. As front fences were not permitted in Canberra, most houses were bordered by hedges. The Department of the Interior maintained these hedges on the condition that they conformed to the species nominated for that particular street. After consulting Fenner, Pryor decided on a layout that responded to the unique footprint of the house, and—in contrast with the predominant pattern—left the site relatively open to Torres Street. In this way, the eastern and western edges of the site were planted with a variety of trees and shrubs to provide privacy and shelter from winds. A 'peninsula of trees' ran out from the north-eastern corner of the house, *Juniperus sabina* was planted to shelter the front terrace, and a broad sweep of lawn to the north of the house extended to the boundary, leaving the major street frontage largely exposed.[27]

The Aesthetic Imperative

If to be 'modern' in post–World War II Australia was to read every international architectural publication that you could lay your hands on, to value creativity and experimentation, and to exhibit a strong interest in contemporary movements in art, music and film, Boyd fitted the bill.[28] As a practising architect and prolific writer, he became one of Australia's leading propagandists for the modern movement during the 1940s and 1950s.[29] His own architecture was experimental, adapting concepts from key figures of modernism—such as Le Corbusier—to suit local contexts. Boyd's first design for the Fenner House—an

---

27 Frank Fenner, 'The Garden at 8 Monaro Crescent, Red Hill', March 1977, Fenner, F. J., FAA (1914–2010), MS 143/8/4H7.
28 It was claimed that the sources of Boyd's architectural education were seminal writings by McGrath, Pevsner, Bertram, Richards, Mumford, Le Corbusier and Giedion, supplemented with an influx of overseas journals and magazines. Boyd's interests in the other arts were demonstrated by numerous conversations he shared with his cousin Arthur in his Murrumbeena studio. For Boyd as a 'Modern', see Serle, *Robin Boyd: A Life*, 55–62.
29 Ibid., 'Preface'.

exploration of vertical space that has been compared with Le Corbusier's two-storey Citrohan living rooms[30]—was described by his client as being 'unusual at the time', 'revolutionary' and even 'unbuildable'.[31]

That Boyd was a modern architect, and had been modernist in inclination from an early stage in his career, is well established. But what of Fenner? What was his position in regard to modernism? As inaugural Professor of Microbiology, Fenner played a key role in establishing The Australian National University in Canberra in the years immediately after World War II. He was particularly well informed in regard to international developments in modern art, architecture and design. Always observant, Fenner recorded extensive notes and diagrams in his travel diaries.

By late 1952, temporary laboratories were set up in Canberra for the John Curtin School of Medical Research, and Fenner—who was based in Melbourne until the facilities were ready—drove with Bobbie and their two children, Vicki and Marilyn, to the capital in a small convoy of Morris Minor and Ford Prefect. They might have had modest transportation, but this was an important milestone in the establishment of the university—and, as it turned out, in the history of the modern house in Canberra. Fenner had been to Canberra before the war—to study Aboriginal skulls at the Institute of Anatomy[32]—but aside from that had no previous connections, and no vested interests, in the city. Arriving with a clean slate, he brought with him a sense of optimism about the future: setting up new laboratories in which to continue his research, building a house for himself and his family, and establishing professional and social connections in a relatively new and rapidly expanding city were all exciting prospects.

Fenner sought to incorporate a number of modernist ideas and concepts into his house. A principal source of influence was the overseas study tour that he undertook in 1953. Fenner flew from Kingsford Smith Airport in Sydney to San Francisco on 23 May 1953, just a few days after signing the contract documents with Schreiner for his Red Hill house. Often flying by Comet, and carrying a suitcase filled with presents including stuffed koalas and books on wallabies, Fenner proceeded to visit the laboratories 'of almost every virologist in the United States'.[33] Throughout the trip, he was frequently invited back to spend the evening, or to stay overnight, with colleagues and their families. Fenner was methodical and thorough. Each evening he recorded in his travel

---

30 Hamann, *Modern Architecture in Melbourne: The Architecture of Grounds, Romberg and Boyd, 1927–1971*, 169–70.
31 Fenner, *Nature, Nurture and Chance: The Lives of Frank and Charles Fenner*, 60; Letter to Geoffrey Serle, 17 June 1994, Fenner, F. J., FAA (1914–2010), MS 143/8/4H5, Box 3.
32 As a medical student from 1934 to 1938, Fenner received a scholarship that allowed him to research Aboriginal skulls held in the Institute of Anatomy in Canberra. He stayed in Beauchamp House (now Ian Potter House, Australian Academy of Science), which was located opposite the institute.
33 Fenner, *Nature, Nurture and Chance: The Lives of Frank and Charles Fenner*, 64–5.

diary details of after-dinner conversations, the houses they had occurred in, the names of the family members, and the presents he had given them. His notes indicate that after a period of 'shop' talk about infectious diseases and antibodies, conversation would invariably turn to contemporary house design.

In Berkeley, he stayed a few days with Bill Reeves from the University of California, and noted that his house was in a 'very pleasant spot in hills. Fine view of San Fran and Berkeley at night.' In Denver, he visited 'Gardiner's house', which was 'contemporary style, very low ceiling, 2 storey but looks like one… sliding doors also used effectively'. In New Jersey, he stayed a few days with a gynaecologist friend, Grogan O'Connell, and his wife, Janet, who had just built a contemporary house in Alpine. Fenner was impressed by the O'Connells' house, and made a number of diary notes and sketches. He described the house as 'modern and attractive, in 2 acres of thick woodland, so that no other house can be seen nearby'. He took several photos of the house, and even made notes of '[f]eatures of the house that we might copy' for his own house. These included details of recessed heaters, light fittings and bathroom cupboards and mirrors. He was particularly interested in a glass-topped, steel-framed table on the terrace that he sketched on two separate occasions, noting that it '[l]ooks the type of thing we could get made at the workshop'.[34]

By 1953, there was evidence of the beginning of a postwar recovery in architecture in North America and Europe, heralded by the completion of a number of seminal modernist buildings. One of these in particular aroused Fenner's interest. On his last day in New York, with his BOAC flight to London delayed, he wandered over to the recently completed Lever House. Designed by Gordon Bunshaft of Skidmore, Owings and Merrill, Lever House in 1953 was 'one of the sights of New York'. A tall, prismatic glass tower supported on Le Corbusier-style pilotis rising from a glass podium, it was the forerunner of the commercial skyscraper, the ultimate in big-business architecture, and, at the time, the epitome of the modern urban structure. As Reyner Banham stated, Lever House was the first architectural expression of a new, postwar age—'a monument to an America whose existence could barely be sensed at the time: Eisenhower America, grey-flannel-suit America, with Madison Avenue only a block away'.[35] The sleek, modern lines of Lever House, derived from International Style architecture, were emblematic of corporate capitalism. But there was another potential interpretation. The ideologies and values that lay behind its repetitive, graph-paper structural grid—including technological advancement and rationalism—could equally apply to the scientific world.

---

34 Fenner, 'Collins Trip Book', 1953. The table represented in the sketch is similar to steel-framed tables designed by Jean Prouve and Le Corbusier.

35 Reyner Banham, *Age of the Masters: A Personal View of Modern Architecture* (London: Architectural Press, 1975), 114. Joan Ockman gives a good account of Lever House in 'Mirror Images: Technology, Consumption, and the Representation of Gender in American Architecture Since World War II', in *The Sex of Architecture* (New York: Harry Abrams, 1996), 191–210.

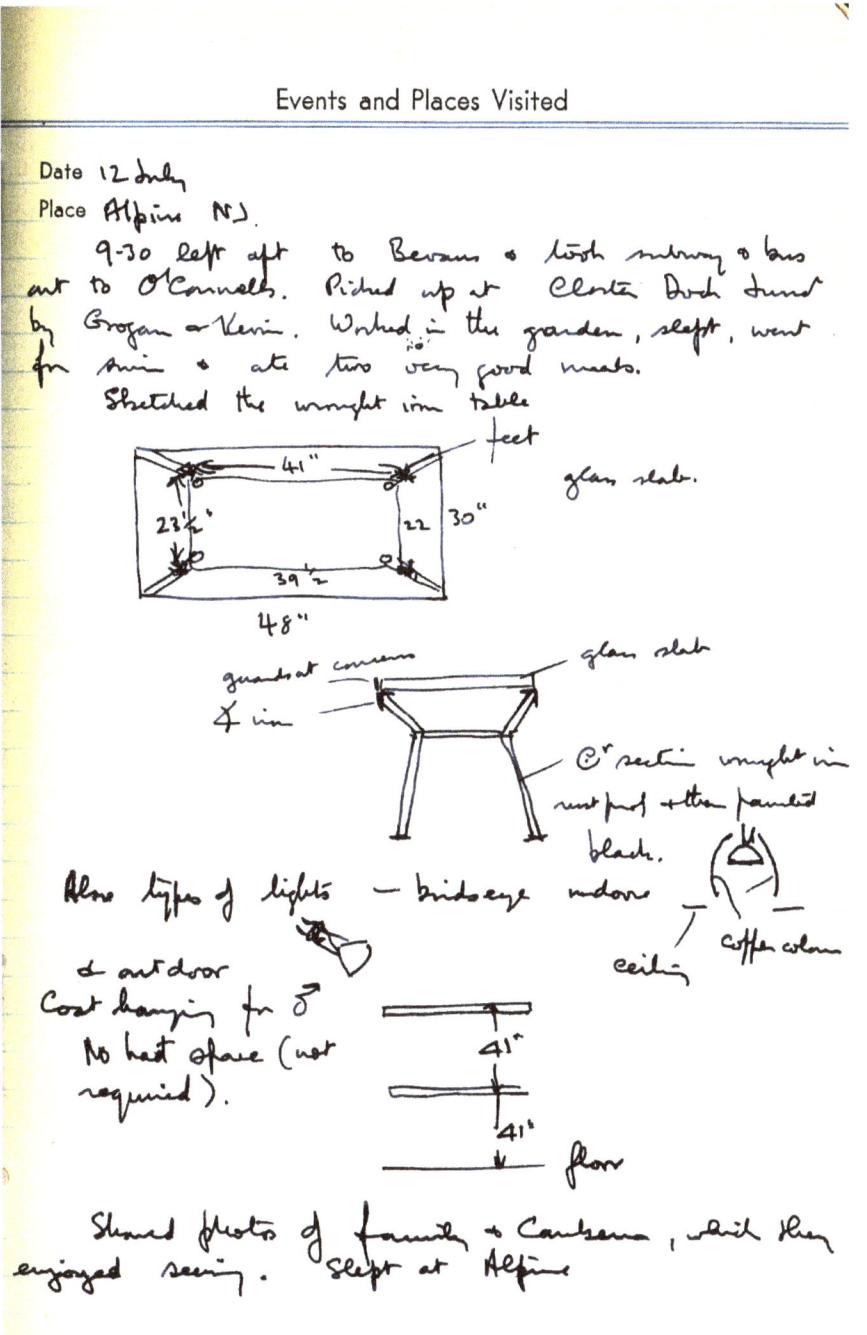

Figure 2.8 Frank Fenner, diary entry for 12 July, 1953

Image: Fenner, 'Collins' Trip Book, 1953. Manuscript Collection, Adolph Basser Library, Australian Academy of Science. Fenner, F. J., FAA (1914–2010), MS 143, Box 22. Courtesy of Marilyn Fenner

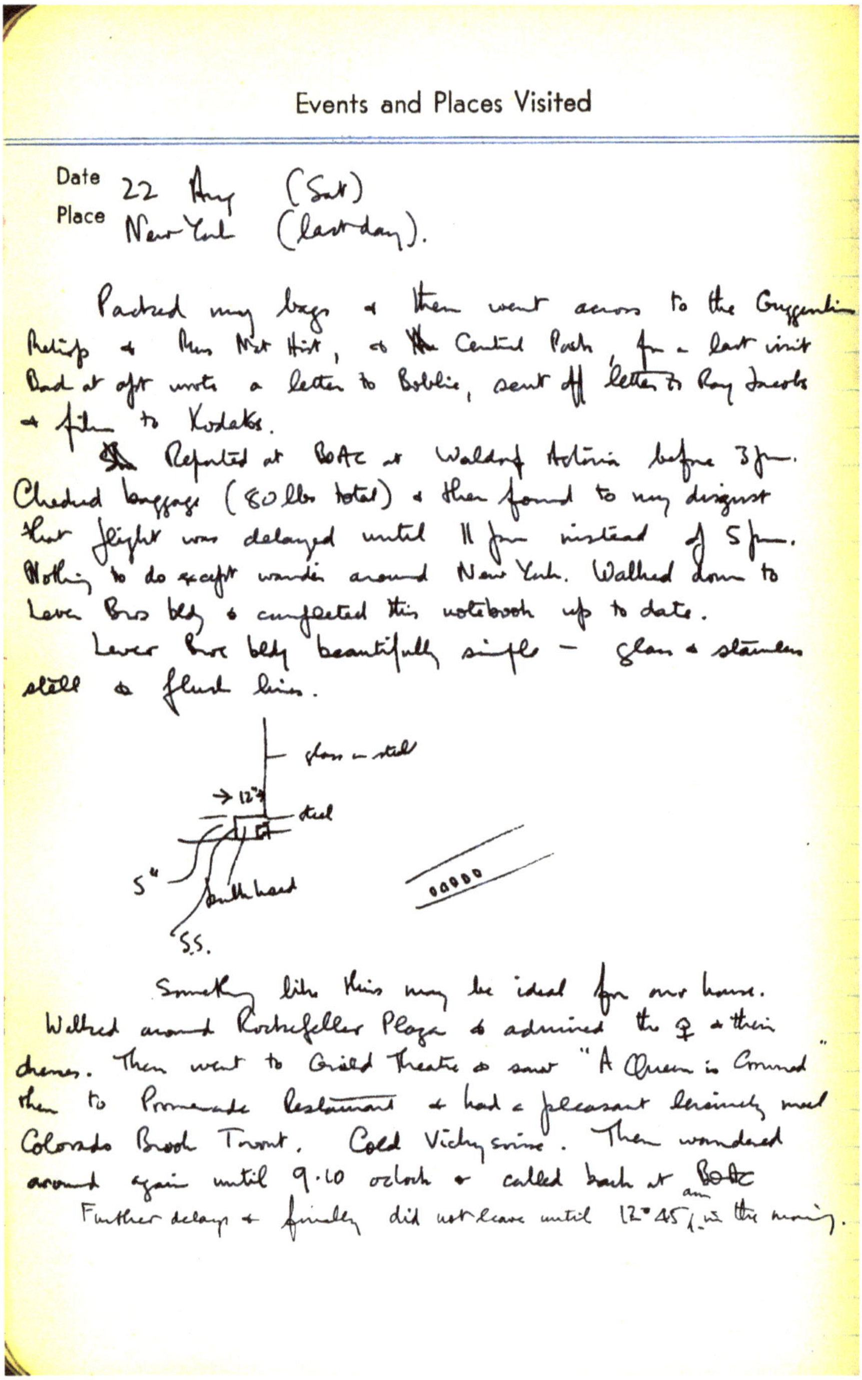
Events and Places Visited

Date 22 Aug (Sat)
Place New York (last day).

Packed my bags & then went across to the Guggenheim Phillips & Mus Nat Hist, & the Central Park, for a last visit. Back at apt wrote a letter to Bobbie, sent off letter to Roy Jacobs & film to Kodaks.

Reported at BOAC at Waldorf Astoria before 3 pm. Checked baggage (80 lbs total) & then found to my disgust that flight was delayed until 11 pm instead of 5 pm. Nothing to do except wander around New York. Walked down to Lever Bros bldg & completed this notebook up to date.

Lever Bros bldg beautifully simple – glass & stainless steel & flush lines.

Something like this may be ideal for our house. Walked around Rockefeller Plaza & admired the ♀ & their dresses. Then went to Guild Theatre & saw "A Queen is Crowned" then to Promenade Restaurant & had a pleasant leisurely meal Colorado Brook Trout, Cold Vichyssoise. Then wandered around again until 9.10 o'clock & called back at BOAC.
Further delays & finally did not leave until 12.45 am in the morning.

Figure 2.9 Frank Fenner, diary entry for 22 August, 1953

Image: Fenner, 'Collins' Trip Book, 1953. Manuscript Collection, Adolph Basser Library, Australian Academy of Science. Fenner, F. J., FAA (1914–2010), MS 143, Box 22. Courtesy of Marilyn Fenner

Figure 2.10 Lever House, New York

Photograph: J. Alex Langley, from Banham, *Age of the Masters: A Personal View of Modern Architecture*, 113

Lever House impressed Fenner because it was 'beautifully simple—glass and stainless steel and flush lines'. Not intimidated by any disjunction of scale, function or context between a New York office tower and a Canberra house, he enthusiastically sketched a detail of the building in his travel diary, noting: 'Something like this might be ideal for our house.'[36] While there is no evidence of any influence of Lever House on the Fenner House—and it is not clear if Boyd was ever shown this sketch—it is highly likely that if Fenner did discuss it with him at the time of his return, the architect might not have approved. At that

---

36   Fenner, 'Collins Trip Book', 1953.

stage, Boyd was not fond of Skidmore, Owings and Merrill's architecture, which he believed was too commercial. He began to change his mind three years later, however, when he saw Lever House for himself, and even became something of a disciple of Skidmore, Owings and Merrill when shown around the Chicago office by Bill Hartmann, with whom he proceeded to get drunk over dinner.[37] It is testament to Fenner's enthusiasm for modernism that he was one step ahead of his architect on this occasion.

In Paris, Fenner found the Musee de l'Arte Moderne 'a superb new building with a wonderful collection and good display'. After arriving in Rome by train, he was equally impressed by Eugenio Montuori's new Main Railway Station. Standing on the polished floor of the main booking hall, under the curved ribs of the vaulted roof, he looked out through the glazed end wall over the city, and described the building as 'a magnificent and very modern structure with beautiful clean lines and fine materials'.[38] In Stockholm, Ragnar Ostberg's earlier Arts and Crafts-style City Hall was appreciated for 'the splendour of the halls, especially the Golden Hall with its mosaics on a gold mosaic background. It is a really impressive building…in position, surroundings, conception, grandeur. Something we might well have somewhere in Australia, but don't.'[39]

Boyd had written that modern architecture was 'inevitably linked with modern art in the public mind',[40] and Fenner was no exception to this rule. During this overseas trip, he regularly visited art galleries in every city, often returning for more than one visit. Descriptions of art and architecture share the pages of his travel diary, and through an examination of these it is apparent that he was particularly interested in modernism and abstraction. In New York, he made frequent excursions to the Sol Guggenheim Collection, to Edward Durell Stone's gleaming white Museum of Modern Art, and to the Metropolitan Museum of Art, whose central, sunken court was a favourite lunch venue. He observed modern paintings in private residences and visited art institutions in other cities such as the National Gallery in Washington, DC, the Baltimore Art Museum and the Musee de l'Arte Moderne in Paris. One exhibition at the Guggenheim contained 'several Kandinsky's Mondrian. Some very good Chagall, an attractive Modigliani nude, and interesting Klee and Seurat'; an apartment in New York displayed 'a wonderful lot of modern originals—Picasso, Rouault etc.'; the

---

37 Serle, *Robin Boyd: A Life*, 168.
38 Assisting Montuori in the design of the Rome Main Railway Station were Leo Calini, Massimo Castellazzi, Achille Pintonello and Annibale Vitellozzi (who went on to design the Palazzetto dello Sport with Pier Luigi Nervi in 1956–57).
39 Fenner, 'Collins Trip Book', 1953.
40 Boyd, *Australia's Home: Its Origins, Builders and Occupiers*, 95.

National Gallery had 'Picasso Derain Dufy Vlamincks' that he had not seen previously 'in original or reproduction', while the Baltimore Art Museum was noted for works by Picasso and Rodin.[41]

Fenner was the ideal client for an aspiring modernist architect. He clearly appreciated modern art and architecture, was well travelled and visually astute. As a scientist, he would obviously have been comfortable with a rational design methodology: an architectural process that recognised specific problems and proceeded to find solutions in a systematic manner. But as a client, Fenner offered—and expected—more from his architect than a rational design process. Underscoring his detailed diary descriptions was a genuine excitement over the visual and tactile experiences of these new, modern objects. His enthusiasm was not based on any apparent rationality as much as it was on an admiration of simple, elegant design, and an appreciation of the materials, colours and details of modern architecture.

The Fenner House became a successful collaboration between an architect and a client who shared a common interest in modernism. When Grounds, Romberg and Boyd were awarded the ACT Chapter Medallion, *The Canberra Times* reported that the house 'contributed much to architectural thinking and contemporary design'.[42] The Fenner House received a four-page spread with colour photographs in the November 1956 edition of *Australian Home Beautiful*. It did not, however, appear on the cover of that edition; television had just arrived in Australia, and the cover displayed an image of a happy family, complete with white poodle, gathered around the latest modernist icon: an upright, timber-veneered Radiola television set, courtesy of Amalgamated Wireless. Boyd, the modern evangelist who had, seven years earlier, placed a mock-up of a television set in his 'House of Tomorrow' in Melbourne because the real thing was not available in Australia, had finally been upstaged by the real thing.[43]

Imitation of Life

> The most expert Artists among the ancients…were of [the] Opinion that an Edifice was like an Animal, so that in the Formation of it we ought to imitate Nature.
>
> — Leon Batista Alberti, *Ten Books on Architecture*[44]

---

41 Fenner, 'Collins Trip Book', 1953.
42 *The Canberra Times* (November 1956).
43 *Australian Home Beautiful* (November 1956).
44 Leon Batista Alberti, *Ten Books on Architecture*, 1755, Reprint (London: Alec Tiranti, 1955), book IX, 194.

> The key to its success will be the determination to allow the human element to become the dominant factor. The biological principle must be paramount. Man is to be the focus for all design; then it shall be truly functional.
>
> — Walter Gropius, 'Reorientation'[45]

> In the new climate beyond the door, a house which better expresses the life and the land may grow more profusely and the scattered seeds spread by creative architects may take abundant root.
>
> — Robin Boyd, *Australia's Home*[46]

Fenner was well informed in regard to the physical environment from an early age, and became increasingly involved in environmental issues throughout his career. Charles was a member of the Field Naturalists Society, and published scientific papers on geology and fieldwork. During the 1930s, he took Frank on overland excursions in an open car across South Australia and Victoria, where he explained 'features of the countryside…geological, botanical, historical, in a fascinating way'.[47] From 1948 to 1949, Fenner studied at the Rockefeller Institute for Medical Research in New York under Rene Dubos. Dubos was a huge influence; Fenner described how he later became 'an environmental guru' and coined the term 'think globally act locally'.[48] Later in his career, Fenner became a member of the Scientific Community on Problems of the Environment, foundation Director of the Centre for Resource and Environmental Studies at The Australian National University and Vice-President of the Australian Conservation Foundation.

There are a number of examples of Fenner's awareness of environmental issues in regard to architecture. In 1949, when he and the other founding professors of the John Curtin School met with Florey in Oxford to plan the new Canberra building, Fenner recalled they 'decided on an H-shape…with the main laboratories on the south of each wing, to avoid direct sunlight'.[49] During his 1953 overseas trip, he made frequent entries in his travel diary describing the details of his surroundings. Flying from London to Paris, he observed '[m]any fruit orchards. Courtyard type farmhouses etc'. While travelling by train down the coast of Italy to Rome, he was '[s]truck by [the] colour of houses in this bright sun, and the manifold measures adopted for keeping out the sun'.[50]

---

45 Walter Gropius, 'Reorientation', in Gyorgy Kepes, *The New Landscape in Art and Science* (Chicago: Paul Theobold, 1956), 97.
46 Boyd, *Australia's Home: Its Origins, Builders and Occupiers*, 278.
47 Fenner, *Nature, Nurture and Chance: The Lives of Frank and Charles Fenner*, 9–10.
48 Frank Fenner, Interview by Ann Moyal, 8 March 2001, 4 April 2001, Canberra, NLA Oral History Section.
49 Fenner, *Nature, Nurture and Chance: The Lives of Frank and Charles Fenner*, 55.
50 Fenner, 'Collins Trip Book', 1953.

2. Paradigm Shift: Boyd and the Fenner House

Figure 2.11 Aerial view of the John Curtin School of Medical Research, The Australian National University, 1957

Photograph: National Archives of Australia. NAA: A1200, L23558

Of all the sciences, it was biology that architects most frequently turned to for analogy. The purpose of the comparison was to facilitate the understanding of new, unknown concepts by connecting them to known ones. Since the eighteenth century, a number of writers have explored the potentialities of biological analogies to inform architectural theory. In the main, these have consisted of the typological analogy, by which specific types are identified with a classificatory system; the ecological analogy, where the appropriateness of a building for its environment is compared with that of plants and animals;[51] the organic analogy, meaning the harmonious relationship of parts to the whole; the anatomical analogy, or relationship between skeleton and structure; and the

---

51 Fenner recalled a scientific anecdote, regarding the 'extraordinary specialisation of the location of insects' in vegetation: 'The ticks that cause tick typhus in New Guinea were always on the margins of the forest, where you had a bit of savannah, a bit of open country, grass and then trees. And it was when troops got into that sort of country that they got scrub typhus. So I am sure, especially for insects, there are relationships of that kind.' Frank Fenner, Interview by the author, 18 October 2007.

Darwinian analogy of evolutionary trial and error.⁵² But the drawing of analogies between architecture and biology is an exercise to be treated with prudence: as architect and writer Philip Steadman warned, buildings are not organisms like plants or animals, but remain 'inert physical objects'.⁵³ Architectural historian Peter Collins argued that the strongest analogical link to architecture was the influence of environment on design—a concept he believed came from Darwinism. But the concept of natural selection was taking the analogy too far, as 'after all, in architecture it is not only the Fittest which Survive'.⁵⁴

Consideration of the formative influence of the environment on design and of the subsequent scientific analysis of building form derives from the notion of biotechnical determinism. Architectural commentator Alan Colquhoun considered this to be an underlying principle of the modern movement, and traced its origins to nineteenth-century cultural-evolutionism philosophy, particularly that of Herbert Spencer. As Colquhoun explained: 'Form was merely the result of a logical process by which the operational needs and the operational techniques were brought together. Ultimately these would fuse in a kind of biological extension of life, and function and technology would become totally transparent.'⁵⁵

There was evidence of this way of thinking in Australian architectural discourse in the immediate postwar years. Anticipating an unprecedented demand for new houses, and faced with a serious lack of funds and building materials, a series of government and private initiatives encouraged designers and builders to construct more-efficient houses. What was required were pragmatic, scientific-based methods of analysis to improve the ways in which buildings related to their environment. Consideration of the effects of the Australian sun and climate was nothing new—this had been a common topic within architectural discourse since the late nineteenth century—but what was different was the process. No longer left to conjecture, the strategies were to be founded on solid, quantifiable research.⁵⁶

---

52 Blondel's *Cours d'Architecture* is frequently cited as the origin of the modern architectural system of typological classification. Nineteenth-century German architect and writer Gottfried Semper based his theory of architectural type on animal and plant morphology. A more recent example is Philip Steadman's *The Evolution of Designs: Biological Analogy in Architecture and the Applied Arts* (Cambridge: Cambridge University Press, 1979).
53 Steadman, *The Evolution of Designs: Biological Analogy in Architecture and the Applied Arts*, 6.
54 Collins, 'The Biological Analogy', *Architectural Review* 126 (December 1959): 305. This was published in 1959 to coincide with the centenary of Charles Darwin's *The Origin of Species*.
55 Alan Colquoun, 'Typology and Design Method', *Perspecta* 12 (1969): 72, cited by Steadman, *The Evolution of Designs: Biological Analogy in Architecture and the Applied Arts*, 1.
56 For instance, in *Sub-Tropical Housing*, Viennese immigrant architect Karl Langer emphasised the need for mathematical calculations in regard to the dimensions of eaves overhangs. Karl Langer, *Sub-Tropical Housing* (Brisbane: University of Queensland Press, May 1944). *Architecture* published details of the 'Heliodon', an instrument devised by the English Building Research Station to replicate, in model form, the motion of the Sun. Working with models of proposed houses, the Heliodon could demonstrate the precise amount— and duration—of sun penetration into a building. *Architecture* (January–March 1945): 137–42. Australia's

But in some instances this belief in determinism—of the potential for scientific analysis to improve the relationship between a house, its occupants and the prevailing climate—extended beyond the considered, incremental modification of building form and veered into pure conjecture. It was this type of naive faith in biotechnical determinism that lay behind Breuer's conception of his binuclear house. Published in John Entenza's *Californian Arts & Architecture* in December 1943, it was, like the John Curtin School of Medical Research building, a 'H'-shaped building comprising two separate wings and a connecting link. One wing was for 'every day's living', while the other was for 'concentration, work and sleeping'. Predicting a model of postwar, suburban lifestyle that would never eventuate, Breuer promoted his house as a form of technological, protective cocoon for his male client: the postwar man would return to a house that was 'heated, protected, insulated, mechanized'. As he would need to enter his 'mechanized world', or place of work, only 'three or four days a week', he would be spending more time in the house and would 'more than ever appreciate his privacy'.[57]

While with the benefit of hindsight, Breuer's projections about postwar work patterns proved to be incorrect, his binuclear plan was inextricably linked to biology. The first connection was semantic: 'binuclear' was a biological term meaning a cell comprising two nuclei, while the second connection related to the splitting of the plan into two separate blocks. In a criticism of open planning that, quite unintentionally, reinforced the binuclear configuration, English biologist and geneticist Conrad Waddington compared the practice of combining different functions in the one general space—kitchen, dining, sleeping—with the form of highly evolved animals. The animals, he pointed

---

Commonwealth Experimental Building Station (CEBS), set up to research construction materials and methods, particularly in relation to house design and thermal comfort, published a series of bulletins titled *Notes on the Science of Building*. An important publication by the station was R. O. Phillips' *Sunshine and Shade in Australasia*, in which sun angles in relation to time and geographic location were mathematically determined. To this publication, Philips appended details of his own Australian version of the Heliodon, which he named the 'Solarscope'. R. O. Phillips, *Sunshine and Shade in Australasia* (Sydney: Commonwealth Experimental Building Station, 1951), Technical Study 23 (D.D.23). Walter Bunning's *Homes in the Sun* included a plea for appropriate planning in relation to solar orientation, and provided plans of 'Suntrap' and 'Solar' houses as exemplars. Walter Bunning, *Homes in the Sun: The Past, Present and Future of Australian Housing* (Sydney: W. J. Nesbitt, 1945). Along with J. W. Drysdale's *Designing Houses for Australian Climates*, this made the Commonwealth Experimental Building Station's information more accessible to the general public. The CSIRO provided further scientific-based analysis by publishing reports such as *Thermal Conductivities of Building Materials* and *The Design and Construction of Solar Water Heaters*. J. R. Barnes, *Thermal Conductivities of Building Materials* (Melbourne: CSIRO Division of Building Research, March 1946), Report No. R. 2; R. N. Morse, *The Design and Construction of Solar Water Heaters* (Melbourne: CSIRO Central Experimental Workshops, April 1954), Report No. E. D. 1. Popular periodicals such as *Australian Home Beautiful* began to cover similar themes, publishing articles such as 'What is a Solar House?', 'For Sydney's Sun' (January 1950), 'Enjoy Our Climate at Home' (August 1950), 'Sited for Sunshine' (March 1951), 'Houseful of Sunshine' (September 1951), 'Comfort or Convention' (February 1952), 'Cool in Summer—Winter Sun Trap' (September 1952), and 'An Asset in the Sunless South' (February 1953). All of these addressed the issue of appropriate design for Australian climates. 'What is a Solar House?' *Home Builders Annual* (1946): 20, 21, 64.

57   *California Arts & Architecture* (December 1943).

out, 'divided themselves into separate blocks, each of which does something to function, liver, kidney, intestine, muscles, brain'. To Waddington, the open plan—comprising various functions within the same block—was 'not sound biology'. In contrast, the binuclear plan—divided into separate blocks—was.[58]

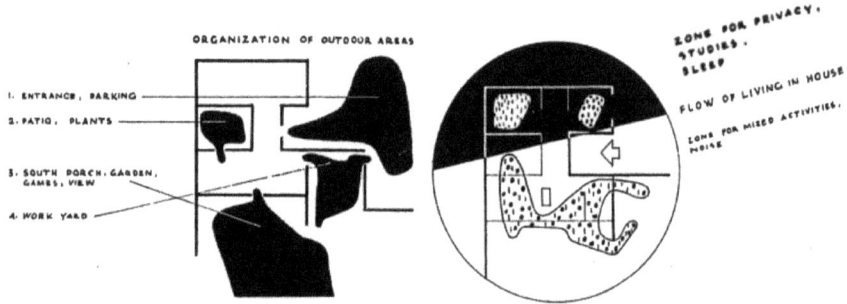

Figure 2.12 Marcel Breuer, 'binuclear' house proposal, 1943

Image: from Blake, *Marcel Breuer: Sun and Shadow, the Philosophy of an Architect*, 149

If Breuer was unwavering in his acceptance of technological progress, Boyd was circumspect. In the first edition of Australia's *Architecture and Arts* magazine, Boyd applauded the pragmatism of science, stating: 'eventually science will answer all the problems. I don't mean just in architecture—I mean in everything.'[59] But he remained wary of some aspects of scientific discourse. When Ernest Titterton, Professor of Nuclear Physics at The Australian National University, delivered an address to the Australian Architectural Convention in Melbourne titled 'Modern Warfare and Australian Cities', Boyd accused him of making the advent of the first '[a]tom bomb sound like a great humanitarian venture'.[60] He was also sceptical about some of the research by the Commonwealth Experimental Building Station, claiming that it 'seemed to justify some of this unscientific sympathy of popular buildings'.[61]

Boyd, like many Australian architects before him, believed that careful consideration of the Australian climate, in particular the sun, was one of the critical factors that needed to be addressed to improve the quality of Australian houses, whose ability to cope with extremes of temperature he found wanting. He was critical of the lack of insulation and heating in houses in the southern states, and the lack of cooling and sun shading in those in the north.[62] He

---

58   Conrad Waddington, 'Biological Form and Pattern', [Talk given to the Architectural Association, London, 1958], *Architectural Association Journal* LXXIV, no. 825 (September–October 1958).
59   *Architecture and Arts* 1, no. 1 (July 1952): 15.
60   Serle, *Robin Boyd: A Life*, 114.
61   Boyd, *Australia's Home: Its Origins, Builders and Occupiers*, 200.
62   'Lack of Comfort Deplored in Modern Homes', *The Canberra Times* (16 January 1953). This article was based on a paper Boyd had delivered to the Australian and New Zealand Association for the Advancement of

applauded Walter Butler's 'revolutionary suggestion' of 1902 that recommended northern orientation for all rooms, and 'an eave of calculated width which would shade the glass only in summer'.[63] Boyd was supportive of Bunning's *Homes in the Sun*, describing its author as 'the best known architectural publicist in the country'.[64] Central to Boyd's position on sun and climate was an appeal to cease fighting against 'the un-English qualities of Australia's climate', and to learn to live with it.[65] While the notion of identifying a particular 'Australian' architecture was controversial at the time—and not an idea that Boyd readily subscribed to—he nevertheless believed that the requirements of the 'modern Australian' were different from those of inhabitants of other countries. It was important to address those specific needs—to 'let these differences rule shapes, forms and details in one's building'.[66]

It was the way in which Boyd allowed the 'difference' of the bright Canberra sunlight to generate specific forms and details that most clearly expressed his ideology, and resulted in the most striking visual aspect of the Fenner House. The north faces of the two rectangular blocks are glazed full height throughout their entire length. Regularly spaced, white-painted mullions extend from floor to roof soffit, broken by a continuous horizontal transom at door head height. The overall effect of these glazed walls is reminiscent of a school classroom or laboratory building from the same period, where the same criteria—maximum admission of northern light—applied. This aspect of the Fenner House is similar to other Boyd houses, including the north-facing glazed wall of the 1952 Darbyshire House in Templestowe, Melbourne.

For Boyd, the glazed wall was impervious in two directions: 'a transparent wall which dissolved the barrier between indoors and outdoors.' As well as admitting 'light, air and view', it also worked in the opposite direction—projecting 'the enclosed space into the open' and extending 'the spatial experience within the room'.[67] In relation to the transmission of light and view, this aspect of the Fenner House worked well, but was less successful for thermal comfort. In keeping with building practice at the time, the entire walls were single glazed, which contributed to high internal temperature fluctuations. In contrast with the glazed northern walls, the eastern and western walls, and the southern wall of the diurnal block, were constructed of solid brickwork with a painted finish. The original colours specified by Boyd were a further method by which he controlled the amount—and quality—of light that entered the interior. Most

---

Science (ANZAAS) conference in Melbourne the previous day.
63   Boyd, *Australia's Home: Its Origins, Builders and Occupiers*, 60. Butler designed buildings in the Federation Arts and Crafts style in Melbourne, including the 1912 Mission to Seamen in Flinders Street.
64   Ibid., 191.
65   Ibid., 93.
66   Robin Boyd, August 1962, NLA Oral History Program.
67   Boyd, *Australia's Home: Its Origins, Builders and Occupiers*, 170–1.

walls were painted white, but surfaces capable of reflecting the intense Canberra light to the interior were painted grey.[68] By adjusting the exterior wall treatment to address the comfort level of the occupants, Boyd clad the Fenner House in a responsive skin.

The roof of the Fenner House was a further physical expression of the moderation of sunlight. A clean, low-pitched gable roof, edged by a continuous fascia line (the gutters and downpipes were concealed), it adjusted in relation to the need for sun protection as it swept around each block. Flush on the south, east and west facades, the roof cantilevered over the north facades to form a deep eaves overhang. The way in which this house admitted the low winter sun, while excluding the majority of summer sun, was an important aspect of Boyd's design. According to the client, Boyd had similarly insisted on wide eaves to the north for the earlier Hotham Crescent proposal.[69]

Figure 2.13 Fenner House, view from north-east

Photograph: Ben Wrigley, 2012

There was, however, a problem with this aspect of the design: the house admitted too much morning sun. Soon after they moved in, Fenner wrote to Boyd, complaining:

---

68   Elinor Ward, 'This House is Canberra's Medallion Winner', *Australian Home Beautiful* (November 1956): 41.
69   'He was extremely keen on a feature of this house which was unusual in the time: that you'd have wide eaves which would keep the sun out in the summer and let it in [during] the winter.' Fenner believed that Boyd, in this way, was advanced in his thinking. Frank Fenner, Interview by the author, 18 October 2007.

The sun through the upper glass of the kitchen at breakfast (before the eaves cut out some—the house faces far enough east to get early east sunlight) is very trying. We were thinking of bamboo blinds or some sort of obstruction to the sun on the upper fixed panes but would like to have your views on this.[70]

Figure 2.14 Fenner House, kitchen

Photograph: Ben Wrigley, 2012

The two separate blocks of the Fenner House, and the additive nature of the plan, created a large footprint, which gave the house a significantly high proportion of external surface area in relation to overall volume. While that high ratio of external surface was an optimum condition for the ingress of heat and light—at times when that was desirable—the opposite applied in regard to heat loss. The additional outer surface area of walls and roof provided more opportunities for loss of heat, via conduction, to the atmosphere. In turn, this created heating and cooling problems, and higher operating costs than that of a standard, more compact, plan form.

Two environmental influences—neither of which was anticipated by Boyd—came into effect after the Fenner House was completed. The cumulative effect of these led to the Fenners experiencing great anxiety and considerable tension with

---

70   Fenner to Boyd, 14 April 1954, 'Fenner House Canberra', Grounds, Romberg and Boyd Records 1927–1979, Manuscript Collection, State Library of Victoria, MS 13363, Box 43/16(a). There is no record of Boyd's reply to this request.

their architect. The first was caused by alternating expansion and contraction of the timber roof sub-frame during Canberra's extreme temperature fluctuations. This caused the Malthoid roofing to stretch and buckle, which eventually created tears in the material and numerous leaks inside the house. The failure of the Malthoid roof was not uncommon—almost all such roofs by Boyd and Grounds suffered the same fate—but the process was accelerated by the high temperature fluctuations between day and night experienced in Canberra's inland, high-altitude location.[71] The cause of the other problem was of a biological nature, but not in the broad sense that has previously been alluded to: this was very specific. To achieve the clean, continuous line of the fascia running around the edge of the roof, Boyd had concealed box gutters within the roof. But these were not designed with correct overflow safeguards, and when the outlets became blocked with leaves from nearby trees, they flooded with water and formed a further source of water penetration into the interior of the house.

At this stage in his career, Boyd had limited knowledge of construction and detailing. While he had many projects under way, the rapid acceleration of his practice had provided minimal post-occupancy feedback—but that would come. His partner Frederick Romberg was known for his attention to detailing. Romberg considered Boyd's house designs at that period to be 'outstanding', but 'a little suspect' in construction.[72] When Boyd travelled to the United States in August 1956—missing the celebration for the award of the Canberra Medallion—he left behind a number of houses at various stages of construction. Problems soon arose, including leaking roofs and chimneys that smoked inside the rooms. Complaints were directed to his partners, who did not let these go by without comment to Boyd. Boyd later complained that his sleep was interrupted by nightmares of 'Dr. Roche, Mrs. Ednie, and the little man from Lemon Street, North Balwyn, shaking their poor, rain-soaked heads at me and disappearing in billows of smoke'.[73] While there was no apparition of the Fenners in his dreams, they had in fact notified the architect that their house leaked as far back as June 1955.[74]

---

71 Graemme Gunn, a former Grounds, Romberg and Boyd employee, attributed the problems of Malthoid roofs to excessive 'expansion and contraction of wood subframes in the extremes of Australian temperature'. Hamann, Modern Architecture in Melbourne: The Architecture of Grounds, Romberg and Boyd, 1927–1971, footnote, 165.
72 Serle, *Robin Boyd: A Life*, 130–1. 'Some contemporaries were eventually to consider that in many respects Romberg was the best architect of the three, especially as a technician and an "administrator" of a building' (p. 143).
73 Hamann, Modern Architecture in Melbourne: The Architecture of Grounds, Romberg and Boyd, 1927–1971, 206–8. Dr Roche was a Canberra client to whom Fenner had recommended Boyd's services in June 1954. Fenner to Boyd, 10 June 1954, 'Fenner House Canberra', Grounds, Romberg and Boyd Records 1927–1979, MS 13363, Box 43/16(a).
74 Letter from Frank Fenner to Robin Boyd, 23 June 1955, 'Fenner House Canberra', Grounds, Romberg and Boyd Records 1927–1979, MS 13363, Box 43/16(a).

Over a four-year period, the Fenners did the best they could to treat the symptoms. But by late 1958, after a series of particularly heavy downpours, they ran out of patience. Fenner made an impassioned plea to his architect to address the cause, writing:

> [W]e have never had a year (indeed hardly a month) in which there were not leaks somewhere…We have decided that the only thing to do is to re-roof the house with something that will not leak…There is no such guarantee and we're up for the whole price of re-roofing—unless you are willing to make a contribution towards it.

Stating that he and Bobbie appreciated 'many aspects of the design of this house', he regretted that 'its complete failure to exclude water makes it impossible for us to leave it even for a week, lest the floor and carpets somewhere else are ruined by water'. At this point, the Fenners were prepared to walk away from their award-winning house:

> Bobbie would like to sell it and live in a rented house because she can no longer put up with dishes and towels all around the floor when it rains; but we can't even sell it with the roof as it is.
>
> Yours sincerely,
>
> Frank.
>
> p. s. Since beginning this letter a new leak has developed in the Drawing-room, so that we now have three dishes on the floor of the family room and one on the cabinet in the drawing room.[75]

A further effect of the ingress of moisture was that timbers began to rot, particularly in the frame of the glazed connecting link. Fenner sent samples of the affected timber to the Division of Forest Products at the CSIRO in Melbourne for analysis. Receiving confirmation that the rot was a fungal infection associated with excessive dampness, he forwarded the information to Boyd for his attention.[76]

In 1960, Boyd engaged Bischoff to act as his representative in Canberra. Bischoff arranged for the Malthoid roof to be replaced with a previously unavailable Swiss-designed aluminium foil, and reported to Boyd: 'Mrs. Fenner reports no leaks recently so here's hoping.' This solution, however, also failed. In July 1961, Grounds, Romberg and Boyd wrote to the roofing company complaining of new

---

75 Letter from Fenner to Robin Boyd, 1 December 1958, 'Fenner House Canberra', Grounds, Romberg and Boyd Records 1927–1979, MS 13363, Box 43/16(a).
76 Fenner to Division of Forest Products, CSIRO, Melbourne, 21 May 1958, 'Fenner House Canberra', Grounds, Romberg and Boyd Records 1927–1979, MS 13363, Box 43/16(a).

leaks.⁷⁷ The roofs to both blocks were eventually re-roofed with continuous steel roof sheeting, which finally solved the problem, but at significant cost. Hamann claimed that each time the roof was replaced, the cost was almost equivalent to the total original building fee.⁷⁸

Riposte

By omitting any consideration of the role of women in his analysis of the 'post-war man', Breuer's methodology was flawed. His whole concept that the functional requirements of a house could be considered purely from the male occupant's needs was deficient, as were many of the reasons for his subsequent advocacy of the binuclear plan type. The Fenner House, as a descendant of that type, retains within its layout atavistic evidence of those same assumptions.

When the Fenner House won the Canberra Medallion, the judges claimed that the plan 'has the merit of separating the sleeping accommodation and children's playroom from the general living and entertainment part of the home'.⁷⁹ But there are a number of comments to be made about this separation of functions. The postwar idea that leisure time would increase had resulted in a growing emphasis on the provision of recreation spaces within the home. Many of the Californian Case Study Houses incorporated such spaces. In some of these, a child's playroom was located adjacent to the kitchen, facilitating supervision from the kitchen, while others provided an adult 'hobby' space near the kitchen.⁸⁰ But in the Fenner House the kitchen and playroom were located in separate blocks, making supervision of young children from the kitchen impossible. When the house was first built, Vicki was old enough to play by herself, but Marilyn would have required supervision. The functional ramifications of this were that both children were left unsupervised at times, that the relatively small dining room doubled as a playroom during the day or that Bobbie sought domestic help for either cooking or child minding.⁸¹ A further issue was the location of the study opening directly off the playroom, making this space impractical while the playroom was being used. The decision

---

77 'Fenner House Canberra', Grounds, Romberg and Boyd Records 1927–1979, MS 13363, Box 43/16(a).
78 Hamann, Modern Architecture in Melbourne: The Architecture of Grounds, Romberg and Boyd, 1927–1971, 165.
79 *The Canberra Times* (November 1956).
80 The 'utility' space that Boyd indicated next to the kitchen in the Fenner House was a combined laundry, pantry and storage area, not a hobby space.
81 The first option was highly unlikely, the second was plausible, but impractical, given the dimensions of the dining room, while the third was also possible, but remains unconfirmed. Joachim Driller made a similar observation regarding the separation of kitchen and playroom in the Geller House I. Joachim Driller, *Breuer Houses* (London: Phaidon, 2000), 150.

to place adults' and children's bedrooms in the same wing was practical while the children were young, but not so desirable as they grew older, when separate parents' and children's zones might have been a preferable option.

It has not been possible to give a full account of the role played by Bobbie Fenner in the story of this house. It is most probable that, as a partner in marriage, she played an equal role to Frank in most respects; however, she died in 1995 and left few written records.[82] On the other hand, Frank, a highly prolific publisher and diarist, left many written accounts of his public and personal lives, and these, plus recorded interviews, form a large part of the documented history of the Fenner House. It is for this reason that the client's perspective has been related through his voice.

The available documentation does reveal, however, that Bobbie was the client contact throughout almost the entire construction phase—a period of six months. Frank departed for overseas study just after the contract documents were signed, leaving Bobbie in charge of 'any problems that might arise' before he returned at the end of October.[83] As it turned out, there were plenty. Boyd initially engaged Tom Haseler (who had previously worked with John Eccles on his house) to supervise construction, and attended site infrequently. Bobbie found Haseler, however, to be 'very conservative', and became concerned that he was making many decisions that were in conflict with Boyd's design. She had 'quite an argument' with Boyd about this before she managed to convince him to 'take over supervision himself and come up more frequently'.[84] During the construction period, there was frequent written correspondence between the Fenners.[85]

The 'sensitive use of colour and texture of materials' was another aspect of the Fenner House that attracted praise from the Canberra Medallion judges.[86] Elinor Ward was impressed by this feature: 'As always with a Robin Boyd house, the colour is exciting and imaginative.' The bold use of colours throughout the house expressed a sense of playfulness. A deep-blue entrance door appeared to 'float' in the glass link, while the living room had teal-blue ceilings, a light-green wall, and chairs upholstered in plum, blue, lemon and yellow fabric. The dining room

---

82   The only available documents consist of personal letters that Bobbie wrote to Frank when he was overseas. Unfortunately, these are from an earlier trip; the 1953 letters, written when the house was under construction, are not available.
83   Fenner, *Nature, Nurture and Chance: The Lives of Frank and Charles Fenner*, 61.
84   Tom Haseler, of 56 Arthur Circle, Forrest, was stated to be the supervisor on 14 September 1953. 'Fenner House Canberra', Grounds, Romberg and Boyd Records 1927–1979, MS 13363, Box 43/16(a). 'At first Robin employed a local architect as supervisor, and came up rather infrequently. However, this man was very conservative, and repeatedly made decisions which went against Robin's ideas and our own. Bobbie had quite an argument with Robin about this, but eventually persuaded him to take over supervision himself and come up more frequently.' Fenner to Serle, 17 June 1994, Fenner, F. J., FAA (1914–2010), MS 143/8/4H, Box 3.
85   Fenner, 'Collins Trip Book', 1953.
86   *The Canberra Times* (November 1956).

was painted deep coral, the kitchen had blue cabinets, scarlet benchtops and black linoleum tiles, while the children's bedroom had grey walls and a citron-yellow ceiling.[87] For stuffy, English-influenced 1950s Canberra—where wall-to-wall floral carpets, pastel-coloured walls, rose-patterned linen upholstery and checked gingham or lace net curtains were de rigueur—this represented a quantum leap into the future. Boyd described the colour scheme as 'varied, but not riotous…which can't result in discords', relying on a 'basic grey neutral' background to provide a foil to the brighter colours. Frances Hutchison believed that Bobbie deserved credit for the interior colours, reporting that the colour schemes were 'worked out by Mrs. Fenner using the children's paint boxes'. It is clear that Boyd liaised with Bobbie on the colours: a letter referring to the colour scheme, and to 'linen colour samples from Miss Hardess', was addressed to Bobbie rather than to Frank.[88]

While the significant contributions of women are hidden within the text, the female presence, from Boyd's point of view, has been visible throughout. To him, the Australian house was strictly women's territory, and feminine in gender. This was not based on his own ideals, but on how he perceived male culture. For the sensitive, artistic Boyd, the conventions of 1950s male comradeship—and related fears of being labelled 'effeminate', 'affected' or a 'pansy'—restricted male involvement in domestic matters to the mere solving of practical problems. Those elements of the house that he believed males were permitted to concern themselves with were thus limited to 'parts that were liable to leak or jam', including 'eaves gutters' and 'sliding sashes'. The woman, on the other hand, was given free rein over everything else: 'the plan, the colours, the fabrics, the shapes.'[89] Boyd's gendered taxonomy of the Australian house revealed two important issues. By building 'male' components, such as gutters and downpipes, within the depth of the roof and wall cavities of the Fenner House, he rendered invisible and inaccessible the very elements that required male attention. And so, when the rainwater system did inevitably fail, for the reasons outlined above, it was almost impossible to rectify.

Boyd's reading of 1950s Australian masculinity needs to be placed in perspective. In a number of articles, he revealed a lack of affinity for what he termed the 'lowbrowism' of the average Australian male—a sentiment that sometimes veered into snobbish distaste. As his biographer, Geoffrey Serle, pointed out, Boyd was 'the very opposite of the good-on-yer-mate backslapper', and in his contempt for 'the mob swilling their beer in squalid pubs' and the 'empty

---

87 Elinor Ward, 'This House is Canberra's Medallion Winner', *Australian Home Beautiful* (November 1956): 40–2, 45. The chairs included a Grant Featherstone-designed Contour Chair.
88 Boyd to Bobbie Fenner, 29 January 1954, 'Fenner House Canberra', Grounds, Romberg and Boyd Records 1927–1979, MS 13363, Box 43/16(a); Frances Hutchison, 'Medal-Winning House', *Australian House and Garden* (November 1956).
89 Boyd, *Australia's Home: Its Origins, Builders and Occupiers*, 266, 272.

arrogant look of the ockers', he might not have sufficiently appreciated some of the decent qualities of the ordinary Australian man.[90] The positive side of this was Boyd's own lack of arrogance and his genuine sensitivity to clients' needs—the very characteristics that had led Fenner to Boyd, rather than to Grounds, in the first place.[91]

The Fenner House was an incremental part of Boyd's search for the appropriate postwar house—for a house that displayed a genuine response to questions of climate, appropriate materials and human comfort. The Fenner House exemplified Boyd's call for simple, practical plans with open living areas and blocks of single-room width. Sited to maximise northern and southern light, and to provide shelter from prevailing winds, these were to be covered by low-pitched roofs whose overhangs responded to seasonal sun angles.

While Boyd had been highly critical of existing domestic architecture in Canberra, believing it to be pretentious and style driven, he still held a genuine respect for the underlying structure of the city: 'despite all the architectural chauvinism, despite architecture itself, Canberra is beautiful'. This, he believed, was mainly due to a combination of Walter Burley Griffin's street planning and Pryor's planting.[92]

Within this context it appears that the Fenner House, with its lack of concession to accepted local convention and absence of historical style, became Boyd's riposte to all that had come before. This was Boyd's opportunity to show how houses *could* be built in Canberra. And the success of the Fenner House in this respect was largely due to the binuclear plan. While there were shortcomings in regard to internal relationships and efficiency, the clear logic of the articulated binuclear plan provided Boyd with an opportunity to break the house down into three smaller, easily manipulated elements. Each of these was then adjusted carefully in relation to criteria such as roof pitch, eaves overhang and fenestration, so that each responded to individual requirements, but still remained part of a coherent whole. There were problems with the implementation of some of this. These were due partly to Boyd's relative inexperience, but also to limitations with available technology—for instance, steel roof sheeting was not available in sufficient lengths to provide continuous coverage.

In spite of the significant technical shortcomings, this was a brave house, and one that—in accordance with Boyd's intentions—departed radically from the kaleidoscope of historical, style-based houses that pervaded Canberra suburbs. Fenner's enthusiasm for the project can be detected in a series of letters he wrote to Florey in Oxford in late 1953. Keeping Florey regularly informed of progress

---

90   Serle, *Robin Boyd: A Life*, 138, 328–9.
91   See Lewis's comments to Fenner regarding the differing personalities of Boyd and Grounds in Chapter 1.
92   Robin Boyd, 'The Functional Neurosis', *Architectural Review* (August 1954).

at the university, Fenner usually concluded his letters with a brief update on progress at his own house. In February 1954, he reported that it was 'going well and the painters are now at work on it. We expect to move in in 2 or 3 weeks. We're very pleased with it and think that it is quite a handsome structure, and will be comfortable too.'[93]

Figure 2.15 Fenner House, living room

Photograph: Ben Wrigley, 2012

Figure 2.16 Fenner House, dining room

Photograph: Ben Wrigley, 2012

---

93 Fenner to Florey, Canberra, 4 December 1953, 18 February 1954, 23 April 1954, Fenner, F. J., FAA (1914–2010), MS 143/19/1 A to G, Box 38.

3. Promoting the New Paradigm: Seidler and the Zwar House

Figure 3.1 Zwar House, 1955, south-east view from Yapunyah Street

Photograph: Brendan Lepschi, 2005

Throughout the history of architecture there have been many pamphleteers, publicists and polemicists who have helped to shift public perceptions of existing doctrines, and to promote the advantages of new ways of thinking. Robin Boyd was one such individual within Australian modernist discourse. Another was Harry Seidler, whose campaign in the early 1950s to introduce modernist ideas gained much publicity. 'High Priest of the Twentieth Century', 'Modern Master: How Harry Seidler Changed the Way We Live', and 'Harry Seidler Preached the Gospel of Modern Architecture to His Adopted Country' were just a few of the headlines he received.[1]

Seidler's campaign attracted the attention of many Australians who followed architecture, art and design. One of these was John Zwar, a young plant physiologist who arrived in Canberra to take up a position at the CSIRO in 1952.

---

1   *People* presented a four-page article on Seidler in January 1951 in which he was ordained the 'High Priest of the Twentieth Century', one whose duty was to persuade 'conservatives that his houses are just right for this modern age'. Seidler was presented as a form of avenging angel who 'wears bow ties, walks on crepe-soled shoes, and talks with an American accent'. *People* (17 January 1951): 17–20. The other references are by Philip Drew, [Domain], *Sydney Morning Herald* (16 March 2006): cover, 8.

One of the first scientists recruited by Frankel to the Division of Plant Industry, Zwar had read many of Seidler's articles, along with those of the architect's mentor, Walter Gropius. He also owned a dining suite designed by Charles Eames. A significant part of Zwar's attraction to Seidler was his reputation as a vanguard of modernism—an individual who was prepared to challenge accepted conventions of taste and design. Zwar, for whom existing domestic architecture in Canberra was moribund—both aesthetically and functionally—saw Seidler as a kindred soul. Here was someone who not only shared his own views about house design, but also was prepared to stand up for his principles. Zwar was impressed by Seidler's well-publicised victories over planning authorities, noting how 'several municipalities had challenged his plans and he'd gone to court and won every one'.[2]

Seidler was aware that some of the interest in his architecture was generated by his growing notoriety and recent successes in the Land and Evaluation Court. But he believed that the principal reason he was in demand was because many clients, like Zwar, saw that it was time for a change: 'a lot of people were genuinely sick of the rather routine brick boxes that were built everywhere at that time, and the place was simply ripe for new things.'[3]

In 1955—the year after he bought an elevated site with a view over the city at 12 Yapunyah Street, O'Connor—Zwar read Seidler's *Houses, Interiors and Projects*. He was particularly impressed by the seven pages of plans, sections and photographs dedicated to the Bowden House in Deakin.[4] He decided to approach Seidler. But the architect's formidable reputation was also a deterrent, and for some time Zwar hesitated in contacting him. Would he accept such a modest commission? And would Zwar be able to get along with the architect who, like his boss, Frankel, already had a reputation as a 'stormy petrel'?[5] Zwar mulled over these issues. Following discussions with his work colleagues, he

---

2 John Zwar, Interview by the author, 26 September 2008. *Australian Home Beautiful* published a proposal for a binuclear house in May 1950, and in September of the following year it published an article explaining how Seidler had become embroiled in 'a three month fight' to obtain a building permit for another house. The Rose Seidler House was published by *Woman's Day and Home* and *Australian Home Beautiful* in 1952, the latter describing how Seidler—'a young man now barely 30, a "New Australian" of a few years standing, who was already one of the most controversial figures in Australian architecture'—had won the 1951 Sir John Sulman Award for architectural merit. In 1954 Seidler's prefabricated steel 'House of the Future', a one-bedroom house for 'a young married couple', was assembled at the Armco factory in Sutherland, NSW, and later erected inside the exhibition floor of the Sydney Town Hall as part of the Architectural and Building Exhibition. The exhibition was opened by Walter Gropius on a visit to Australia. Details and photographs of the house, which had been drawn by Colin Griffiths, were published in *The Australian Women's Weekly* and other publications.
3 Harry Seidler, Interview by Hazel de Berg, 13 January 1972, National Library of Australia, Oral History Program. As Philip Drew wrote, these new clients were responding 'to the clarity and rationalism of Modernism' that Seidler promised. Kenneth Frampton and Philip Drew, *Harry Seidler: Four Decades of Architecture* (London: Thames and Hudson, 1992), 19.
4 Harry Seidler, *Houses, Interiors and Projects* (Sydney: Associated General Publications, 1954), 52–8.
5 'His stormy-petrel idealism has won him admiration'. *People* (17 January 1951): 19.

was eventually persuaded to contact the architect. But he was disappointed with the response: Seidler was grateful to receive the inquiry, but would not be able to accept, due to other commitments. At this point, Zwar was ready to concede defeat, but his colleague suggested that he visit Seidler in person and try to talk him into accepting the commission. With nothing to lose, Zwar drove to Sydney, picked up another friend for moral support, and went looking for Seidler's Point Piper office.[6]

Figure 3.2 Bowden House, view from south-west, 1954

Photograph: Max Dupain, from Seidler, *Houses, Interiors and Projects*, 53

After parking outside 4 Wolseley Crescent, Zwar descended a long flight of steps and arrived at a solid, blue-painted door. The door was set, off-centre, in a Mondrian-like pattern of square, horizontal and vertical glazing panels. Looking through those panels, Zwar could see right into the office. Behind Seidler, who was already getting up from his desk on the right, there was a freestanding open bookcase that separated the front office from the living area

---

6   As was the case with the Fenner House, with the Zwar House, it is difficult to establish the role that Zwar's wife, Heather, played in the process. John said that she did not travel to Sydney with him to meet Seidler. When asked how much she was involved in discussions regarding the house, he said 'Oh, a bit'. John Zwar, Interview by the author, 26 September 2008.

to the rear. The modulated compartments of the bookcase—containing books, architectural models and other objects—formed a composition that countered the glazed panels of the entrance wall. When viewed together, the patterns of these surfaces created visual tension across the depth of the space and formed a coherent spatial composition.[7]

Figure 3.3 Harry Seidler's Point Piper Studio at night

Photograph: from *Art and Design*, no. 1, 1949, 26

The visual interplay experienced by Zwar was an example of what Seidler referred to as 'counterpoint'—a musical term he borrowed to describe an interaction between contrasting elements. Seidler believed that counterpoint—an ideal composition containing the right balance between opposing characteristics such as solid against void, vertical against horizontal, curved against straight or dark against light—was capable of invigorating a work of art or architecture.[8]

---

7 The Point Piper office was described in *People* (17 January 1951): 18; Seidler, *Houses, Interiors and Projects*, 124–5; and more recently by Philip Goad, 'An Interview with Penelope Seidler, The Architect's Studio, 1948–49', in Ann Stephen, Philip Goad and Andrew McNamara, *Modern Times: The Untold Story of Modernism in Australia* (Melbourne: The Miegunyah Press, 2008), 114–19.
8 'Visual opposition will give life to environment. Not all transparency and not all solidity, not all soft and not all hard, but a skilful visual interplay between opposites; planes opposing each other, verticals against horizontals, solid opposed by void, hard-rough texture against soft-smooth, dark against light, cold colour against warm, curve against straight line, and above all in Australia's climate sunlight against shadow.' Harry Seidler, 'Notes on Architecture', in Harry Seidler, *Houses, Buildings and Projects 1955/63* (Sydney: Horwitz, 1963), 11.

The effect was further enhanced by the use of colour. The side and rear walls, carpet, ceiling and freestanding bookcase were all grey, while the curtains were yellow. Contrasting with this were small highlights of strong colour: doors and cushions of bright blue, red and yellow, and a cantilevered, black wall unit. Zwar found the overall effect of this composition impressive—as had Seidler's first Australian client, who requested the exact colour scheme for her own house.[9]

Believing that Seidler was out of his league, and that he, as a young scientist on a modest income, would not be able to impress him, Zwar opened the discussion on safe territory. He said that he liked the Bowden House, and described his Yapunyah Street block—photographs of which he had previously sent to Seidler's office. Confident that the conversation was going well, Zwar decided to make his pitch. In his matter-of-fact manner, he explained that his budget was £5000, and added: 'That's the amount of money. I want a house—the sort of house you design. What can we do for that?' Perhaps it was Zwar's enthusiasm that impressed Seidler, because he soon agreed to take on the project. A brief discussion followed, during which it was decided that Seidler would design a basic module that could be added onto as the family grew. The architect added that he knew a good firm of builders in Canberra—Primmer and McPhail, who had constructed the Bowden House—and said that he would talk to them once the plans were ready. Some time later, Primmer and McPhail's quote of £4600—comfortably within Zwar's budget—was accepted.[10]

Zwar met Seidler in Canberra on a number of occasions, both prior to and during construction of the house. He found that, in spite of his architect's reputation for being difficult, he was 'a charmer'—the easiest man to get along with. But he was aware of the reason for this: he agreed to almost everything his architect suggested. Had that not been the case, Zwar believed the situation might have been quite different.[11]

---

9   *People* (17 January 1951): 18. The studio was linked, via an intellectual framework of European modernism, to Seidler's first studio in New York. There, at 222 Riverside Drive on the Upper West Side, he had decorated the walls with a Mondrian-like pattern of black and yellow lines. As Penelope recalled, Mondrian was 'the connecting thread between both of Harry's apartments'. Philip Goad, 'An Interview with Penelope Seidler, The Architect's Studio, 1948–49', 117.
10 The final cost of the house was closer to £5000. John Zwar, Interview by the author, 26 September 2008. Rather than going to open tender, Seidler preferred to cultivate a select group of builders who were familiar with his working methodology and could be trusted to maintain his high standards of workmanship. Once the documents were ready, he negotiated a price with them. There were other advantages in maintaining relationships with builders: through McPhail, Seidler obtained a commission to design the South Canberra Bowling Club in Austin Street, Griffith. It is possible that Seidler returned the favour in kind: the *Harry Seidler Collection of Architectural Drawings, 1948–1987* contains sketch plans of a proposed house in Ryrie Street, Campbell, for Miss June McPhail.
11 In this respect, Zwar cited John Philip, the subject of a later chapter, as an example of a client who would not have been as compliant as he was. John Zwar, Interview by the author, 26 September 2008.

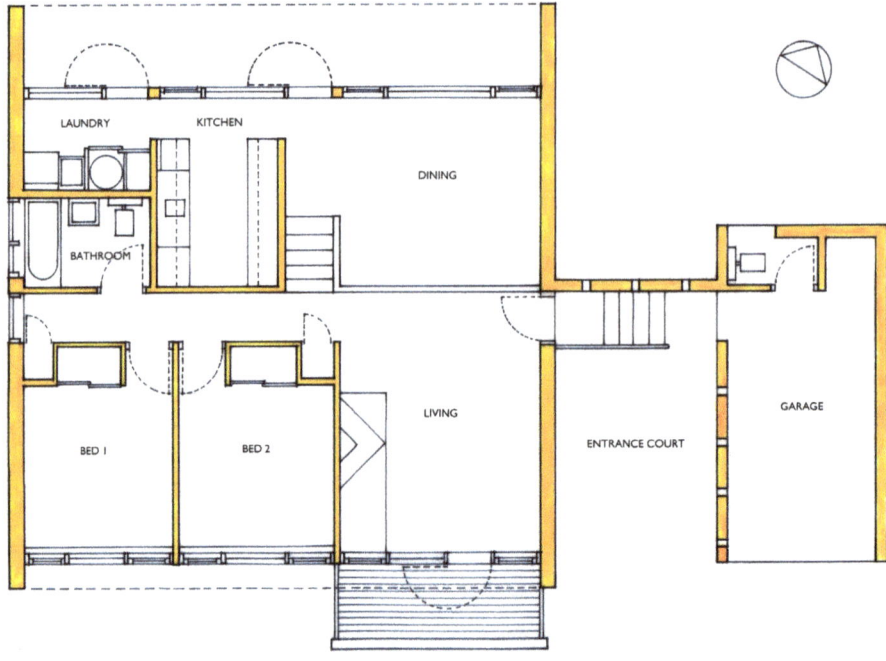

Figure 3.4 Zwar House, floor plan

Image: redrawn by the author from Harry Seidler

Seidler personally prepared the colour scheme for the Zwar House. He specified colours and finishes for all external and internal surfaces, including fabrics for curtains, upholstery and cushion covers, and stipulated where the various items and materials could be purchased. Zwar visited Rene's in the Strand Arcade in Sydney to find a black-and-white curtain fabric that Seidler had selected, and followed his architect's instructions as much as his limited budget would allow. When the house was finished, Zwar was criticised by his friends for following his architect's colour scheme so faithfully: 'What, you're letting your architect dictate your taste?' They thought he was mad.[12]

Nearly 50 years later, when his wife, Heather, had died and his family had grown up, Zwar decided that it was time to sell the house. Before he did so, he rang Seidler. Zwar explained that he had been 'very happy with the house', and recalled that they had a pleasant conversation. Seidler, who remembered Zwar and the house, said that he appreciated the call. As Zwar noted, it was not long after that when the architect passed away.[13]

---

12 Ibid.
13 Ibid.

Point Piper Laboratory

> Harry always liked to do houses because it was sort of his laboratory—you were always searching for types…they were experiments, there were versions that never went anywhere, but somehow [they] became the launching pad for other variations.
>
> — Colin Griffiths[14]

In mid-1955, Colin Griffiths was briefed by Seidler and began to prepare the sketch plans for the Zwar House.[15] Griffiths was one of Seidler's first employees, having joined the office at the beginning of 1954 to replace Don Gazzard, who had travelled overseas.

The Zwar House, a 'one-box', square house measuring approximately 11.6 m by 11.6 m (excluding the garage block and bedroom extensions), conformed to a particular type of small house that Seidler and Griffiths were continually developing and adapting: a compact, minimum, low-cost model that could be manipulated to respond to the topography and solar orientation of various sites. Griffiths recalled that the small houses presented a constant challenge, particularly in finding the right builders and keeping within budget. They were simple brick houses with a mono-pitch, 'shed' roof of corrugated, 'Super Six' asbestos. Usually square in configuration, they often incorporated a split in level to accommodate the slope of the site. The square form was partly based on the rationale that the lowest budget was obtained through the most compact plan form, and that any attenuation of that basic form increased the wall areas and material costs. But this plan type was also influenced by Bauhaus aesthetics. Griffiths recalled how it was based on the Bauhaus idea of beginning with a pure, platonic form that was then manipulated as required. Internal spatial variations were explored, while the external form was modulated by puncturing voids, or by pushing out or recessing various elements.[16]

Sometimes referred to by Seidler as 'ring plan' houses,[17] the first of these compact models was a proposal for a house in Beecroft. The Marcus Seidler House in Turramurra, of 1949–51, was an enlarged version, as was another in Gordon. The standard Universal House proposal, designed by Seidler for the Small Homes Bureau of the Royal Australian Institute of Architects—and drawn by Griffiths—was a further variation. The 1956 Heyden House in Miranda, the 1956 Breakspear House in Clontarf, a 1958 house in Kangaroo Point, the 1958

---

14 Colin Griffiths, Interview by the author, 31 October 2008.
15 The sketch plan is dated 4 August 1955.
16 Colin Griffiths, Interview by the author, 31 October 2008.
17 Seidler, *Houses, Interiors and Projects*, xvii.

Experiments in Modern Living

Luursema House in Castlecrag, the 1958 Bland House in Coogee and exhibition houses in Pennant Hills of 1960 and Carlingford of 1962 were all variations of the same theme.[18]

Seidler used the split between the two levels, which divided the house into two equal rectangles, for two functions: to follow the natural site slope and to separate the house into functional zones. In the Zwar House, the bedrooms and the living area were placed on the lower level, while the dining room and 'service rooms'—kitchen, laundry and bathroom—were located on the upper level. It was the nexus between the way in which the internal plan was split according to the functions and the need to provide a change in level to correspond with the natural site conditions that provided Seidler with an opportunity to achieve one of his principal goals: maximum spatial effect for minimum use of material. The split-level configuration of the Zwar House provided a higher volume through the central area, which dramatised the experience of the house at key points.

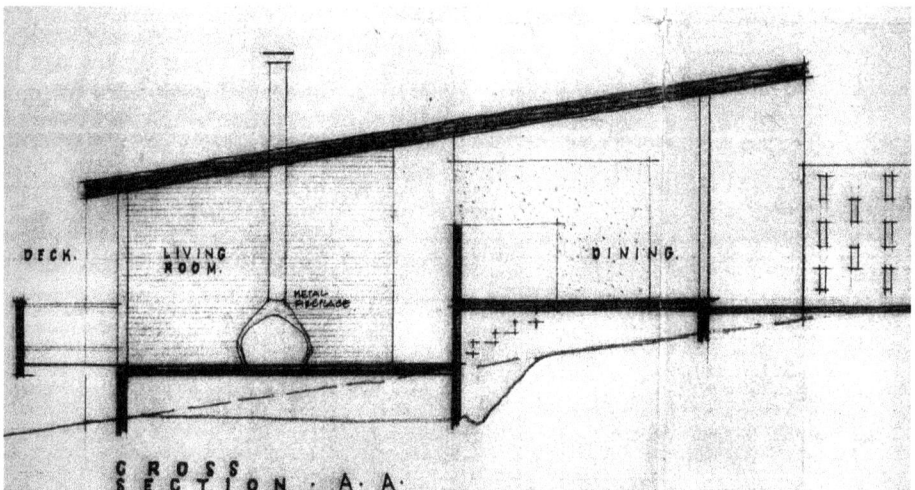

Figure 3.5 Zwar House, cross-section

Image: from 'John Zwar House, Lot 68 Yapunyah O'Connor ACT', drawn by Colin Griffiths for Harry Seidler, 4 August, 1955. John Zwar Collection

But the corridor, which divided the plan across the centre and separated the bedrooms and living room from the rest of the house, also conceptually divided the Zwar House from Seidler's other variations on the square, compact house type—none of which contained a corridor.[19] While it is clear that the main reason

---

18 Details of these houses are included in ibid.; Seidler, *Houses, Buildings and Projects 1955/63*; and Frampton and Drew, *Harry Seidler: Four Decades of Architecture*.
19 The one exception was a short section of corridor in the 1960 Pennant Hills exhibition house.

for the central passage in the Zwar House was to accommodate the proposed main bedroom addition to the south-west, other houses in the compact series solved that problem without providing a separate corridor.

Seidler's overall approach to the production of design and documentation was one of extreme efficiency. Fundamental to this was the establishment of archetypal solutions that functioned well, and the adaptation and reuse of these for future projects. Griffiths described his former employer as a 'performance-based operator' who 'didn't muck around with the design' once it was accepted. Seidler saw no advantage in arriving on a Monday morning with a new scheme and starting all over again, and if a solution was successful it was reused.[20] Proof of this can be seen in the 1958 Bland House in Coogee, which was demolished in 1988. This house utilised virtually the same plan as the Zwar House, even though its orientation was turned through 90 degrees. The main differences between the houses consisted of adjustment of fenestration, roof form and sun shading. Even the built-in joinery units separating the dining area from the entry and living spaces were similar.[21]

Seidler's methodology had to be streamlined in order to function within the small office that he shared with Griffiths. Seidler sat at a desk perpendicular to the front wall, while Griffiths was stationed nearby at a collapsible drawing table. They worked on all aspects of projects together. When they discussed a drawing Griffiths would turn around and kneel on the floor with his arms resting on Seidler's desk. In that way they were able to work on a drawing together, and turn it around to view the composition from alternative angles. The confined space meant that Griffiths worked a lot from memory: 'there was no layout space, so you devised the plan, and you kept that and all its dimensions and that was put aside and you put another piece of paper [on the drawing board] and you started the sections and elevations by recalling all that.'[22]

While Seidler's office was efficient in operation, there was no lack of information in the documentation. In spite of the modest budget and scale of the Zwar House, the working drawings consisted of seven drawings of approximately B1 size.[23] In addition to the standard floor plans, sections and elevations, there were subfloor, roof-framing and electrical plans, and a comprehensive series of details, many of which were drawn full size. These covered all aspects of the kitchen, laundry, bathroom, bedrooms, built-in furniture and fireplace. This

---

20   Colin Griffiths, Interview by the author, 31 October 2008.
21   Seidler, *Houses, Buildings and Projects 1955/63*, 45.
22   Colin Griffiths, Interview by the author, 31 October 2008.
23   The tracings measure approximately 925 x 725 mm; B1 size is 1000 x 707 mm. *Harry Seidler Collection of Architectural Drawings, 1948–1987*.

was possible because of the reuse of standard details from previous projects. For example, Seidler developed two types of freestanding metal fireplaces: a conical version and a triangular version, with the latter specified for the Zwar House.

Figure 3.6 Portrait of Harry Seidler with Walter Gropius

Photograph: Max Dupain, 1954. National Library of Australia. nla.pic-an12660573

A number of parallels can be drawn between the way in which Seidler practised architecture and the way in which scientists operate. Seidler was committed to what might be termed a 'scientific approach' to all aspects of the design, documentation and construction phases. One manifestation of this was the extreme efficiency of his operation. Another was the importance that he attached to the science of building. Griffiths recalled that they regularly consulted the Commonwealth Experimental Building Station (CEBS) reports and studies.²⁴ To step back from the details of Seidler's houses and look at the bigger picture, it could be argued that his primary motivation for practising architecture was essentially the same as those that led scientists, such as Zwar, to practise science. Underlying the CSIRO's separate research areas were a number of common ideologies. Many of these—the ideas of working for the public good to improve the human condition, and faith in scientific rationality and in knowledge transfer between disciplines—were shared by practitioners of modern architecture.²⁵ After attending Gropius's Master Class at the Harvard Graduate School of Design in 1945 and 1946, Seidler wrote how Gropius had instilled in him 'the firm belief that we are to bring about vital changes to the physical environment—to better the man-made world'.²⁶

But the most important similarities between Seidler's methodology and that of scientists were not related so much to his 'scientific' use of technical data, or to his primary motivations, as much as they were to his modus operandi. Conrad Waddington, a scientist who spent a large part of his career exploring the overlapping territories between his own field, biology, and those of art and architecture, identified a potential link between Seidler and scientific procedure. In *The Nature of Life*, he examined the key differences between scientific and artistic methodology. Waddington described how one of the central tenets of scientific research was that it was never the work of one individual—or even a succession of individuals—but was based on cooperative effort. To illustrate this point, he employed a constructional analogy:

> An individual man can, of course, add a brick to the structure, or even lay out the plan of a new room, but his brick must be added to a wall which others have already partially built, and his new room must join on and communicate with the rest of the whole palace of knowledge.²⁷

Waddington believed that science, more than any other cultural activity, was built on the foundations set down by previous research. While there was generally an uneasy relationship between tradition and originality in the arts— painting, poetry and literature—no such suspicions were aroused in the field of science. As Waddington explained, if a work of art displayed obvious references to previous examples, the artist would probably be dismissed as derivative. But in scientific work, unless the scientist could demonstrate understanding and

---

24 Colin Griffiths, Interview by the author, 31 October 2008. The publications included J. R. Barnes, *Report No. R. 2: Thermal Conductivities of Building Materials* (Melbourne: CSIRO Division of Building Research, March 1946), and R. O. Phillips, CEBS Technical Study 23 (D.D.23), *Sunshine and Shade in Australasia* (Sydney, 1951).
25 Brad Collis, *Fields of Discovery: Australia's CSIRO* (Crows Nest, NSW: Allen & Unwin, 2002), xii–xiii; Boris Schedvin, *Shaping Science and Industry: A History of Australia's Council for Scientific and Industrial Research, 1926–49* (North Sydney: Allen & Unwin, 1987), 287, 355–6.
26 Frampton and Drew, *Harry Seidler: Four Decades of Architecture*, 390.
27 Conrad Waddington, *The Nature of Life* (London: George Allen & Unwin, 1961), 14–15.

respect for the work of predecessors, he or she would not be taken seriously. This 'communal, co-operative nature of scientific endeavour', Waddington believed, was one of its main strengths.[28] While disputes still arose in the scientific world regarding individual authorship—it was widely known, for example, that Fleming, Florey and Chain had a falling out over that very issue in regard to penicillin—Waddington had a valid point, and one that, although he did not identify it himself, applied as much to architecture as it did to art or literature.

If Seidler's approach to architecture is considered in regard to Waddington's statements, a number of issues come to light. Seidler saw his domestic architecture in Australia as being a logical continuation of the modernist houses that Breuer was building on the east coast of North America. Between 1946 and 1948, Seidler had prepared working drawings for a series of Breuer's houses in the architect's New York office.[29] The experience had left a lasting impression on Seidler's design philosophy and work practice, leading architectural writer Philip Drew to describe Seidler's architecture as 'East Coast Modern, the American idea of the Bauhaus idea restated by Breuer'.[30]

The opportunity to design a house for his parents in Sydney had lured Seidler away from Breuer to set up his own practice in Australia. Within a week of arriving, Seidler recalled how he 'drove around Sydney and looked for large areas of land like we built on in Connecticut while working for Breuer'. As his biographer, Alice Spigelman, explained, he was thinking of 'the houses Breuer and Gropius had built in the rural settings of Cambridge'.[31] After the family settled on a 6 ha bushland site in Clissold Road, Turramurra, Seidler set about designing his first house, which became known as the Rose Seidler House, after his mother. Designed and built between 1948 and 1950, it was the precedent for the Zwar House, which Seidler would design some five years later.

Seidler was quite open about the international origins of this house: 'It was probably…a direct transplantation of European through Eastern United States developments in architecture centred in Cambridge, Massachusetts, just plonked straight into the North Shore of Sydney.'[32] He was not exaggerating: what he 'plonked' onto his parents' site was in fact a previous design that he had prepared in Breuer's office in 1947. In association with Rolland Thompson, the son of the

---

28 Ibid.
29 'Anyway in the two years that I spent in Breuer's office I did most of the drawings for the houses he built between 1946 and 1948, including his own, well-known cantilevered timber house—which has been very much publicized in the world—in New Canaan. He had a great influence all round on me, obviously my total…coming to grips with a building, from design right to the finish, was really experienced in his [Breuer's] office, and that had an influence on me, particularly in the early years of my practice in this country.' Harry Seidler, Interview by Hazel de Berg, 13 January 1972, NLA Oral History Program.
30 Philip Drew, in Frampton and Drew, *Harry Seidler: Four Decades of Architecture*, 15.
31 Alice Spigelman, *Almost Full Circle: Harry Seidler, A Biography* (Rose Bay, NSW: Brandl & Schlesinger, 2001), 171–2.
32 Harry Seidler, Interview by Hazel de Berg, 13 January 1972, NLA Oral History Program.

client, Seidler had designed the Thompson House for a site overlooking a lake in Foxborough, Massachusetts. While that house was never built, Seidler retained the model and brought it to Australia with the rest of his belongings. When it came to designing his parents' house in Turramurra, Seidler took the Thompson House and turned it through 180 degrees to relate to the southern hemisphere location. Aside from that, the house remained substantially unchanged; in fact, the designs were so similar that the scale model Seidler presented to his parents for their house was actually the original model of the Thompson House.[33]

It was not important to Seidler that his Australian houses were 'original' works of art. But it was vital that they originated from a sound pedigree—that they were linked genetically to established architectural forebears. Seidler made no secret of the origins of his architecture—and made no apologies for it. By propagating the ideologies and forms of Gropius and Breuer, he believed that he was spreading the word and showing Australians the correct way to build.

Of course, Seidler was not the only Australian architect to borrow overseas models. Boyd, for instance, had taken Breuer's binuclear house plan and reproduced it on two different sites in Canberra. But when the work of Boyd is considered in its entirety, these direct transplantations were isolated examples. Boyd's house designs varied significantly throughout his career, and he frequently incorporated input from a number of sources. Seidler, on the other hand, stayed true to his original mentors. This is not to say that he repeated exactly the same forms and spaces as Breuer's originals. Over time he tinkered with, adjusted and improved aspects of these transplanted designs. But in spirit and ideology, they remained European modernist—via east coast North America—in origin.

Seidler's process of incremental modification began at an early stage. As with most architects' first houses, with the Rose Seidler House, there were problems. Seidler was unaware of the strength of the Australian sun and had to retrofit heavy curtains on the window of his parents' bedroom to block out the morning sun.[34] The Rose Seidler House, and other early houses with flush glass facades, weathered badly in the harsh Australian conditions. Seidler 'felt so guilty' about some that he and Griffiths would visit them on weekends to 'caulk joints and paint window frames'. But Seidler learnt quickly from his mistakes and adapted his designs to suit local conditions. Observing that 'the sun used to come in and fade curtains', he began to avoid east and west orientation for windows, and introduced more substantial eaves overhangs, or recesses in the house form, to provide protection from sun and rain. At the same time, he ceased to construct

---

33 Drew described what he termed the 'minor changes' to the Thompson House. Frampton and Drew, *Harry Seidler: Four Decades of Architecture*, 20.
34 Spigelman, *Almost Full Circle: Harry Seidler, A Biography*, 178.

houses of lightweight, timber-framed external walls, clad with asbestos cement sheets—which provided poor thermal insulation—and adopted masonry construction.[35]

In relation to Waddington's theory of scientific practice, the strength of Seidler's Australian houses was not that they were isolated, independent structures, but that they constituted fragments of a bigger picture—fragments that both acknowledged the existence of international architectural discourse and claimed their place within that community. Building on the solid foundations of previous research, Seidler made clear and explicit references to previous work by Breuer. While, in Waddingtonian terms, these aspects of Seidler's approach were his strength, to many observers those same aspects were his biggest weakness. Seidler was often accused of being derivative and of not attempting to address the Australian context. These were criticisms that Seidler—who did not believe in either the existence of or the need for a unique 'Australian' culture—usually dismissed with contempt. One commentator who saw Seidler's lack of connection to Australian culture as a problem was Drew. Citing Seidler's formative years at Harvard, Drew wrote: 'the universals which animate Seidler's work are European not Australian...The price of sticking to the task of faithfully enlarging Modernism was the exclusion of Australian content.'[36]

Underscoring the debate about Seidler's possible lack of Australian substance was an ongoing debate regarding regionalism that can be traced back to the Gropius House at Lincoln, Massachusetts, designed by Gropius and Breuer in 1937 and 1938. In 1954 Sigfried Giedion cited that house to be an exemplar of the 'New Regionalism'. For Giedion, the concept and structure of the Gropius House placed it firmly within the canon of contemporary architecture, yet aspects of its design also displayed empathy with the 'natural conditions of its region'. These latter aspects included a reworking of the traditional New England front porch and its traditional timber frame clad with white-painted weatherboards. In fact, the only difference that Giedion claimed to see between this house and its more traditional New England neighbours was that the weatherboards ran vertically rather than horizontally.[37]

But what Giedion failed to comprehend were the considerably more significant dissimilarities: the floor plan was not based on traditional New England models, nor was the flat roof. Joachim Driller believed that, rather than being an example of a 'New Regionalism', the Gropius House was nothing more than an

---

35 Colin Griffiths, Interview by the author, 31 October 2008.
36 Philip Drew, 'The Migration of an Idea 1945–1976', in Frampton and Drew, *Harry Seidler: Four Decades of Architecture*, 81.
37 Sigfried Giedion, *Walter Gropius: Work and Teamwork* (New York: Reinhold, 1954), 71. The regionalism debate was taken up later by Frampton, who coined the term 'critical regionalism'. Kenneth Frampton, 'Critical Regionalism: Six Points for an Architecture of Resistance', in Hal Foster, ed., *The Anti-Aesthetic: Essays on Post-Modern Culture* (Port Townsend: Bay Press, 1983), 16–30.

amalgam of Gropius's and Breuer's previous European buildings and projects. This, he believed, was confirmed by the Gropius House's lack of a southern roof overhang to protect it from the sun. If Gropius and Breuer had been genuinely attempting to consider the natural conditions of New England, he asked, why would they have made such a fundamental omission?[38] Breuer's first house, located just down the hill from the Gropius House,[39] suffered from a similar lack of regard to local weather conditions and poor detailing. Six months after it was completed, the majority of the window frames leaked; after two years so did the flat roof, and there were ongoing problems with the oil-fired central heating.[40]

It was this area—the failure to adequately address local climatic conditions—that created serious flaws in the regionalist argument. This was also where Seidler was most frequently criticised—and where the problems with the Zwar House began.

The Dilemma of the Universal Paradigm

Everywhere you go you always take the weather with you

— Neil Finn and Tim Finn[41]

In overall concept, the precedent for the Zwar House was the Rose Seidler House, designed and built some five years earlier. Like its predecessor, the Zwar House was a fragment of international modern architecture. Precise and hard edged, it stood detached from its site and was only notionally site specific: subject to hemispheric solar orientation and repositioning of internal steps to traverse the slope, it could just as easily have been located, with varying results of human comfort, on any site in Sydney, North America or Europe. Which it was: Seidler admitted that his houses stretched 'from one side of the United States to the other', and he had no hesitation in building a second 'Zwar House' in Coogee three years after the Canberra version.[42]

---

38   Joachim Driller, *Breuer Houses* (London: Phaidon, 2000), 106–7, 114–15. In 1967 Giedion wrote: 'Yet neither its flat roof, its screened porch…its vernacular weatherboarding…[or its] large windows could be said to mark any notable divergence from the local New England building idiom.' Sigfried Giedion, *Space, Time and Architecture: The Growth of a New Tradition* (Cambridge, Mass.: Harvard University Press, 1967), 502. (The first edition of *Space, Time and Architecture*, published in 1942, contained no references to Gropius's American work.)
39   The Gropius and Breuer Houses were funded by Mrs James Storrow, who donated the land and paid for the construction. Driller, *Breuer Houses*, 104, 125.
40   Ibid., 130.
41   *Weather With You*, Words and music by Neil Finn and Tim Finn, 1991.
42   This is a reference to the Bland House—see earlier. Seidler was proud that '[h]omes to the specification of my plan stretch from one side of the United States to the other'. Harry Seidler, Quoted by Peter Emmet, *Rose Seidler House, Wahroonga 1948–50: Conservation Plan* (Sydney: Historic Houses Trust of New South Wales, 1999), 92.

In his 1954 *Houses, Interiors and Projects*, Seidler published details of buildings and projects completed during the first five years of his Australian practice. Almost all of his commissions were in and around Sydney—a location that he termed 'South East Australia', where he believed inhabitants enjoyed a climate 'comparable to that of some Mediterranean countries or of California'. Seidler claimed that 'few countries in the world' were blessed with the mild conditions of south-eastern Australia, where there were no extremes, and where temperature variations between summer and winter were so minor that, if a building took into account 'special local conditions' (whatever that meant), no heating or cooling would be required.[43]

Houses, Interiors and Projects also included houses for contexts outside Sydney: a sheep station at Quirindi, in country New South Wales, the Bowden House in Canberra, and two projects for standardised houses for various locations.[44] The binuclear Quirindi farmhouse design represented a departure from Seidler's Sydney houses. Designed to accommodate the 'intense summer heat and bushfire danger' of its specific location, it contained a force-ventilated roof cavity. A similar roof form was evident on the 1959 Paspaley House in Darwin, NT, which incorporated additional measures to address the tropical climate.[45]

Seidler did not, however, appear to consider the specific conditions of the national capital as much as he did those of Quirindi or Darwin. Except for a small courtyard recessed into the north-eastern facade for shelter, the Bowden House was not substantially different to the architect's Sydney houses of the same period.[46] The problem most likely originated from Canberra's geographical location. Relatively close to Sydney, and technically within the region of south-eastern Australia, Canberra nevertheless experiences vastly different climatic conditions from Sydney due to its high elevation and inland location. These differences include higher daily and seasonal temperature fluctuations, and frosts. Canberra's climate is certainly not benign, and not Mediterranean. In winter, temperatures at night drop to –6° Celsius, making some form of heating essential. Although Seidler visited Canberra on a number of occasions, it is possible that, due to time constraints, he returned to Sydney the same day and did not experience the overnight drop in temperature for himself.[47]

Seidler made a number of further generalisations about the Australian climate. On one occasion, he claimed that heating was more of a luxury than a necessity,

---

43   Seidler, *Houses, Interiors and Projects*, xii, xvii.
44   These last examples included a 'Universal House' to be 'used on any reasonably flat site regardless of its orientation', and a prefabricated house.
45   Seidler, *Houses, Buildings and Projects 1955/63*, 33–5.
46   Seidler, *Houses, Interiors and Projects*, 52–8.
47   Zwar recalled that Seidler visited Canberra on 'two or three occasions' in regard to his house. He did not think that Seidler stayed overnight. John Zwar, Interview by the author, 26 September 2008, and In discussion with the author, 7 December 2008.

and conflated survival with comfort: 'In this country…people are just simply uncomfortable. It's not as bad as it is in Europe where…you have to protect yourself from the cold otherwise you can't exist.'[48] To Seidler, the fireplace—which he included in almost every one of his houses—was a symbolic and formal device more than a functional item. Like the Zwar House, most of Seidler's houses were divided into two zones: bedrooms and living. In the centre of the living zone was a fireplace that he believed marked the geometric and spiritual centre of the house: 'Although anything but an efficient method of heating', Seidler wrote, 'the psychological warmth of the sitting group around the open fire is still the centre of the present-day home'.[49] Seidler's fireplaces were divided into two basic types: masonry or metal. In houses of more than one level, the former type, which usually originated on a lower level and extended through the floor to the main living area above, formed an additional formal and aesthetic function: a device that visually and tectonically anchored the house to its site.[50]

Perhaps it was Seidler's view of fireplaces as being mainly symbolic and visual that contributed to a common lack of functionality in their design. Griffiths remembered how there was 'a long history of unsuccessful fireplaces in the houses', with a number of them discharging smoke into the living room. In an anecdote reminiscent of Boyd's nightmares of rain-soaked clients disappearing into billows of smoke, one client refused to pay his final fees instalment because Griffiths and Seidler could not prevent his fireplace from smoking inside the house.[51]

While Zwar was generally very happy with the house, he found the fireplace to be quite inadequate. One of Seidler's standard, triangular-section metal fireplaces welded together by a boilermaker from 6 mm thick mild steel plate, it required constant stoking to maintain an effective temperature.[52] In the late 1960s, Zwar removed the fireplace in order to demolish the internal dividing wall between the living room and bedroom. Heating was then supplied by a rudimentary oil heater, which he installed on the north-eastern living room wall. Left on almost permanently in the colder months, it succeeded in keeping only some of the chill off, and was replaced with an electric unit in the 1980s.[53]

---

48 Harry Seidler, Interview by Russell Henderson, 21 April 1986, 21 May 1986, NLA Oral History Program.
49 Seidler, *Houses, Interiors and Projects*, xv.
50 See, for instance, Rose Seidler House, Turramurra (1949–50), Marcus Seidler House, Turramurra (1949–51), and Harry and Penelope Seidler House, Killara (1966–67).
51 John Zwar, Interview by the author, 26 September 2008.
52 Ibid.; and John Zwar, Interview by Brendan Lepschi, 2005. Brendan Lepschi, 'Canberra Post-War Houses Project, No. 12 Yapunyah Street, O'Connor', November 2005. Griffiths agreed with Zwar's reservations, admitting that, in Canberra, a single fireplace was not appropriate. He confirmed that, although Seidler's early training and experience were in North America, he was not aware of the coldness of some Australian locations, and did not install sophisticated heating systems into his houses well after the Zwar House. Colin Griffiths, Interview by the author, 31 October 2008.
53 John Zwar, Interview by the author, 26 September 2008; and John Zwar, Interview by Brendan Lepschi, 5.

Seidler was aware that a compact building such as the Zwar House was the most thermally stable. He was also cognisant of the implications of various materials, stating: 'Light and open construction is thermally unstable. A solid, heavy building will have a desirable heat storage capacity, ready to dissipate heat in our cool evenings.'[54] But these issues were not particularly well resolved in the Zwar House. The entire north-western wall and a large proportion of the south-eastern wall were single-glazed, providing large surface areas for heat to escape. The two remaining external side walls, although constructed of double brickwork, provided minimal heat storage due to their orientation. Additionally, the timber-floored house was particularly vulnerable to heat loss through that perimeter. To minimise heat loss from the downstairs living area, which was originally separated from the dining and family rooms by a half-height wall only, a full-height wall was installed between the passage and living room in the late 1970s. Constructed of alpine ash boards with glazed panels above, it incorporated a sliding door for access.

Seidler also understood the importance of providing adequate protection from the heat of the sun. In 1963 he wrote: 'It is impossible for us to live comfortably in buildings which admit too much of the sun's heat.'[55] Zwar recalled that Seidler was particularly concerned about that aspect of the house, and believed that he generally got it right. But there was one problem: before the upstairs bedroom was added in 1967, the glazed north-western wall admitted too much sun in late afternoon when the western sun came in low over O'Connor Ridge.[56] When the addition was added, Seidler placed a timber screen to shade the upper part of the windows, but Zwar found that it was largely redundant in that location.[57]

Counterpoint

With the benefit of more than half a century of hindsight, Zwar looked back on his approach to obtaining a site, choosing an architect and building a house, and decided that he must have been 'pretty naive'. Perhaps that was partly true. But it was a combination of his youthful optimism and quiet determination that resulted in this small but significant house being built. The relatively young age of the major contributors was significant: in 1955, when he commissioned Seidler, Zwar was twenty-eight years of age, Seidler was thirty-two, while Griffiths was barely twenty.

---

54 Harry Seidler, 'Notes on Architecture', in Seidler, *Houses, Buildings and Projects 1955/63*, 11.
55 Ibid.
56 As Zwar recalled, 'the sun did come in a bit, in the autumn…when it's getting round to the west…It was all right in the middle of the day when the sun was high, but it…could get quite warm'. John Zwar, Interview by the author, 26 September 2008.
57 Zwar believed that might have been because of the shade provided by a nearby tree. Ibid.

The notion of counterpoint, which was so central to Seidler's architecture, entered the story of the Zwar House well before that day in 1955 when the client stood, apprehensively, outside the blue door and peered into Seidler's Point Piper office. In fact, it was the search for a counterpoint to Canberra's 1950s architecture that led Zwar to that destination. Modest and unassuming by nature, he claimed little credit for his role, saying that it was essentially limited to providing the site and stipulating the maximum budget. Yet without Zwar's pursuit of Seidler—a quest that he followed with some determination and tenacity, given his limited means—the house would not have eventuated. Fundamental to Zwar's attempt to engage Seidler was his desire to build a radical modernist house in the national capital as a counterpoint to the existing architecture—including the Black Mountain Laboratories where he worked.

When the Council for Scientific and Industrial Research decided in 1929 to establish two lines of research—economic botany and entomology—in the federal city, Bertram Dickson, a mycologist,[58] was made Chief of the Division of Economic Botany (later renamed the Division of Plant Industry). Establishing these divisions was a long and drawn-out process that tested the patience of those involved. Many scientists felt isolated and cut off from the rest of the scientific community, regarding themselves as 'outcasts in a scientific and social wilderness'. To make matters worse, the Canberra location was far from ideal for entomology—the severe winters and barren soil were quite unsuited to botanical work—and there were long delays in completing the laboratories and glasshouses.[59] As a result, the long, grey facades of the classically inspired Black Mountain Laboratories became a symbol of lost opportunities for Dickson, who sardonically compared them with 'Queen Hatshepsut's funeral buildings at Dayr al-Bahre in the Valley of the Kings of Ancient Egypt'.[60]

Zwar considered the existing domestic architecture of the national capital to be mundane and functionally deficient. The government-owned Tocumwal House, at 2 Todd Street, O'Connor, which he and Heather rented from when they married in 1954 until their new house was built, was one of about 100 almost

---

58 A botanist who studies fungus.
59 To a large extent, the delays were unavoidable. The Federal Capital Commission was attempting to complete a large number of buildings in time for the relocation of Parliament and the Public Service. Henry Rolland recalled that the deadline for the completion of Parliament House was so tight that on the opening day, 9 May 1927, he still had carpenters working in the building. Henry Rolland, *Over the Years: An Autobiography of H. M. Rolland, OBE, FRAIA* (Hawthorn, Vic.: 1971), 15. But, for Dickson and his staff—who were temporarily housed in the Botany School in Sydney and then in the upper floor of the entomology wing—the prolonged disruption to their research was a constant source of frustration.
60 Schedvin, *Shaping Science and Industry: A History of Australia's Council for Scientific and Industrial Research, 1926–49*, 87–90. Dickson's own house was a cottage at 22 Balmain Crescent, Acton, designed by Thomas Robert Casboulte, Chief Architect of the Federal Capital Commission's Housing Department, in 1928–29. <http://heritage.anu.edu.au>

identical houses lined up in rows. Each house was oriented to a street front, regardless of solar orientation. Windows were generally small and the houses were dark and cold.

Sheena Jackson described what it was like living in Todd Street: 'a row of fibro and wood boxes perched on the rotary-hoed clay in the wettest winter for years, no trees or shrubs anywhere and sheep paddocks and flies at the end of the street. It was a real shock after the gentle, manicured streets of Melbourne.'[61]

The idea of counterpoint was followed through in many aspects of the built fabric of the Zwar House. Although it was not elevated above the landscape like its more illustrious predecessor, the Rose Seidler House, the Zwar House was a constructed, geometric object that sat starkly in a field of grass, with no attempt at mediation between nature and artifice. Zwar claimed that he, like Seidler, had little time for or interest in gardening.[62]

The external walls comprised two types: bagged and painted brick walls running parallel from north-west to south-east, and infill cross walls that were mostly glazed. The fenestration of the cross walls continued the interplay of contrasts: small window openings were punched through large, solid walls on the south-western facade, while the brick walls to the garage and courtyard were peppered with small, vertical slots to form grilles. The infill walls were subdivided into studied compositions of squares and rectangles—the latter with alternating horizontal and vertical thrust. The counterpoint effect was further highlighted through the use of complementary colours: teal blue, lemon yellow and salmon pink.

The play of opposites continued through to the interior of the Zwar House, with colour juxtapositions and contrasting window proportions. The interior contained extensive areas of timber. These included alpine ash floors and vertical boarding to selected walls, alpine ash door and window frames, and a combination of solid ash and Canadian plywood to built-in joinery units. The warm hue of these surfaces, coated in clear polyurethane, contrasted with the adjacent painted walls. Yet in spite of these visual contrasts, the overall result was a coherent and homogeneous internal space, mainly due to consistent detailing and the repetitive use of a family of fixtures, fittings and materials.

---

61   Sheena Jackson, 'Remembering Todd Street', in *The Tocumwal Archive* (Canberra: ACT Heritage Library, Woden Library). Tocumwal Houses are now appreciated by many in the Canberra community.
62   John Zwar, Interview by the author, 26 September 2008.

Figure 3.7 Zwar House, view from south

Photograph: Brendan Lepschi, 2005

Figure 3.8 Zwar House, view from dining area

Photograph: Brendan Lepschi, 2005

Neighbours and visitors did not know what to make of the Zwar House, as was the case with the Fenner House. The plain lines and lack of traditional ornamentation reminded some of austere government buildings of the time, prompting tradesmen to ask if it was a 'guvvie' (government house)—presuming that no-one in their right mind would actually choose to live there. To others, it appeared out of place, like a small beach house that had somehow been washed up on a Canberra hillside.[63]

Economy

Zwar, like Fenner, saw modern architecture as a potential solution to practical problems. Yet both scientists were just as attracted to the visual appearance of this new phenomenon—to the details, forms, materials and colours. What fascinated them was how modern architecture combined these material aspects to become a physical manifestation of a new world—a modern, postwar world whose emergence and progress were so intimately tied to their own fields. When Zwar paid Seidler for his design and documentation services, he was essentially purchasing a modernist artefact that reflected these aspirations as much as he was commissioning a house to provide shelter for his family. This aspect of the transaction between client and architect was summarised by the fact that Seidler presented his client with a print by the Bauhaus student and teacher Josef Albers to hang on the wall of his new house. Titled *Seclusion* and dated 1942, it now hangs in Zwar's new residence in the Canberra suburb of Pearce. With Zwar having sold the Zwar House in 2003, and the new owners demolishing it to make way for a much larger residence, *Seclusion* is the only surviving element of Seidler's comprehensive vision for an affordable small house in the national capital.[64]

The house that Seidler designed for John and Heather Zwar represented a return to one of the earliest tenets of modern architecture: response to social need. Unlike Breuer's houses, which increasingly exemplified a consumerist notion of modern architecture as an expensive and fashionable commodity, the modest Zwar House was a demonstration of affordability. Seidler was aware of this distinction, writing how different his first Australian clients were to Breuer's in New York, 'who were wealthy and wanted modern houses mainly for elitist-visual reasons'.[65] Just how affordable the Zwar House was is evident when the cost—£5000 in 1956—is compared with that of other houses. The Rose Seidler

---

63 Neighbouring resident of Yapunyah Street in discussion with Brendan Lepschi, 19 January 2009.
64 Zwar was surprised, believing that Seidler usually sold these to his clients. John Zwar, Interview by the author, 26 September 2008.
65 Frampton and Drew, *Harry Seidler: Four Decades of Architecture*, 394.

House had cost approximately £8000 to build in 1948–50,[66] while the cost of the Fenner House was £8500 (excluding heating) in 1954. Breuer's first house in Lincoln, Massachusetts, cost about US$10 000 as far back as 1939, while the monumental Frank House in Pittsburg, designed with Gropius, cost a mammoth US$250 000. Breuer's averaged-sized house, Geller House I, which Seidler documented between 1946 and 1947, had a budget of US$25 000, while his relatively modest House II of 1947–48, which Seidler also draughted, cost more than US$17 000.[67]

After 1955—the year the Zwar House was designed—Breuer rarely built any house for less than US$100 000, and many cost significantly more than that.[68] While average salaries were higher in the United States than they were in Australia at the time, it was clear that Breuer was not designing houses for average clients. And when he attempted to do that, he failed miserably. His demonstration 'House in the Museum Garden', built in the grounds of the Museum of Modern Art, New York, in 1948–49, was intended to be a display house for clients on average incomes. But the cost—between US$20 000 and $27 500, depending on the choice of variations—placed it out of reach of those for whom it was supposedly designed.[69]

Seidler's entire approach to domestic architecture was informed by Gropius and Breuer. From Gropius came the desire to build a better world by making modern design available to people of average incomes, and the will to promote modernist principles.[70] From Breuer came the design and documentation methodology— the idea that each house was part of an integrated, coordinated process limited to a few recurring set pieces: standard floor plans and universal details combined in various permutations.[71]

That Seidler never departed far from the underlying themes and ideologies of his mentors' original doctrines when he designed houses in the Australian context was not, in itself, a problem. Nor was it a problem that he chose to do that instead of pursuing a uniquely 'Australian' architectural vocabulary— in the form of references to the vernacular or to traditional ways of building. By importing an established ideology on which to establish a local architecture, Seidler avoided such issues, and had no need to invent a new architecture from scratch. Instead, working on a sound intellectual platform, he could build on the knowledge of others within the international architectural community.

---

66   Emmet, *Rose Seidler House, Wahroonga 1948–50: Conservation Plan*, 100.
67   The costs of houses are all based on figures that were current at the time of their construction.
68   Driller, *Breuer Houses*, 20, 125.
69   Ibid., 186.
70   Frampton and Drew, *Harry Seidler: Four Decades of Architecture*, 395.
71   Driller, *Breuer Houses*, 39; Frampton and Drew, *Harry Seidler: Four Decades of Architecture*, 391.

By testing, analysing and modifying those established models, Seidler approached Waddington's description of the way in which scientific knowledge is advanced through publishing, sharing and building upon earlier research.

But as described earlier, the Zwar House contained some technical flaws. Principally associated with inadequate heating and cooling, these problems seem to have arisen from a lack of accuracy in the methodology. It is possible that information regarding sun angles and temperature fluctuations was not adequately considered in relation to details of the roof overhangs, the sun screening, the type of heating or the thermal properties of materials. The lack of any true scientific analysis of these factors seems to have occurred because of a form of blindness on the part of Seidler—an affliction from which Gropius and Breuer also suffered. Problems that were already inherent in their New England houses were further compounded when Seidler imported the same minimalist white boxes to Australia, and failed to adequately adjust them to suit prevailing conditions.

In spite of the rhetoric about the age of science that was often discussed in the popular architectural and design journals of the time, a true scientific approach was not implemented to adapt these houses to local conditions at any stage of their migration from Europe to New England, Sydney and Canberra. Seidler, like his mentors and their supporters such as Giedion, were blinded by the visual qualities of these icons of modernism. This was a self-inflicted form of blindness that came from being seduced by the formal qualities of the crisp, modern forms that had come to represent the modern world. It was not simply that they were naive. The problem they faced was that the formal qualities of this new architecture that they so vigorously espoused were entirely dependent upon a few set pieces: minimalist, sharp-edged, white boxes in various combinations.

And so the image of the house, and what it represented, became more important than its ability to function as a series of comfortable, habitable spaces. Although Seidler tinkered with aspects of his houses, he was reluctant to modify the inherited designs beyond a certain point. The archetypal clean, crisp box was easily lost once the multifarious requirements of a fully functional house—roof eaves to provide shade and protection from the weather or recessed doors to form transitional spaces between inside and outside—were considered.

But these same limitations enabled Seidler to operate so efficiently, and to produce affordable, modern houses such as the Zwar House. While not as well known as some of his other buildings, the Zwar House was part of an ongoing experiment into the compact, modern house type, in which Seidler sought to inject the maximum amount of modern design for the minimum cost. In this respect, the Zwar House exemplified an outstanding commitment to intellectual rigour, and to the pursuit of what an affordable postwar house could be.

4. Form Follows Formula: Grounds, Boyd and the Philip House

Figure 4.1 Philip House, view from north-east

Photograph: Ben Wrigley, 2011

John Philip was brought to Canberra as part of Frankel's ambitious postwar recruitment program, and was appointed head of a new agricultural physics group at the CSIRO. Regarded as Australia's leading environmental physicist, he was elected a Fellow of the Australian Academy of Science in 1967. His wife, Frances ('Fay'), was an accomplished artist who was related to the Boyds via the Mills and à Becketts, and had attended the Murrumbeena State School in Victoria with Mary and Arthur Boyd. Many of Frances's portraits of Australia's leading scientists and academics—including Sir Mark Oliphant, Doug Waterhouse, John Jaeger, William Rogers, Patrick Moran and Manning Clark—are held in the collections of the Australian Academy of Science and The Australian National University.

The Philip House, at 42 Vasey Crescent, Campbell, is one of three adjacent houses by Grounds, Romberg and Boyd that are known collectively as the Vasey Crescent Group. The other two houses in the group are the Blakers House and the Griffing House. Grounds and Boyd were both involved with these houses. All three were designed by Grounds, who arranged initial briefings, recorded the clients' requirements and prepared sketches from late 1959 through to early 1960. Boyd met with the clients in January 1960, and took control of the houses from May of that year as Grounds prepared for a three-month overseas trip.[1]

The Philip House is important for two reasons. The first is because of its status as part of a group. This signals a shift away from a focus on the house as a singular, artistic statement—an edifice that is complete in its own right. The Philip House, as one member of a group of three adjacent houses, provides an opportunity to discuss a more collaborative approach to residential design. The second reason for studying the Philip House is to examine the extraordinary contribution made by John Philip. It could be argued that his involvement in the design process, and his impact upon the built form, was equal to that of Grounds or of Boyd. But unlike his capital-city predecessors in architectural patronage—Fenner and Zwar—Philip was not primarily motivated by the visual iconography of modern architecture or design. What drove him instead was a relentless pursuit of the optimum way in which the house, as a habitable structure, could address function and human comfort.

A Collaborative Ethos

It was through a series of fortuitous events that the Vasey Crescent Group came to be planned as a coordinated series of houses by one architectural firm. On 21 July 1959, the three blocks were sold by the Department of the Interior at public auction in Albert Hall. The bidding for Block 9 (number 42) proceeded for some time before Philip raised his hand, doubled the previous bid, and purchased the lease for £1010. Number 44 was purchased by Bruce Griffing—a quantitative inheritance geneticist who also worked under Frankel—and his wife, Penny. Gordon Blakers, a senior public servant, and his wife, Catherine, bought number 46. The day after the auction, *The Canberra Times* reported on the front page that 'some of the highest premiums ever offered for residential leases in Canberra were paid in keen bidding', and that 'Mr. J. R. Philip of Lyneham' had paid the highest premium for his site.

The views to be obtained from the elevated location were part of the attraction of Campbell. Philip explained to *The Canberra Times* that he and Frances were 'pleased with the view from the land and they might even see the Lakes in

---

1   Grounds' departure, and Boyd's subsequent involvement from the early documentation phase through to completion, resulted in Graeme Gunn—who prepared drawings for the Philip and Griffing houses during July and August 1960 under Boyd's direction—having no recollection that Grounds had ever been involved. In addition to Gunn, other architects and draftsmen who worked on the Philip House included James McCormick, Pat Moroney and H. R. Stafford. Conrad Hamann, Modern Architecture in Melbourne: The Architecture of Grounds, Romberg and Boyd, 1927–1971 (PhD dissertation, Visual Arts Department, Monash University, 1978), 186, footnote.

the future, "if we crane our necks"'.² Although Philip and Griffing knew each other through work, they had not arranged to attend the auction together. Nor had they agreed to buy adjacent sites. Neither of them knew the Blakers. The first time the three owners met was when they went to inspect their sites, where they discussed general ideas for their houses.³ Over the ensuing months all three Vasey Crescent owners independently approached Grounds to design their house: the Blakers shortly after the auction, the Griffings in August 1959, and the Philips in December.⁴

It was largely due to Frances that the Philips commissioned Grounds. With her father and brother both architects, hiring an architect seemed the normal thing to do. Having seen a house in Melbourne that attracted her attention, Frances knocked on the door to inquire if Grounds had designed it. Receiving confirmation that he had, Frances and John contacted the architect and visited his office—a converted terrace at 340 Albert Street, East Melbourne. There they were greeted by Grounds, who descended the stairs with open arms and announced—with 'great pomp and ceremony and drama—"ah, The Philips! Do come in. So you want me to do your house!"'⁵

While it was a genuine coincidence that led to all three clients choosing Grounds, it was not altogether surprising given the influence of his Australian Academy of Science building. The critical acclaim the academy received greatly enhanced the reputation of Grounds, Romberg and Boyd in both Melbourne and Canberra contexts: the Griffings, for instance, considered them to be 'the leading architectural firm in Australia' at the time.⁶ The academy building also played another role, becoming a regular location for Grounds and Boyd to meet their scientist clients when visiting the capital city.

Although the idea of coordinating a unified approach to the three houses appears to have originated with Grounds, it was an opportunity that all clients welcomed. Philip was aware of the significance of the venture. In 1960 he wrote to the Department of the Interior stating that 'the prospect of three adjacent private houses designed by, and built under the supervision of, Roy Grounds is surely a chapter in domestic architecture unique not only to Canberra, but, indeed, to Australia as a whole'. He was also cognisant of the challenge that lay

---

2   *The Canberra Times* (22 July 1959): 1. At that time Lake Burley Griffin did not exist. Some details of the auction were obtained from Candida Griffiths, Interview by the author, 27 June 2008.
3   Eric Wilson, 'Good-Mannered Houses', *Australian Home Beautiful* (December 1963): 5.
4   Hamann, Modern Architecture in Melbourne: The Architecture of Grounds, Romberg and Boyd, 1927–1971, 186, footnote.
5   Candida Griffiths, Interview by the author, 27 June 2008. Details of the meeting with Grounds were compiled from information from this interview and from Geoffrey Serle, *Robin Boyd: A Life* (Melbourne: Melbourne University Press, 1995), 192.
6   'Griffing House, 44 Vasey Crescent, Campbell, Canberra', Papers of John Philip (Manuscript), National Library of Australia, MS 9801, Box 1 (author not noted, but most likely Bruce or Penny Griffing).

before them: 'the need for the three adjoining houses to be planned, to some extent, in concert...has demanded the resolution of the conflicting requirements of three separate families.'[7]

While the Vasey Crescent clients were from professional backgrounds—scientists, a senior public servant and an artist—they shared a common concern for budget. Other traits were a disdain for the average postwar house—the Philips, in particular, were 'fairly scathing about the typical suburban box'[8]—a preference for modern architecture and design, an interest in gardening, and a strong commitment to environmental concerns, including passive solar design. In this way, the Vasey Crescent clients shared many attributes with those who commissioned postwar modern houses in North America, such as the Case Study House clients.[9]

An opportunity to design three adjacent houses for well-informed clients who were sympathetic to the tenets of modernism was rare in architectural practice. It was an opportunity that Grounds was equal to. Informed by his experience on previous houses, he began by establishing a 'kit of parts' to work with. This allowed him the freedom to express the individual requirements of each house, yet retain an overall consistency of architectural language. The most fundamental element of the kit was a simple rectangular prism constructed of unpainted concrete block-work, and protected by a low-pitched, metal deck roof with deep eaves overhangs. This appears to be an element that Grounds arrived at early on: an undated 'thumbnail' sketch alongside notes from his first meeting with the Philips indicated such a form. Added to the basic kit were vertical, black-painted timber posts to support cantilevered floors and roofs, timber planked eaves soffits, and large, timber-framed windows. In formal architectural terms, the compatibility and ultimate success of the group were due to Grounds' skill and dexterity in manipulating this limited range of components.

Grounds proceeded to arrange these elements on the three sites in various permutations. Conrad Hamann explained how the three houses were 'conceived as elementary groups of two rectangles. In the Blakers' house, the rectangles were juxtaposed. In the Griffing house, they were placed one in front of the other;

---

7   John Philip to J. N. Rogers, Assistant Secretary (Lands), Lands and Survey Branch, Department of the Interior, Canberra, ACT, 9 April 1960, 'Philip House Canberra', Grounds, Romberg and Boyd Records 1927–1979, Manuscript Collection, State Library of Victoria, MS 13363, Box 61/1(b).
8   Candida Griffiths, Interview by the author, 27 June 2008.
9   Kevin Starr described these clients as 'progressive professionals who preferred modern architecture and the ideas and life style it embodied to that associated with the standard, traditionally-styled, suburban tract homes that proliferated in the postwar period...intellectual and sophisticated in taste if not in income'. Kevin Starr, 'The Case Study House Program and the Impending Future, Some Regional Considerations', in Esther McCoy, 'Arts & Architecture Case Study Houses', *Blueprints for Modern Living: History and Legacy of the Case Study Houses* (Cambridge, Mass.: MIT Press, 1990), 163.

in the Phillip house they were stacked on top of each other'.[10] The end result was that each house was able to respond to the individual owners' requirements in terms of internal accommodation and facilities, resulting in varying internal room dimensions, plan types and overall form, while the whole group resembled a coherent architectural composition. Grounds considered the houses as a group from very early on: at the same time that he was holding preliminary discussions with the Philips about their house, all three clients were presented with a composite sketch layout that showed the footprints of the houses.

The means by which Grounds achieved a coordinated group were twofold: first, by creating a seamless visual flow across the site, and second, by maintaining and optimising views from each house. The house sites were located on a spur running in an east–west direction from nearby Russell Hill, which ended in a steep fall on the western boundary of the Philips' site. The Blakers' site was on the highest point of the spur, the Griffings' in the middle, and the Philips' at the lowest point. In the other direction, all sites sloped down from Canberra Nature Park at the rear towards Vasey Crescent. To achieve the optimum siting for the houses, Grounds radically departed from the normal practice of setting houses 7.6 m back from the street line. Instead, by setting each house progressively further back from its immediate neighbour, he allowed all three houses to follow the same hillside contour. In this way the Blakers House was located in the centre of its site, the Griffing House behind the centre line, and the Philip House right to the rear of its site. As the Blakers and Griffing houses were essentially 'L'-shaped, the resultant composite site plan appeared as a continuous line of building, stepping back up the hill, broken only by the two intermediate boundary lines.[11]

By stepping the houses in this way, Grounds achieved three objectives. The first was that all ground floors were virtually on the same level, which created visual continuity. And although the Philip House—at two storeys, with a basement partly below ground level—was the tallest structure, because it was the most recessive of the three, it did not dominate its neighbours. The third result of the stepping configuration was that views from each house were preserved and enhanced. All three enjoyed potential uninterrupted views towards Mount Ainslie to the north, and towards the city centre and proposed lake to the west. Again, had either the Philip House or the Griffing House been set at the standard 7.6 m from the street boundary, the scheme would not have worked, as western views from the other houses would have been obscured. The clients appreciated the placing of the houses on the sites in such a sympathetic manner. Catherine Blakers wrote to Grounds stating that 'we very much like the sketch plans and

---

10 Hamann, Modern Architecture in Melbourne: The Architecture of Grounds, Romberg and Boyd, 1927–1971, 239.
11 Eric Wilson described the design in 'Good-Mannered Houses', 5–7.

the placing of the three houses on the block', while the Griffings appreciated 'the pattern made by the three houses and are pleased that each family has a view from its living area'.[12]

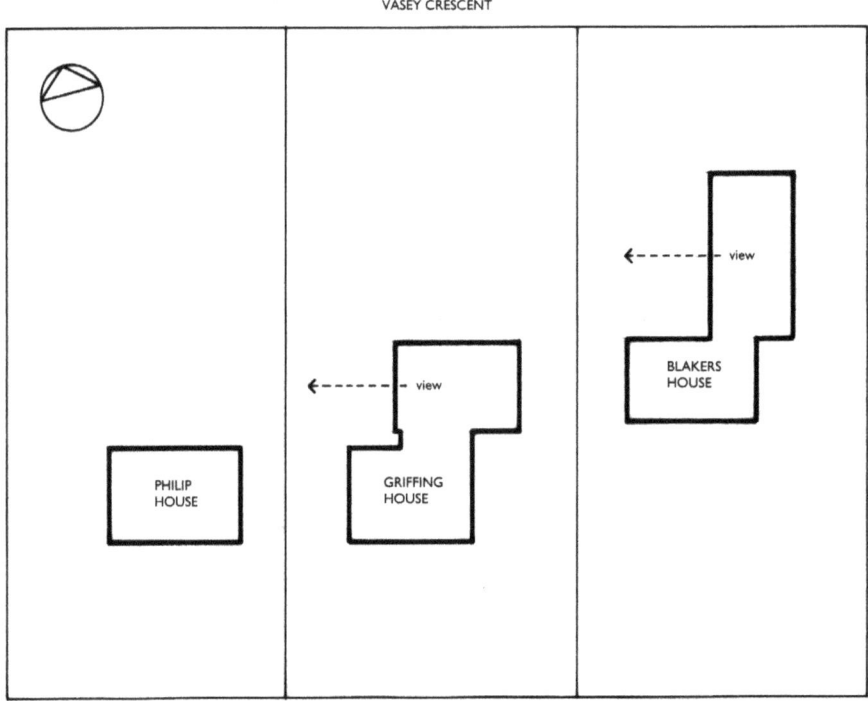

Figure 4.2 Vasey Crescent Group, site plan

Image: redrawn by the author from Grounds, Romberg and Boyd. Courtesy of Victoria Grounds and the Robin Boyd Foundation

But Grounds' carefully resolved site planning would have been negated had traditional, individual garden plans been implemented by the Vasey Crescent owners. With front fences banned by the Department of the Interior, the common solution was for individual owners to plant hedges or thick foliage along the front boundaries of their properties. The Philips, Griffings and Blakers realised from early on that this would not be an appropriate solution, and decided to coordinate an integrated landscape plan. Frances had long held a keen interest in

---

12 Catherine Blakers to Grounds, 2 December 1959, 'Blakers House Canberra, Correspondence', Grounds, Romberg and Boyd Records, 1927–1979, MS 13363, Box 63/2(b); Bruce and Penny Griffing to Grounds, 4 December 1959, 'Griffing House Canberra, Correspondence', Grounds, Romberg and Boyd Records, 1927–1979, Box 63/1; 'Griffing House, 42 and 44 Vasey Crescent, Campbell, Canberra', Papers of John Philip (Manuscript), National Library of Australia, MS 9801, Box 1.

cultivating and growing Australian native plants, and took a leading role in the discussions.[13] The Vasey Crescent Group owners decided to aim for consistency by planting native gardens to present a 'continuum' to passers-by. While each garden was to be designed by its owners, it was expected that 'individual talent and enthusiasm' would provide diversity.[14] Eric Wilson, writing for *Australian Home Beautiful*, noted how this undertaking had 'involved a great deal of discussion, mutual consideration and effort on the part of the three families'.[15]

The Philips believed that it was important to maintain an Australian theme in the street planting. Upon hearing that planners from Parks and Gardens were intending to plant pinoaks in Vasey Crescent, John contacted them to say that the three houses 'were being planned to have a certain unity which might have a distinctly Australian flavour about it', and that the owners believed that Australian trees such as *Eucalyptus maculosa* would be more appropriate. Having received confirmation that their preferred trees would be planted in the street, Philip wrote to Grounds to inform him, adding: 'I hope this does not conflict with your ideas!'[16]

There was, however, disagreement between the clients over one planning issue. The Philips proposed combining all three driveways into one road that followed the site contours. In March 1960, H. R. Stafford from Grounds, Romberg and Boyd prepared a site plan showing how this might work, and sent it to the Blakers and the Griffings for consideration. But, to Philip's disappointment, the proposal did not meet with his neighbours' approval, mainly because of uncertainties over the arrangement if any of the houses were sold in the future.[17]

Another form of collaboration in the Vasey Crescent Group was that the three houses were constructed from a unified palette of materials, colours and textures, all of which adopted characteristics of the adjacent bushland of Canberra Nature Park.[18] Wherever possible, Grounds and Boyd specified natural, 'rough' materials, finishes and colours for the exterior and interior of the houses, as described by Hamann:

> The interiors of all these houses mirrored the exterior. Walls were left unplastered and unbagged…Ceilings were of the most elaborate mitred

---

13 During the 1930s, while still a child, Frances established an early native garden at her Melbourne home, propagated from seeds obtained from her aunt's property in the Gippsland hills. She maintained a glasshouse, and trips to the country were punctuated with diversions to local nurseries to supplement her collection.
14 'Griffing House, 42 and 44 Vasey Crescent, Campbell, Canberra'.
15 Wilson, 'Good-Mannered Houses', 7.
16 John Philip to Grounds, 17 March 1960, Papers of John Philip.
17 'It seems that our future neighbours are unimpressed with the virtues of the combined drive, and that this proposal will be abandoned. Personally, we think that an excellent opportunity for unified site treatment is thus lost; but we can see that the combined drive has practical disadvantages for the other houses, particularly the Blakers.' John Philip to Grounds, 28 March 1960, 'Philip House Canberra'.
18 Roy Grounds, De Berg Tapes, National Library of Australia, Recorded in Melbourne, 11 October 1971.

planking, varnished and running through the window walls to connect with the soffit areas outside. Paintwork was virtually absent. The Canberra houses had black painted iron posts running up to the fascias, but it is difficult to recall paintwork anywhere else on these designs. Where wood fittings occurred, they were either varnished or limed.[19]

Figure 4.3 Philip House, living room, looking east

Photograph: Candida Griffiths (daughter of Frances Philip and John Philip)

Affinity with the landscape and the belief that buildings should be 'an extension of nature' were common themes in Grounds' domestic architecture. The origins of this approach can be traced back to a number of sources. One of these was his knowledge of the appearance of surfaces and colours in sunlight. When Japan entered World War II, Grounds joined the Royal Australian Air Force. From 1942 to 1943, he was Area Camouflage Officer with HQNEA Unit. His Reporting Officer stated that, in addition to having 'tremendous drive' and being 'smart and punctilious on matters of discipline', Grounds 'possessed a very intimate knowledge of the requirements of the area' and was 'a good officer in Works on Camouflage duties'.[20]

---

19   Hamann, Modern Architecture in Melbourne: The Architecture of Grounds, Romberg and Boyd, 1927–1971, 62–4, 239.
20   Royal Australian Air Force Record, 'Grounds R. B.', National Archives of Australia, NAA: A9300, Grounds R. B., 27, 31, 32.

The art of camouflage, or concealment through deception, was a multidisciplinary activity that combined knowledge and skills from science and the arts. Zoologists studied camouflage patterns and disruptive colouration in the animal world, physicists examined the physical effects of light and colour, while chemists experimented with dyes and paints. Camouflage was especially suited to architects, artists and photographers, with a number of these working in this area during World War II.[21] One of these was Walter Bunning, who, like Grounds, prepared working drawings of camouflage installations.

Recurring themes throughout Grounds' life were the strong emotional link that he forged with natural settings and places, and the desire to spend time there to recuperate from stress. Immediately after returning from active duties, he spent two years working as an orchardist and dairy farmer in country Victoria.[22] Grounds claimed that his affinity with nature became stronger in later years because of his association with scientists on the Academy of Science building. That was when he purchased 'Penders', a coastal property on the NSW South Coast with 'nearly five miles of waterfrontage', to which he escaped 'for a week every month, and a month in the summer'. Part of the appeal was the seclusion: writing to Philip, Grounds explained how he and Betty had 'just returned from a month's vacation in complete isolation in our forest'.[23] The other attraction to Penders was his desire to return the land to its natural state: Grounds claimed that he 'bought it to prevent subdivision and to return it back to the wonders of nature, a part of Australia that would for all time remain that way'.[24] After his death in 1981, Grounds' remains were returned to his coastal retreat, in accordance with his wishes.[25]

While Grounds' reasons for merging these houses into their natural settings are clear, the same cannot be said for Boyd, who, after all, had based his polychromatic colour scheme for the Fenner House on Vicki and Marilyn's paintboxes. It is possible that he had mellowed in his approach to colour by the time he took over the Vasey Crescent houses from Grounds. Another factor was that Betty Grounds—who had been involved with the interiors of the Academy of Science building—seemed to have the final say on colours for the

---

21 Among the architects were Walter Bunning, John D. Moore and Leslie Wilkinson, while those from art backgrounds included William Dobell, Eric Ernest Joliffe, Daryl Lindsay, Keeper of the Prints, National Gallery Melbourne, and Lewis McCubbin, Director, National Gallery of Adelaide. The photographer Max Dupain was another camouflage officer. National Archives of Australia, NAA: A5954/69, NAA: A453/1, 1942/28/2298.
22 Hamann, Modern Architecture in Melbourne: The Architecture of Grounds, Romberg and Boyd, 1927–1971, 45.
23 Grounds to John Philip, 29 January 1969, Papers of John Philip.
24 Roy Grounds, De Berg Tapes, National Library of Australia, Recorded in Melbourne, 11 October 1971.
25 'At Penders, the spirit of Sir Roy Grounds still roams at large. In the moody surroundings of his beach retreat on the New South Wales South Coast, strange upturned tree sculptures stand guard like pagan charms. With single stone eyes, they watch the spot where Grounds's ashes were sprinkled in March, and the unoccupied house, a stylised tee-pee of fibreglass and nylon sailcloth which has stood for 12 years.' Geoff Strong, 'Centre of Contention', The Age (8 August 1981): 19–20.

Vasey Crescent houses. At one stage, Boyd wrote to Penny Griffing, stating: 'Mrs. Grounds was not enthusiastic about any of the colours in the carpet range you mentioned.'[26] But whether it was due to those reasons, or simply because he wanted Grounds' design intent to remain intact, Boyd exerted as much control over colour as his partner. Most of Boyd's efforts on the Vasey Crescent houses seemed to be concerned with maintaining visual continuity between the three houses, and between them and the adjacent bushland. A large part of the success of this venture can be attributed to the persistence of John Philip, who regularly checked with Boyd to ensure that the houses would present an integrated appearance.

Immediately after signing the building contract, Philip wrote to Boyd—who had formally taken over responsibility for the Vasey Crescent houses from Grounds—expressing his concern about details that he believed might affect the external appearance of the houses. One of these was the colour of the mortar. When visiting houses under construction in Canberra, the Philips had observed that the predominant mortar colour was mustard, which they thought would clash 'quite horribly with the pale grey of Besser blocks'. They asked Boyd if there was any way of adjusting the mortar colour to provide a closer match.[27] Writing to Dalheim Constructions the next day to confirm that they were the successful tenderers, Boyd wasted no time in asking them to

> [p]lease be careful to match the finishes, especially in the Besser block work, with those on the Griffing House next door, which has started a little ahead of yours. Also the colours when we finally get around to them will be matched. We would be grateful if, all along, you would keep in mind that the three houses in the row should present a unified appearance.[28]

Boyd replied to the Philips that he knew 'the normal colour in Canberra is bad, due to the yellow-brown colour of the sand', but regretted that there was no way of changing this without resorting to expensive colour mixes. He recommended that, as the Griffing House was already under construction, it was more important to match the mortar colour to that.[29] The Philips stated that they were happy with this solution—as long as their mortar did in fact match that of the Griffings'. To see if this was the case, the Philips inspected another house in Vasey Crescent that was being constructed by Dalheim Constructions, and noted that the mortar there was more mustard in colour than that mixed

---

26 Boyd to Penny Griffing, 13 December 1960, 'Griffing House Canberra'. Betty Grounds had previously been involved in the interior of the Australian Academy of Science building, for which she had selected light fittings.
27 John Philip to Boyd, 25 August 1960, 'Philip House Canberra'.
28 Boyd to Dalheim Constructions, 26 July 1960, 'Philip House Canberra'.
29 Boyd to John Philip, 29 August 1960, 'Philip House Canberra'.

by Meli and Eglitis, the builders of the Griffing House.[30] Boyd wrote to Dalheim Constructions again, stressing the importance of matching 'the effect of the Besser block work with Griffing's', and also 'the colour of the mortar which, of course, depends on the colour of the sand'. He instructed Dalheim Constructions to check with the other builders as to 'what sand they used, and endeavour to get the same'.[31]

In keeping with the rigour imposed on the exterior, the interior colours of the Philip House were limited to a few tones. Great care was taken to ensure that nothing would clash with the exterior, or with the natural tones of the bushland setting. Carpet and tiles were a soft teal blue, walls were unpainted concrete blocks or blond-coloured vertical ash boarding, and ceilings were ash. Much of the furniture consisted of natural materials: the Robin Day-designed steel-framed chairs, for instance, were covered in leather hide. Eric Wilson, writing for *Australian Home Beautiful*, noted that the only accents of colour to the interior were the satin chrome light fittings, copper flue and pans, white porcelain dishes and coffee pots, and books.[32]

Figure 4.4 Philip House, living room, looking south-west

Photograph: Candida Griffiths

---

30 John Philip to Boyd, 31 August 1960, 'Philip House Canberra'.
31 Boyd to Dalheim Constructions, 5 September 1960, 'Philip House Canberra'.
32 Eric Wilson, 'Style is Timeless', *Australian Home Beautiful* (December 1963): 11.

Experiments in Modern Living

This coordinated approach to natural and muted colours, with an emphasis on a blue–grey theme, was continued through the interiors of all the Vasey Crescent houses. Boyd reminded Penny Griffing that '[t]he building itself will be, of course, grey and natural-timber', and that '[g]rey on the floor will maintain this background scheme'. The Griffings were instructed to 'keep to greys in all floor coverings and to blues and greens in all your furnishings—throughout the whole house'. And in case she still did not have the message, he repeated that the colour scheme was: 'BACKGROUND: Grey and light natural timber. FOREGROUND: Blue-Green and dark natural timber.' Such was the control exerted by the architects that the clients were further instructed to 'banish reds, oranges, golds', but were permitted to introduce these colours 'accidentally' into the spaces in the form of ephemeral items such as 'flowers or books or a dress'![33]

Physics at Home

> In the lovely austere world of mathematics there are no uncertainties. There are no people, no classes, no warm or cold, no hate or spite, no time, no death. There are only numbers.
>
> — Norman Mussen, Structural Engineer, Philip House[34]

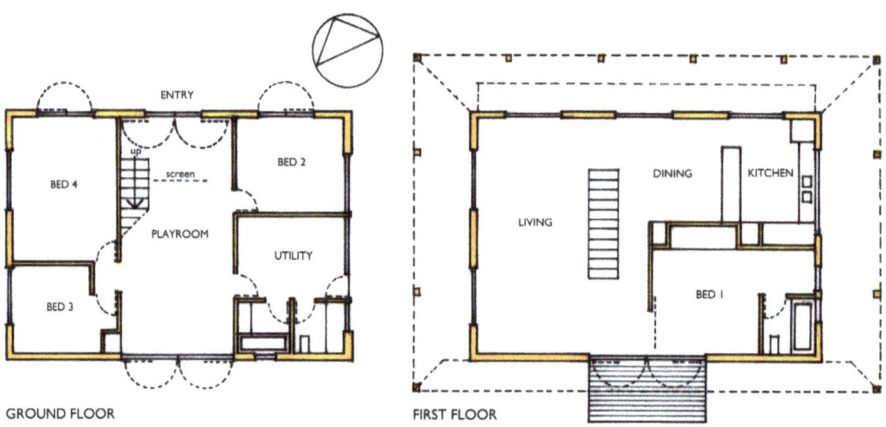

Figure 4.5 Philip House, floor plans

Image: redrawn by the author from Grounds, Romberg and Boyd. Courtesy of Victoria Grounds and the Robin Boyd Foundation

---

33 Boyd to Penny Griffing, 13 December 1960, 'Griffing House Canberra Correspondence'.
34 Norman Mussen, 'There are Only Numbers', *Architecture and Arts* 1, no. 1 (July 1952): 23. Mussen was a structural engineer and senior lecturer in the School of Architecture at Melbourne University during the 1950s. He was the structural engineer for the Philip House. See Fritz Suendermann to Boyd, 23 March 1962, 'Philip House Canberra'.

As an environmental physicist, John Philip was perfectly capable of discussing how transformations of matter and energy in the material world related to house design, but his input did not stop there. Philip had no hesitation in discussing any aspect of architecture that he believed warranted his attention. Writing to brief Boyd—who was about to come to Canberra to meet with the Philips—that their 'sometimes difficult' client was fired up about the window heads not being flush with the ceiling, Grounds, Romberg and Boyd's supervising architect, Fritz Suendermann, warned Boyd that '[u]ndoubtedly you will have the pleasure of being lectured by John Philip on various aspects of architecture, ranging from "Spec-Builders' Aesthetics" to "Beaumaris Romantic"'.[35]

In the 1950s, Philip was one of a small number of scientists across the world who realised the potential of mathematical physics to contribute to environmental issues. His research, through which he revolutionised scientific understanding and became a world authority, involved thermodynamics: the way in which water moves through soil. By providing the key physical concepts and mathematics required for a unified understanding of hydrological principles, Philip presented a generation of scientists and engineers with clear sets of principles to maximise the use of available water. His work was especially important in dry countries such as Australia, where he studied unsaturated soil, whose pores contained both air and water.[36]

Philip was a child prodigy and an outstanding mathematician. Qualifying for university at the age of thirteen, he was considered too young to attend, and, after filling in two more years, attended the University of Melbourne and graduated as a Bachelor of Civil Engineering at age nineteen. In 1960, he was awarded a Doctorate of Science (physics) by the same university. David Smiles recalled that mathematics provided Philip with 'both his language and his logic'.[37] Earlier in his career the problems he was working with were too complex for computers of the time, so Philip developed his own methodology using a simple hand calculator. He never used a modern computer and had a habit of performing extremely complex calculations while lying on the floor. His daughter, Candida Griffiths, described how her father viewed mathematics 'as a very beautiful thing: as you or I might think of something that we've just drawn as very beautiful, he really, really saw great beauty in his calculations'. She also recalled her father's delight in the momentary observation of a 'beautiful number' on the speedometer of the family car.[38]

---

35 'I accept all your explanations for Philip's queries and I know he can be very difficult'. Boyd to Suendermann, 20 June 1961, 'Philip House Canberra'; and Suendermann to Boyd, 6 June 1961, 'Philip House Canberra'.
36 One practical outcome of his theoretical work was the practice of planting trees in dry locations to improve local climates.
37 David Smiles, John Philip's Commemorative Gathering, Australian Academy of Science, 18 July 1999, Papers of John Philip.
38 Papers of John Philip; Candida Griffiths, Interview by the author, 27 June 2008.

But for Philip, numbers reached profound significance as tools for investigating order in the physical world:

> The great task of science reduces ultimately to the search for order: to discern the regularities in the bewildering universe around us—firstly so that we may gain understanding of it and our place in it; and secondly so that we may use this understanding to manage both our world and ourselves more wisely.

That this quest for order was common to both physics and biology was exemplified, for Philip, by the fact that the 'two great generalisations' of science—in physics, the second law of thermodynamics, and, in biology, the principle of evolution by natural selection—both represented a search for order. Philip's summary of Charles Darwin's theory of natural selection described it as 'the process whereby organisms automatically evolve into ever more highly ordered forms of ever-increasing complexity…The organism with the talent of coping with the environment automatically inherits the environment; the one without it automatically disappears'.[39]

Philip displayed a keen interest in the arts, listing his hobbies as 'reading, writing, architecture, cooking'. John and Frances were both involved with the commissioning of Ken Woolley's F. C. Pye Laboratory at the CSIRO, Black Mountain. John's description of the completed building indicated how he viewed architecture: 'It also seems to us to be unique in other, more human, senses. It is a delight to work in this building. It is a pleasure to the eye and satisfying to the mind to find oneself in a building combining beauty and logic, humanity and efficiency.'[40]

In the late 1980s, Fellows of the Academy of Science became concerned by reports that the concrete domed roof of Eero Saarinen's Kresge Auditorium at the Massachusetts Institute of Technology in Boston was beginning to fragment due to a continuous cycle of freezing and thawing in winter. Believing that the cold nights and sunny days of Canberra might have the same effect on Grounds' dome, the academy asked John Philip to investigate. Philip organised the installation of temperature and water-content sensors in the roof, and, through data obtained from these, he established that 'the temperature in the

---

39 John Philip, Undated draft script for 'Insight', ABC 'Physics and Biology', National Library of Australia, 'Philip House Canberra'.
40 John Philip, 'The Elements—Earth, Air, Fire, Water', [Special feature on Ken Woolley's F.C. Pye Laboratory], *The Canberra Times* (30 August 1966). Candida Philip and Toss Gascoigne (a former CSIRO employee) both recall that the basic configuration of the F. C. Pye Laboratory was first sketched by Frances Philip. Candida Griffiths, Interview by the author, 27 June 2008; and Toss Gascoigne, In discussion with the author, 2008.

concrete ceiling below the copper roof never dropped below 5°C during the frostiest nights'.[41] Philip's passion for architecture resulted in an invitation to be a Sulman Award jurist in 1964.[42]

Philip approached the design of his own house with the same combination of passion and exactitude that he displayed in other endeavours. Absolutely nothing was taken for granted, or left to chance. Every possible physical aspect of the house was calibrated, recorded, compared and discussed with the architects to achieve, from Philip's point of view, the optimum result in terms of aesthetics, human comfort and the most efficient use of resources. His energy, commitment and level of engagement throughout the entire design process were extraordinary. In late 1959, before they had engaged their architect, Philip had already fired off a number of letters to the National Capital Development Commission, offering his comments on the planning of tennis courts and preschool centres in Campbell, and to the Department of the Interior to seek their assurance that a tree in Vasey Crescent would not be damaged by footpath construction. Throughout the design and documentation phases, he wrote long, highly detailed letters—many containing alternative sketches and extensive lists of items for consideration—to Grounds, Romberg and Boyd on a weekly basis.[43]

Candida Griffiths attributed her parents' decision to build on an elevated site to Frances Philip's childhood memories of holidays in the Gippsland hills. The sloping land of Campbell was ideal for the Philips' requirements, and they walked 'the length and breadth' of the suburb investigating possible sites. One street that aroused their interest was Vasey Crescent, which at that time was just a dirt track. On one site they propped a ladder against an old yellow-box tree to confirm potential views of the future lake. At a later stage in the design process, Frances persuaded Boyd to climb a ladder to confirm the views that would be obtained from the upper level.[44]

There is no record that Grounds—who Frances thought was 'a bit of an arrogant so-and-so'[45] compared with the more approachable Boyd—was ever asked to perform such tasks. With his Academy of Science building having just won the Sulman Medal, and with a string of commissions for scientists in Canberra on

---

41 Ross Taylor, John Philip's Commemorative Gathering, Australian Academy of Science, 18 July 1999, Papers of John Philip.
42 'D. J. Philip' was listed as a member of the Sulman Award jury in 1964. Presumably this referred to John Philip, whose initials were actually 'J. R.'. Andrew Metcalf, *Architecture in Transition: The Sulman Award 1932–1996* (Sydney: Historic Houses Trust of New South Wales, 1997), 96.
43 Letters dated August 1959, Papers of John Philip.
44 Candida Griffiths, Interview by the author, 27 June 2008. The reference to Boyd climbing the ladder is from Serle, *Robin Boyd: A Life*, 192.
45 Serle, *Robin Boyd: A Life*.

his drawing boards, Grounds was carving out a niche in the scientific world.[46] It is important to note, however, that in spite of his growing connections to the scientific community, Grounds remained suspicious of those within his profession who believed that science represented the future of architecture. Rather than welcoming scientific progress as a source of new opportunities and directions, he saw it as a potential form of control. Worse still, he believed that the obsession with science was an indication that architects had lost touch with their principal purpose: to design spaces for people.[47]

Grounds thought that Le Corbusier never really believed a house was 'a machine for living in'; it was only 'a nice catch phrase' that had caught on with a lot of people. For Grounds, the logical outcome of Le Corbusier's aphorism was that architecture was a form of scientific experiment on humanity, whereas, in reality, humanity was made up of a variety of individuals, each with their own specific requirements. Moreover, these requirements, in spite of technological progress, were 'much the same today as they were about two thousand years ago'. Emphatically rejecting popular scientific jargon, Grounds claimed that clients 'want to be left alone and not pushed around by a group of scientific architects who are trying to use clichés which have not a great deal to do with a human being but have a great deal to do with a scientific attitude gone pseudo'.[48]

For Grounds, consideration of the individual client's needs was more important than the application of overarching scientific principles. But what did this mean in practice? Grounds perceived his domestic architectural consultancy as being akin to that of a neighbourhood physician—a situation reinforced by his belief that clients went to an architect only when they were 'in trouble', wanting to do something that they were not capable of doing for themselves:

> You go to a doctor when you're ill, you go to a solicitor when you're in trouble and you go to a dentist when you've got a toothache, you go to an architect when you want something done that you'd like to do yourself but you can't. You're in pain, you need help, you need advice, you need assistance, so you've got to act like a doctor to help them over a hurdle, they'd do it themselves, otherwise.[49]

Grounds was a specialist who would listen to clients' needs and attempt to solve them. In an interview with Hamann, he described himself as a 'sociologist', interpreting people's needs and 'painting pictures' of his clients in wood, stone,

---

46 Other commissions in Canberra that followed the Australian Academy of Science building were a group of townhouses in Forrest for 'Academics Anonymous' (which included Grounds), the Phytotron Building at the CSIRO, Black Mountain, and the botany and zoology buildings at The Australian National University, Acton.
47 'Three Sided Debate', *Architecture and Arts* 1, no. 1 (July 1952): 13.
48 Ibid.
49 Roy Grounds, De Berg Tapes, National Library of Australia, Recorded in Melbourne, 11 October 1971.

brick or concrete. This was essentially how Grounds saw his role on the Academy of Science project, describing himself as 'the instrument of [the scientists'] needs, the professional instrument of their hopes, their wants, their needs'.[50] And, in spite of his strong personality and reputation for being something of a bully, Grounds treated his consultations with clients seriously. He would arrange an initial meeting, often asking the whole family to attend. During this he would take copious notes, and make a determined effort to ascertain their individual requirements, such as household routines and entertaining patterns. This initial consultation was often followed up by a phone call from Grounds, or even a subsequent, unannounced visit. These could occur at any hour: some clients recalled him phoning them late at night, another received a visit at 2 am, while others woke up to find their newly commissioned architect standing outside their front door before breakfast, notebook in hand, ready to study their morning routines.[51]

The first Canberra 'consultation' with the Philips took place in late 1959 in a house they were renting at 22 Longstaff Street, Lyneham. At that meeting Grounds recorded the names and ages of the children, and the family's hobbies, lifestyle and requirements, in a small, lined writing pad. These notes, later typed up back in the office, included the following:

One car

Mr[s]. Philip is a painter

Mrs. Philip enjoys work in a 'no work' studied carelessness garden

Mr. Philip avoids gardening, but is a good cook—and does it—most of it

Likely to entertain over meals

Table tennis—in a Rumpus Room

Radio, TV, etc.—quite incidental

Up to 2 cars in basement

+ table tennis

+ a workshop (future)

+ access to kitchen

---

50 Roy Grounds, Interview by Conrad Hamman, January 1978, cited by Hamann, Modern Architecture in Melbourne: The Architecture of Grounds, Romberg and Boyd, 1927–1971, 53; and ibid.
51 Hamann, Modern Architecture in Melbourne: The Architecture of Grounds, Romberg and Boyd, 1927–1971, 51–3.

One of the first questions that Grounds asked his new clients was how much money they had. In the Philips' case, this amounted to £9000—or, depending on how John's CSIRO salary details eventuated, possibly only £8500. For this reason, economies of scale and materials were of primary importance.[52] The compact design of the Philip House seems to have been established from that first meeting: Grounds' notes describe a '2½ to 3-storey house towards the rear of the site', and contain four 'thumbnail' sketches of a rectangular, two or three-storey house roofed by a shallow gable. Calculations of the floor area—'19.76 plus porch and garage'—resulted in a preliminary estimate of £10 700. The Philips explained how they were embarking on this project five years before they could really afford it, but they did not want that to prejudice the size of the house. They hoped to be able to build the 'bare bones' first and add on later.[53]

A short time later, the Philips received preliminary sketch designs, drawn by James McCormick. These were very similar in layout to the thumbnails. The Philips' response, sent in December 1959, was a portent of what was to come. Ten pages long, it was extremely detailed and included calculations of sun angles and heating costs and alternative plans—the last drawn by Frances and notated by John.[54] The clients told Grounds that they appreciated the architecture on aesthetic principles, but believed that there were 'quite formidable practical objections to the concept' as it stood. They requested major alterations, implementation of which would 'demand quite radical changes from the present plan'.

The changes were informed by John's belief in the importance of the sun, from which, he wrote, 'all life on earth depends ultimately on…for its supply of free energy and order'.[55] They were grouped under two categories: 'The Roof, the Balcony and the Sun', and 'Relocation of Activities Within the House'. All proposed changes were based on the idea that passive solar design should provide adequate levels of comfort without resorting to artificial heating or cooling.

The cantilevered eaves were the first area of criticism. While Boyd in his two designs for the Fenner House had incorporated significant eaves overhangs on the northern side of the blocks, Grounds had proposed 1.8 m deep eaves on all sides of the three Vasey Crescent houses. As there was no functional requirement for such a deep overhang on the south side, and limited requirements on the east and west where the sun is predominantly at a low angle, it appears that the protective nature of the roof was a symbolic gesture more than a practical solution.

---

52 Candida Griffiths, Interview by the author, 27 June 2008.
53 'Philip House Canberra Correspondence'.
54 Candida Griffiths, Interview by the author, 27 June 2008.
55 John Philip, Undated draft script for 'Insight', ABC 'Physics and Biology'.

John Philip was concerned that the continuous 1.8 m wide eaves would not only 'make the house inordinately gloomy and chilly', but would also result in 'a very serious and continuing economic loss which results from the neglect of winter heat supply from the sun'. He calculated that, in regard to the north wall, 'there would be no penetration of sun into the house at midday between about August 25 and April 17', while '[e]ven in mid-winter (June 21) at midday only the bottom half of the window would receive the sun'. Philip provided evidence of the savings that would be incurred by reducing the depth of the eaves:

> It is, for example, easily shown that 20 square feet of sunlit window supply, on the average, 1 kilowatt of heat [1 radiator bar]. Reducing the northern overhang from 6 feet [1.8 m] to 2 feet [600 mm] would save of the order of £70 per annum in winter heating bills *without* admitting more summer sun into the house than we should desire.[56]

The Philips were not the only ones to object to the deep roof overhang. In early December 1959, all three Vasey Crescent clients wrote to Grounds requesting that the cantilever be reduced in depth. The simultaneous timing of their requests indicates collaboration between the clients on this issue, and it is most likely that John Philip—whose submission was the most detailed and scientific—played a key role in orchestrating their coordinated responses.[57]

The second major issue raised by the Philips was the location of activities within their three-storeyed house. At the initial meeting with Grounds, they had discussed a traditional configuration with living areas on the lower levels and bedrooms above. But after considering the preliminary sketches, John Philip's scientific background prevailed, and he asked for the layout to be amended. As Candida Griffiths explained, 'my father was a physicist, and very aware of the fact that heat rises, and wanted to use the physics of the way heat worked rather than working against it'. This meant placing the living areas, where the family spent most waking hours, in a position to benefit from that principle. 'So they said to Grounds "no, that's not what we want, we want it to be an upside-down house". And Roy Grounds said, "well I suppose you know what you're doing", and wasn't particularly thrilled, but I suppose realised he had to back down, because they knew what they wanted.' Philip no doubt felt that his insistence was justified when an article in *Australian Home Beautiful* titled 'Sun Keeps Heating Bills Low' described the success of the passive solar design:

---

56   John Philip to Grounds, 4 December 1959, 'Philip House Canberra Correspondence'.
57   A letter from the Griffings to Grounds was dated the same day, while Catherine Blakers wrote on 2 December 1959. 'Griffing House Canberra Correspondence'; and 'Blakers House Canberra'.

'On bright midwinter days the temperature on the top floor can top 70 deg. without any warmth from the oil heater. This contribution from the sun has had an important part in keeping the Philip fuel bill low.'[58]

A later innovation, introduced by John Philip after the house was completed, was related to the same principle. Aware that the combination of rising warm air and solar heat gain through the metal roof would make the upper level—where the family was primarily located during the daytime—intolerably hot in summer, Philip installed a sprinkler system on the roof to cool the surface temperature. This was not, however, a success; on the hottest days, many neighbours operated sprinklers in their gardens, and the increasing demand placed on the water supply lowered the pressure to a level where the cooling system was ineffective.[59]

In January 1960, Grounds thanked his clients for their 'very orderly tabulation of criticisms', and explained how they had substantially revised the plans in accordance with most of their objections, whilst 'maintaining the essential character and reducing the cost'.[60] Revised drawings, prepared by Pat Moroney, showed the activities relocated to specific levels according to the Philips' instructions. Grounds reminded his clients of the subsequent, unorthodox result—that the entrance to the house was now through the children's playroom on the lower level. The Philips had already decided that they would solve this problem by installing an operable screen to block off the playroom when they invited guests over for dinner parties.[61]

In accordance with the clients' instructions, the revised sketch drawings showed a reduction in the roof eaves overhang on the northern and the southern elevations from 1.8 m to 900 mm.[62] In spite of this, however, Grounds, Romberg and Boyd were reluctant to change this detail on the working drawings, and retained the eaves at a consistent 1.8 m depth all around, with a cut-out opening over the northern windows. Philip persuaded the architects to increase the size of this aperture to extend beyond the width of the windows to allow for the angle of the sun, resulting in the final configuration where the cut-out extended to the line of the return walls. He also convinced Grounds, Romberg and Boyd to reduce the overhang to 900 mm on the southern elevation.

---

58 Eric Wilson, 'Good-Mannered Houses'. The Blakers and Griffing houses also followed passive solar design principles. The Griffings discussed their house in this regard under 'Heating, Griffing House, 44 Vasey Crescent, Campbell, Canberra', Papers of John Philip.
59 Candida Griffiths, Interview by the author, 27 June 2008.
60 Grounds to John Philip, 15 January 1960, 'Philip House Canberra Correspondence'.
61 A double-hinged screen, constructed of an ash frame with Japanese-style blind, was hinged on one side to the stringer and handrail of the stair. This was rolled across to screen off the playroom—which was essentially a second living area—on occasions when guests were arriving at the house via the 'formal', front entry. On most days, the screen was folded back, and the Philips entered the house through the laundry to the east. Candida Griffiths, Interview by the author, 27 June 2008.
62 'Philip House Canberra Correspondence'.

The Philips then focused their energies on the resolution of various details—and errors—in the revised plans. These included the optimum utilisation of internal space to avoid waste—for this, they specified dimensions down to 10 mm—provision of adequate natural light to all rooms, acoustic treatment to avoid noise transmission via the internal staircase, installation of a prefabricated acoustic phone booth, provision of impermeable sills to cope with condensation on windows, and the inclusion of adequate insulation. John Philip noted the incorrect orientation of north points on three of the plans, reminding the architects that 'the block faces slightly east of north, not west of north'.[63]

A number of concerns expressed by the Philips related to aesthetic principles, particularly to maintaining visual compatibility between the three houses. After examining a preliminary site plan of the Vasey Crescent houses, the Philips noticed that there was a difference of 300 mm between the proposed floor level of their own house and that of the Griffing House next-door. John Philip asked Grounds if this disparity would be obvious—'for example, via the non-alignment of window levels'. A reply from Grounds, Romberg and Boyd reassured their increasingly obsessive clients that, due to the relative locations of the houses on their sites, the 300 mm difference would not cause visual conflict. Having already expressed a preference for the concrete-block external walls to be laid in a 'stack bond with the long emphasis vertical' to provide a 'rather desirable vertical emphasis to the house'—presumably to match the verticality implied by the timber posts—the Philips further stated that they preferred the blocks to be hollow Besser blocks because they were 'both cheaper and better thermally'.[64] Another issue that concerned the clients was how their architects intended to treat the detail where the eaves—to be constructed from timber boarding—reduced in width from 1.8 m to 900 mm.[65]

But by early 1961 the Philips' robust, 'hands-on' approach had so exceeded normal levels of client involvement that it began to be interpreted by their architects as interference. In January 1961, Suendermann wrote a file note instructing that 'Philip [was] to be told not to discuss anything with builder!' Later that year Suendermann's patience finally ran out when he received a phone call from Frances on a Sunday evening:

> [L]ast Sunday, 8.15 pm Mrs. Philip rang, saying the whole of the first floor construction has been done wrongly, the whole house is now a mess and John was stamping up and down the floor, cursing Grounds, Romberg and Boyd. When I found out that they had these detail drawings since

---

63 John Philip to Grounds, 15 February 1960, 'Philip House Canberra Correspondence'.
64 John Philip to Grounds, 28 March 1960; Grounds, Romberg & Boyd reply, 31 March 1960; Pat Moroney's file notes after speaking to Philip on the telephone, 12 April 1960, 13 April 1960, 'Philip House Canberra Correspondence'.
65 The solution was a part–45-degree mitred joint that squared off in line with the return wall.

August last year, I could not help but blowing my top and telling them one or two things that have been on my mind for a long time. But after that mild storm we are all good friends again.[66]

Conflating the Paradigms

There is no record that Grounds ever discussed the Vasey Crescent houses in regard to architectural style. But there was nothing unusual about this: he rarely talked about such issues. Grounds' overall attitude towards architecture was based on a 'commonsense', 'workman-like' approach to problem solving that had been instilled early in his career.

Returning to Australia in the early 1930s after living overseas for four years, Grounds saw the architecture of his native country with an increased awareness: 'I saw it with a fresh eye completely and I couldn't understand why people didn't build buildings according to the climate and our own materials instead of aping buildings that had been done in England or in France or in Italy.'[67] Associated with this was his realisation that some earlier Australian buildings functioned well in relation to the local climate. This reinforced in Grounds a preference for tried and true, traditional building forms, and he began to adopt a select group of these elements—gabled roofs, verandahs, vertical posts, pergolas and louvred timber shutters—to incorporate within his domestic architecture. As a result, many of Grounds' houses from the late 1930s through to the 1950s established subtle visual connections to 'old colonial Georgian and rural vernacular' buildings.[68]

Grounds' commonsense attitude to domestic design extended through to building construction, for which he favoured well-established, traditional practices such as bricks, timber-framed windows and 'V'-jointed timber boarding. For him, new materials and building techniques made no sense when existing methods did the job adequately—and often for less cost.[69] It was all about finding the right balance between tradition and modernity: too much of one or the other and the integrity of the idea was lost.

One of the challenges facing Grounds—and other architects with modernist inclinations—was how to convince their clients to accept new aesthetic paradigms. Hamann saw a tactical advantage in the way in which Grounds sometimes disguised certain modernist ideas and innovations—ideas that would

---

66 Suendermann to Boyd, 6 June 1961, 'Philip House Canberra Correspondence'.
67 Roy Grounds, De Berg Tapes, National Library of Australia, Recorded in Melbourne, 11 October 1971.
68 Hamann, Modern Architecture in Melbourne: The Architecture of Grounds, Romberg and Boyd, 1927–1971, 67.
69 Ibid., 55.

have been too radical for some clients—'among warm and traditional forms and materials'.[70] Grounds had no need to resort to such tactics with the Philip House or with the Vasey Crescent Group in general. The clients for these houses were receptive to modern aesthetics and materials, and the raw concrete-block walls of all three houses were anything but traditional. But this dialectic between 'traditional' and 'modern' is evident throughout the Philip House. Although it is generally regarded to be a 'modern' house, the Philips nevertheless believed that it was informed, to some extent, by historical precedents. John and Frances Philip were 'very much attracted to the look of the old pub, and…liked the honesty of the old rural outbuildings…the posts, the veranda'.[71] They saw connections between these structures and the house that Grounds and Boyd designed for them. They also saw parallels between the way in which country homesteads were approached and the way that their house—set back some distance from the street—was approached. The Philips' postwar experience of living in an old hospital building in Deniliquin, NSW, had some bearing on the matching pairs of wide double doors that allowed the ground floor of their house to be opened up.[72]

There are three formal aspects of the Philip House that could be compared with historical architectural precedents, particularly with those of nineteenth-century Georgian buildings. One was the use of simple, rectangular building forms and symmetrical facades. A further characteristic was the row of vertical timber posts around the perimeter of the roof and floor cantilevers. These created the impression of a colonnade—like the posts supporting verandahs on buildings such as Rouse Hill House. The third reference to Georgian precedents was the way in which Grounds ordered the fenestration by vertical alignment of the openings through the ground and first-floor levels.[73]

It is indicative of the subtlety of Grounds' designs for the Vasey Crescent houses—and of the fine line that existed in his domestic work between modernist interpretation of historical themes and outright stylism—that the Philips made various comments in this regard that, on the surface, appear to conflict. They initially acknowledged that certain stylistic influences existed in their house. Directly after receiving McCormick's preliminary sketch design drawings, John Philip wrote to Grounds, saying: 'We appreciate your imaginative and poetic scheme to provide a unity to the three houses by means of the roof forms with

---

70   Ibid., 56.
71   Candida Griffiths, Interview by the author, 27 June 2008.
72   Griffiths recalled how the 'Australian building that was an old hospital really influenced them, and the fact that the doors opened and they went straight out onto the veranda, that was something of enormous importance'. Ibid.
73   Hamann refers to the use of these devices to produce a 'Georgian allusion' in the houses of both Grounds and Boyd. Hamann, Modern Architecture in Melbourne: The Architecture of Grounds, Romberg and Boyd, 1927–1971, 298.

their suggestions of both Colonial Australia and the Orient.'[74] One year after the house was completed, however, the Philips claimed to be opposed to any sense of historical style, stating that 'because of its simple form, the house would avoid any suggestion of architectural stylism, and would remain timeless in this age in which most houses are classified by "periods"'.[75] The key to their satisfaction with the house in relation to the question of style would appear to be the word 'suggestion'—indicating the existence of inscrutable visual references to the past that are implicit rather than explicit.

Figure 4.6 Frances Philip, Painting: Philip House from north, 1988

Image: Candida Griffiths Collection

---

74   John Philip to Grounds, 4 December 1959, 'Philip House Canberra Correspondence'.
75   'Style is Timeless', [Author not noted, but possibly Eric Wilson], *Australian Home Beautiful* (December 1963): 10.

The Philip House became an embodiment of one of Grounds' major strengths as a house designer: his ability to skilfully fuse historical and modernist elements into an integrated whole. By juxtaposing the familiar with the unfamiliar in a way that was essentially new, Grounds—and his co-designer, Boyd—created a modern and original house that incorporated subtle traces of architectural precedents within the massing, proportion and detail of its fabric.

Boyd described how this worked in an analysis of earlier houses by Grounds:

> [T]he materials looked new because they were put together in a new way. They looked squarer and lighter and there were fewer lines, ridges and pockets…they were ordered into more precise shapes and they seemed to cohere better, making a simple but vigorous little pattern of every house.[76]

But it was in this refinement process that the correct balance between traditional techniques and the modern aesthetic was sometimes lost. The reductive approach that Grounds and Boyd both applied to architectural massing—where they took a form and pared it down to its simplest and most elemental state—had its drawbacks when it came to detailing. Of particular concern was Boyd's preference for concealing roof gutters, as demonstrated by the Fenner House. The Vasey Crescent Group houses did not fare much better, with the box gutters becoming blocked with leaves, resulting in water penetration into the interiors during heavy downpours.[77]

After it was completed in early 1962, the Philip House attracted a lot of interest from the public. This was something that it shared with the Fenner and Zwar houses—but with one major difference. The attention was now due to the fact that there was not just one modern house that stood out, but three in a row. Griffiths remembered seeing many cars slowing outside the house, and the drivers and passengers stopping to look. She imagined that many of them were shocked by the 'three ugly houses' set back so far from the street, made out of besser block, with their large windows and flat roofs.[78]

It was the fact that this was a group of modern houses that polarised opinion about the Vasey Crescent Group. Writers such as Eric Wilson and Morton Herman were enthusiastic in their appraisal. Wilson wrote that the group was

---

76   Robin Boyd, *Australia's Home: Its Origins, Builders and Occupiers* (Melbourne: Melbourne University Press, 1952), 175.
77   While there is no evidence of problems with the Philip House in this regard, the other two both leaked. 'Vasey Residences. Saw Bruce Griffing Sunday after a very heavy downpour, and both his and Blaker's houses leaked badly. Water seemed to fill gutters and run back up under roofing and distribute itself over ceiling boards leaking through at every crack. Large amounts at windows running down inside face of walls.' Lou Gerhardt (Grounds, Romberg and Boyd representative in Canberra) to Boyd, 26 October 1962, 'Philip House Canberra Correspondence'.
78   Candida Griffiths, Interview by the author, 27 June 2008.

an excellent example of an alternative to the 'anarchy' of 'uncontrolled design and speculative building' that was taking over new suburbs. Most houses in Canberra, he believed, were 'a chaotic mixture of the conventionally dull and stridently gimmicky'—houses that were similar to those found in other cities, but 'out of character with the generally conservative architecture of Canberra'. The Vasey Crescent houses, however, provided 'harmony with the landscape and with each other', were appropriate for the dignity of the national capital, and demonstrated many of Walter Burley Griffin's ideals in regard to the planning of private houses.[79] Herman wrote how the three houses were vastly different in design, but were given 'harmony of appearance' through similar materials. Because the contours of the sites were largely unchanged, the houses displayed a 'very natural relationship between buildings and ground'.[80]

But the strengths of the Vasey Crescent Group, viewed through the eyes of their critics, were also their main weakness. Traditionalists, opposed to modern design, thought that these houses signalled too great a departure from what they were used to: brick-walled bungalows with tiled, hipped roofs—the sort of houses that had established a foothold in the capital city back in the 1930s. The key to their disenchantment was the underlying threat implied by the uniformity of the houses—as Wilson described it, 'the hint of regimentation' that they detected in the unified designs. Critics saw this as a dangerous precedent, a potential imposition on freedom of choice, and asked: 'who would want to live in a city of homes all designed by Grounds, Romberg and Boyd, or Griffin, or any other architect for that matter?'[81] There was, of course, no possibility that such an event would ever have occurred, and a city of uniform house design was never the intention of Grounds, Romberg and Boyd—or of Griffin. Rather, the Vasey Crescent Group was a unique opportunity for an experiment in the coordination of three adjacent houses. It was an opportunity that Grounds, Boyd and all three clients fully exploited.

In a cheeky note to John Philip that Grounds left under the front door of the Philip House when he passed through Canberra, he wrote: 'Betty and I are in Canberra just for today, so I brought her upstairs here to see as much as I felt I could walk into of what I believe to be the loveliest example of architecture in Canberra.'[82] Boyd believed, however, that the real significance of the Vasey Crescent Group was not as a series of individual houses, but as a group. In August 1962, after a period of friction between the partners—generated by Grounds' decision to break away from the firm and carry out the National Gallery of Victoria project on his own—the firm of Grounds, Romberg and Boyd

---

79 Wilson, 'Good-Mannered Houses', 5–6.
80 Morton Herman, 'Is YOUR House in the Upper Ten?', *The Australian* (3 August 1964): 10.
81 Wilson, 'Good-Mannered Houses', 6.
82 Grounds to John Philip, Undated, Papers of John Philip.

was liquidated, and the new firm of Romberg and Boyd was founded. During the following month, Grounds, following requests from the Philips and the Blakers, entered the Vasey Crescent Group into the Royal Australian Institute of Architects single-family residence award. Boyd did not agree with this decision, writing:

> I think it is a pity that these houses were entered in the competition. I don't think that they are likely to win. I am proud of them as a group and I think they prove something—as a group. But individually nobody has ever pretended that they are very remarkable houses, and the competition is for individual houses.[83]

The response from Grounds, via Lou Gerhardt, was ambivalent: 'We can cancel out now if either firm wishes…Mr. Grounds said that he has no feelings pro or con, and would leave it to you.' He did add, however, that the clients could have entered on their own behalf if he had refused.[84] Against Boyd's wishes, the entry was not withdrawn, and the houses failed to receive an award.

Essentially, Boyd was correct. The ultimate significance of the Philip House resides in the contribution it makes to the Vasey Crescent Group. While it is difficult to talk of the significance of the Philip House as a separate entity, some issues stand out above others. There was an extraordinary amount of correspondence between the clients and the architects throughout the design and documentation phases. Considerable thought was given to every detail and to every decision that was made. In this regard, the Philips deserve credit for their energy and enthusiasm, and the architects for their patience in dealing with clients who were so intimately involved. John Philip's enthusiasm for architecture and boundless energy for what became his pet project, coupled with his application of scientific theory and complete inability to accept refusal for his ideas, were major contributions.

John Philip's passion for architecture continued to the end of his life. In July 1999, he was tragically run over and killed by a car after stepping off a tram in Amsterdam. Candida Griffiths recalled—with some trepidation—how her father was most probably on his way to visit an exhibition of Frank Lloyd Wright's work at the time.[85]

The final house design reflected many of John Philip's aspirations and ideals—particularly in regard to passive solar design. The emphasis he gave, however, to this aspect over and above all other criteria created problems in regard to the

---

83   Boyd to Lou Gerhardt, 24 September 1962, 'Philip House Canberra Correspondence'.
84   Grounds (per Gerhardt) to Romberg and Boyd, 28 September 1962, 'Philip House Canberra Correspondence'.
85   Candida Griffiths, Interview by the author, 27 June 2008.

way the house was used. The decision to place the kitchen and living spaces on the upper level meant that it was necessary to carry grocery items up two full flights of stairs from the basement car space, and it physically detached the living spaces from the garden. In regard to the former issue, early drawings indicated that a dumb waiter was to be installed between the basement and kitchen, but this was later deleted to save cost. The Philips did not regret this decision, as they viewed negotiation of the stairs as part of their daily exercise regime.[86] The physical separation of the living spaces from the outside, however, remained a significant shortcoming that was alleviated, to some extent, by the provision of a small balcony. Shared by bedroom one, this overlooked the nature reserve to the south.

Finally, the architectural character of the Philip House represents the idea that it is valid for a new architectural paradigm to incorporate ideas and concepts from the previous version. In this way, the house became a conceptual bridge spanning the incommensurability between the 'old' and the 'new' paradigms. Unlike Seidler, Grounds and Boyd saw no need to discard previous ways of designing and building houses in the search for a radical new solution. In the Philip House, they endeavoured to construct a house that was a genuine amalgam of the best of both worlds: a delicate balance between known and established techniques and contemporary approaches.

---

86 Ibid.

Figure 4.7 Frances Philip, Painting: Philip House and children, 1965. Left to right: Peregrine, Candida and Julian

Image: Candida Griffiths Collection

5. Where Science Meets Art: Bischoff and the Gascoigne House

Theo said, 'What a great house it is…but it takes two people to build a house: an architect and a client—and you have been very good clients.' And I was pleased to hear that.

— Ben Gascoigne[1]

Figure 5.1 Gascoigne House, view from north

Photograph: Bill Lyristakis, 2010

Sidney ('Ben') Gascoigne chuckled and leaned across the dining table, placing his hand near a small groove on one edge of its otherwise pristine surface.

> Do you see that saw-cut there? Rosalie made that! She used to put bits of wood on the table and saw them, you see. And when I came home one day and she showed it to me, I said, 'Well, we're not going to fill that, not for anybody—this was made by Rosalie Gascoigne!'

It was late November 2007, and I was interviewing Ben in the dining room at 3 Anstey Street, Pearce—a house that Theo Bischoff designed for the Gascoignes

---

1 Ben Gascoigne, Interview by the author, 26 November 2007.

in 1967 and 1968. This was the last week that Ben was to spend in the house. Rosalie, his wife of 56 years and one of Australia's most highly regarded artists, had died eight years previously, and he was about to move into a smaller property. Many of her artworks had been prepared on the table around which we were sitting. Now they were going to new homes: to Ben's apartment, to the National Gallery of Australia or to other family members' houses.[2]

But the courtyard of the house, where Rosalie stored the raw materials for her assemblages, was still cluttered with ephemera that she had accumulated over 30 years of fossicking: dozens of old porcelain dolls' heads, stacks of sun-bleached animal vertebrae, piles of weathered timber slabs from old soft-drink crates, worn enamelware bowls and teapots, fragments of road signs, rusted iron, metal fans, bicycle seats, wire grilles and assorted kitchenalia.

Ben and Rosalie were both born in New Zealand, and emigrated to Australia during World War II when Ben took up a position at the Commonwealth Solar Observatory on Mount Stromlo. During the war, Ben worked on optical munitions: one of his first projects was designing a sighting telescope for anti-aircraft guns.[3] In the postwar years, he began observing stars in the Magellanic clouds, two small galaxies 170 000 light years away. He explored the photometry of faint stars and the maximum effectiveness of telescopes, and was instrumental in setting up the Anglo-Australian Telescope at Siding Spring.[4] Ben's observations and research contributed to the understanding of galactic distance and evolutionary theory. A Fellow of the Australian Academy of Science, he was the first Australian to be elected as Associate Member of the Royal Astronomical Society.[5]

The Anstey Street house (hereinafter referred to as 'the Gascoigne House') was the third of three houses in the Australian Capital Territory that the family lived in. The first was Residence 19, a staff house on Mount Stromlo, where they lived between 1943 and 1960, while the second was a house in Deakin, owned by The Australian National University, which they leased from 1960 to 1969.

Ben and Rosalie both contributed to the house. Ben's brief to Bischoff was the most comprehensive and detailed of any client in this book, and was based on an analysis and critique of problems that the family had experienced with their

---

2   Ben Gascoigne passed away in 2010.
3   Vici MacDonald, *Rosalie Gascoigne* (Paddington, NSW: Regaro, 1998), 13; Tom Frame and Don Faulkner, *Stromlo: An Australian Observatory* (Crows Nest, NSW: Allen & Unwin, 2003), 81.
4   'Some Recent Advances in the Optics of Large Telescopes', *ANU News* 1 (October 1964): 12; *Quarterly Journal of the Royal Astronomical Society* (1968): 9, 98–115; Stephen Foster and Margaret Varghese, *The Making of The Australian National University 1946–96* (St Leonards, NSW: Allen & Unwin, 1996), 98–9.
5   Ragbir Bhathal, *Australian Astronomers: Achievements at the Frontiers of Astronomy* (Canberra: National Library of Australia, 1996), 48.

first two houses. Rosalie added to Ben's criticisms of the previous houses, and became more involved with the project when she could see that it was becoming a reality.

In comparison with his distinguished clients—and with the other architects featured in this book—Bischoff remains a little-known architect outside Canberra. Many of his houses were published in *The Canberra Times*, *The Australian* and other publications in the 1960s soon after they were completed, and a few were included in J. R. Conner's *A Guide to Canberra Buildings* of 1970, but very little has been published on his work during the intervening decades.[6] His well-crafted, modernist houses, however, have stood the dual tests of time and of changing architectural fashion, and are today held in high regard by those in Canberra who are aware of his work. Most of his houses have been retained—many preserved in near-original condition—while others have been restored or extended.[7] When the Marshall House at 86 Morgan Crescent, Curtin—originally designed by Bischoff for the ANU microbiologist Ian Marshall and his wife, Kathleen—was advertised for sale in 2007, the real estate agent attempted to explain the reasons for its enduring appeal: 'Theo Bischoff's timeless architecture is as relevant today as it was when he designed the single level residence almost forty years ago. Extensive timber joinery and the simple detailing of natural material and finishes are evident throughout… and are so evocative of the sixties.'[8]

---

6   J. R. Conner, *A Guide to Canberra Buildings* (Sydney: Angus & Robertson, 1970). No work by Bischoff appears on the Royal Australian Institute of Architects' *Register of Significant Twentieth Century Architecture*, or on the institute's *Map of Significant Canberra Architecture*. Bischoff's work is not included in Andrew Metcalf's *Canberra Architecture* (Sydney: Watermark Press, 2003), and he is mentioned on Martin Miles' *Canberra House: Mid-Century Modernist Architecture* web site only as being project architect for the Frankel House in Campbell and a partner in the firm Scollay, Bischoff and Pegrum. Martin Miles, *Canberra House: Mid-Century Modernist Architecture* (Canberra: Martin Miles and Canberra House), <http://www.canberrahouse.com>

7   Toss and Lyn Gascoigne live in a house at 56 Vasey Crescent, Campbell, designed by Bischoff in 1964 for medical practitioner Dr Aubrey Tow. This house is in original condition. Other Bischoff houses include the Clarke House at 212 Dryandra Street, O'Connor (1958); the Bischoff House at 47 Carstenz Street, Griffith (1959); the Watson House at 13 Waller Crescent, Campbell (1961); the Cleland House at 33 Godfrey Street, Campbell (1961); the Benson House at 61 Quiros Street, Red Hill (1962); the Homer House at 25 Chermside Street, Deakin (1963); the Dr Andrea House at 32 Holmes Crescent, Campbell (1965); the Kellow House at 11 Rason Place, Curtin (1965); the Dr Horniblow House at 15 Theodore Street, Curtin (1965); the Marshall House at 86 Morgan Crescent, Curtin (1966); and the Pike House at 2 Garsia Street, Campbell (1966). Some of these—including the Andrea, Marshall and Pike houses—have had sympathetic additions or alterations.

8   Raine and Horne advertisement, agent Mary Debus, [Domain section], *The Canberra Times* (18 August 2007).

Residence 19, Commonwealth Solar Observatory

In 1905, in the midst of post-Federation debate over where to locate Australia's new federal city, Australian astronomer Geoffrey Duffield approached the Australian Government with a proposal. But, unlike many others who were lobbying the Government at that time, his proposition had nothing to do with the location of the capital city. Instead, Duffield wanted the Government to establish a solar observatory, the function of which would be to provide an Australian connection in a global network. He believed that an Australian observatory would fill a gap in the system between existing observatories in the British colony of India and the United States.[9]

Like many architects and planners of his time, Duffield was interested in the sun from a climatic point of view.[10] New instruments allowing observation of the sun's atmosphere had revealed luminous clouds that were larger than sunspots. Believing that there might be a connection between sunspots, magnetic fields and rainfall, he hoped that the study of solar phenomena might provide a greater understanding of terrestrial meteorological conditions and assist with weather forecasting and anticipation of drought.[11]

In 1908 the Australian Government decided to locate the Federal Capital Territory in the Yass–Canberra region, and in the following year confirmed that an observatory would be located within the Territory. Duffield's environmental criteria for the observatory included large numbers of sunny days, low average rainfall, low wind velocity, steady barometer readings, clearness of atmosphere, good elevation, and the presence of vegetation and foliage to prevent excessive radiation. A number of elevated sites within the capital Territory were considered, and Mount Stromlo—the highest peak in a 1.5 km-long ridge, situated 11 km to the west of the proposed federal city and approximately 200 m above its general level—was selected.[12] Plans for a full-scale observatory were put on hold during World War I, however, when the principal activity on Mount Stromlo

---

9 Solar Physics Committee of the Australasian Association for the Advancement of Science, *Memorandum upon the Proposed Solar Observatory in Australia* (Adelaide, 1909), 6.
10 English planner and theorist Charles Reade (writing as 'Ebenezer Howard') endorsed the importance of the sun in relation to urban planning by identifying sunlight as an essential element of his 'Garden City' concept. Reade's Garden City ideal, with its explicit debt to scientific thought, was an important influence on later planners and architects of the federal capital such as John Sulman and John Murdoch. Ebenezer Howard, *Garden Cities of Tomorrow* (London: Faber, 1946), originally published as *Tomorrow: A Peaceful Path to Real Reform* (1898). In 1908, English-trained architect Robert Haddon's *Australian Architecture* attempted to address the Australian climate and sun. Robert Haddon, *Australian Architecture: A Technical Manual for all Those Engaged in Architectural and Building Work* (Melbourne: E. W. Cole, 1908).
11 Frame and Faulkner, *Stromlo: An Australian Observatory*, 16.
12 Surveyor Charles Scrivener met the government astronomers of New South Wales and Victoria, plus the Commonwealth Meteorologist, in the Federal Capital Territory on 1 March 1910. They inspected potential

consisted of the planting of a *Pinus radiata* ('Monterey pine') plantation by the horticulturalist Charles Weston. This forest, which was ostensibly introduced to get rid of rabbits, stabilise the soil and improve atmospheric conditions in accordance with Duffield's guidelines, spread over the mountain in the ensuing decades and eventually reached the ridgeline.[13]

When the Government finally committed to the establishment of a full-scale observatory in 1923, attention was focused on the layout of the complex, including the location of staff houses. The Commonwealth Meteorologist believed that 'the crest of the Mount Stromlo ridge' was 'an ideal site for a scientific community', but was concerned about the location of staff accommodation: 'The exclusion of the dwellings, which would be situated on the slopes without the compound, is also important as difficulties are always liable to arise from purely personal reasons, particularly where the families of married officials are concerned.' He added that 'the roofs of dwelling houses should not rise above the level of the crest of the hill, and the houses themselves should be situated preferably on the south-eastern slopes'.[14] In July 1923, Duffield, Henry Rolland (Works Director to the Federal Capital Advisory Committee) and Colonel Percy Owen (Director-General of the Department of Works and Railways) met on site to discuss the siting of the observatory buildings. Afterwards they confirmed that the staff housing would be located on the eastern side of Stromlo ridge to provide shelter from the prevailing winds.[15]

It was determined that houses would be required for the Director, two assistants and possibly one senior mechanic, while single accommodation would be needed for research fellows, clerks, a professional officer, apprentice, janitor, chauffeur and cook.[16] During the 1920s the Federal Capital Commission's Architect's Department, under Rolland, designed and built a community of eight staff residences on Mount Stromlo. Termed 'cottages' in the English tradition by the commission, these were similar to the standard houses provided for civil servants in Canberra at the time. Constructed of double brickwork, stuccoed on the exterior and smooth-plastered inside, they had low-pitched, tiled roofs and timber-framed doors and windows. Their simple forms rejected elaborate ornamentation, but contained passing references to Mediterranean and Georgian styles.

---

observatory sites at Black Mountain, Mount Mugga, Mount Ainslie, the Cotter–Murrumbidgee River junction and Mount Stromlo. Of these, some were considered too small, while there were concerns that Black Mountain would be affected by the glare from city lights. Ibid., 23–5.
13   Ibid., 29–30.
14   Ibid., 31.
15   Henry Rolland, Interview by Donald Brech, 29, 32; and ibid., 32.
16   Commonwealth Department of Works and Railways, 'Commonwealth Observatory Mount Stromlo Erection—Notes on Projected Commonwealth Observatory, Stromlo, Federal Territory', 19 February 1923, National Archives of Australia, NAA Series A199, Item FC 1926/206.

The Mount Stromlo cottages followed contemporary planning principles, including accommodation of families without servants, and more efficient, less formal planning. They also incorporated new technology such as plumbing, sanitation and electricity. For these reasons they would have been considered up-to-date at the time they were built.[17] They were not, however, particularly well equipped to deal with the extreme climates on the exposed slopes of Mount Stromlo.

Figure 5.2 'Residence 19', Mount Stromlo Observatory, 1926. This would become the Gascoignes' first house

Photograph: National Archives of Australia, NAA: A3560, 1820

Ben Gascoigne arrived at the Commonwealth Solar Observatory in August 1941, and moved into the Bachelors' Quarters. Rosalie, who had met her future husband in Auckland in 1933, remained in New Zealand for the time being. Arriving in Sydney by flying boat in January 1943, Rosalie transferred to Canberra and travelled on to Mount Stromlo.[18] Ben and Rosalie married in early 1943 and moved into one of the staff cottages, known as Residence 19.

Rosalie's first impression of her new environment was the intense colour: 'Green, orange and blues. It was terribly coloured.' And the fact that 'the sun came out like a hammer. As soon as you stepped out the door—bang!'[19] But by winter of her first year on the mountain, she was convinced that the house had been designed with little appreciation of local conditions: 'that big open cold "built

---

17   For a description of the Federal Capital Commission houses, see Ruth Daniell, 'Imported Styles: Some Origins of Federal Capital Architecture', in Peter Freeman, ed., *The Early Canberra House: Living in Canberra 1911–1933* (Canberra: The Federal Capital Press of Australia, 1996), 91–106.
18   Martin Gascoigne, *New Zealand Lives: The New Zealand Families of Rosalie Gascoigne and Ben Gascoigne* (Canberra: Private publication, 2005), 316.
19   MacDonald, *Rosalie Gascoigne*, 13.

on the south side of the hill" house that we had…It was cold. And the air hung purple like that, purple in the passages.' She recalled that on some days it was warmer outside the house than it was inside. When inside, she found it was too cold to go down the passage to get a handkerchief, and preferred to huddle around the fuel fire in the kitchen.

But Rosalie found ways to pass the time indoors. In an indication of what was to come, during 'one drab winter', she began constructing a patchwork quilt:

> While the wind howled among the pines and hurled itself against the side of the house and my husband went up to work I used to sit patching flowery hexagons together, and the colour and the cheerfulness of the materials never failed to bring company into the room for me.

The darkness of the winter months in the Mount Stromlo house had other repercussions. The Gascoignes began buying modern art prints from Ben's friend Carl Plate, an abstract artist who ran the Notanda Gallery in Rowe Street, Sydney. But the lack of natural light inside the house became a problem: one of the prints, a Braque in a green frame, 'was too dark for their gloomy house'. Rosalie began to dread the arrival of winter, when 'all colour vanished from the garden and the hill was bitter with meager grass and stones'. Finding the colours of the landscape barren, she would search desperately 'for any kind of visual excitement'.[20]

The problems inside the house were aggravated by Weston's pine forest and by the way in which the house was sited. Although the trees had been cleared in patches to accommodate clusters of observatory buildings, they still obscured views to the south. Because the house was located on the south-eastern slope of the mountain and was cut into a bank on the north side, it was in shade for most of the day. For an astronomer who was able to see further than anyone else into the night sky through a telescope, it was frustrating for Ben to return to his own house, further down the mountain, and find that the potentially wonderful views over the Molonglo Valley were obscured by a wall of pine trees.[21] Rosalie remembered the oppressive denseness of the plantation, how the 'pine clad mountain closed in on her as she drove back up from town'. It was a memory that stayed with her: when she eventually moved down from the mountain to live in the suburbs of Canberra below, she gave a radio talk for

---

20 Ibid., 13–16; Rosalie Gascoigne, Interview by Robin Hughes, Australian Biography Project, 12 November 1998, <http://www.australianbiography.gov.au/subjects/gascoigne/interview>
21 Gascoigne recalled that '[we] didn't get any view…we couldn't see through these pine trees'. Ben Gascoigne, Interview by the author, 26 November 2007.

the Australian Broadcasting Corporation about her Mount Stromlo experiences. Titled 'Too Many Pine Trees', it contained numerous references to her memories of the dark and gloomy forest.[22]

Ben recalled how the pine trees—until they were decimated (for the first time) by fire in 1952—shaded their house from what little sun was available: 'we didn't get the winter sun until ten or eleven in the morning, not properly, and there'd be a frost on the southern side of the house—frost there all day sometimes.' To combat the cold, Residence 19 was equipped with no less than five separate fireplaces, a wood stove and a copper for heating water. At a later stage, Ben arranged for oil-fired heating to be added.[23] While the house was virtually sunless, Ben found another problem: any heat that was generated inside quickly dissipated through the external fabric. Following advice from The Australian National University—which had taken over administration of the observatory from the Department of the Interior in 1957[24]—Ben arranged for ceiling insulation to be installed at his own expense. This amounted to £91.4.2—a significant amount at the time. Two years later, when they moved to the Canberra suburb of Deakin, he wrote to the university asking if they would purchase the insulation back from him, stating that 'ceiling insulation can now be regarded as standard practice in Canberra'.[25]

More than 40 years later, the same pine forest played another, more deadly role, providing fuel for a massive firestorm that gutted most of the buildings on Mount Stromlo—including Residence 19 and the Director's Residence—and devastated Canberra's western suburbs.

'A Feeling of Space and Air'[26]

Rosalie's contribution to the Gascoigne House is best approached through an analysis of the ways in which space was important to her work. Descriptions of her art and influences contain many references to space, as do the artist's own accounts. These can be divided into two principal types of space: the external environment that Rosalie explored on foot—and later by car—and the internal

---

22 MacDonald, *Rosalie Gascoigne*, 14–15.
23 Ben Gascoigne, Interview by the author, 26 November 2007.
24 In 1957 Mount Stromlo was formally transferred from the Commonwealth Department of the Interior to The Australian National University and renamed the Department of Astronomy in the Research School of Physical Sciences. Foster and Varghese, *The Making of The Australian National University 1946–96*, 99; Frame and Faulkner, *Stromlo: An Australian Observatory*, 131.
25 Ben Gascoigne to Registrar, ANU, 12 July 1960, Papers of Ben Gascoigne (1938–2007), Manuscript Collection, National Library of Australia, MS Acc08/33, Box 4 (House).
26 Edmond Capon, 'Preface', in Deborah Edwards, *Rosalie Gascoigne: Material as Landscape* (Sydney: Art Gallery of New South Wales, 1998), 5.

spaces of her houses and studio.[27] An appreciation of how each of these spatial typologies impacted on Rosalie's creative process is critical to an understanding of her art—and, consequently, to an appreciation of the role that her domestic environment played in that work.

Rosalie spent a lot of time exploring Mount Stromlo and the wider area of the Monaro region, becoming intimate with these environments and collecting raw materials and found objects. Many writers commented on how something of the essence of these spaces was captured in her assemblages of objects. Edmund Capon wrote about how her art was 'inspired by the surroundings of her immediate landscape, the spacious grazing lands of the Monaro region near Canberra. Reflecting that inspiration, a feeling of space and air echoes eloquently through her work.'[28] Kelly Gellatly described how one of Rosalie's largest works, *Monaro*, a sprawling 4.6 x 1.3 m composition of fragments from yellow soft-drink containers, 'seems to hold the effect of wind rippling across sun-drenched grasslands at its very surface'.[29]

It was the apparent barrenness of the unfamiliar Mount Stromlo environment that trained Rosalie's perception: 'Through that sort of poverty with things, your eye gets very sharp.' In the beginning, Rosalie was observing out of pure necessity—a desperate attempt to fill a visual void: 'I had to have things that I found interesting. There wasn't any stimulation of the eye. You fed your eye as much as you could.' Studying her new landscape in detail, she learnt to identify 'every sort of gravel on that mountain, every sort of grass'.[30] When she found time between domestic duties, Rosalie created a flower garden on the steep land behind the house. Closely related to Rosalie's observation of her surroundings was the desire to pick up objects that interested her and take them home: 'I used to go out, which I liked doing, and I'd take anything that was beautiful…I'd gather that home.'[31] She began collecting Australian native plants, and learnt how to preserve flowers and grass. Gathering roadside grass in spring, she would tie it in bundles and hang them in the garage. An indication of how serious Rosalie was becoming about her interests, and how keen she was to acquire technical information, was her 1960 paper on plant properties, drying methods and the impact of seasonal changes.[32]

---

27   The Gascoignes bought their first car 'from the people across the way' in 'about 1948'. MacDonald, *Rosalie Gascoigne*, 16.
28   Capon, 'Preface', 5.
29   Kelly Gellatly, 'Rosalie Gascoigne: Making Poetry of the Commonplace', in Kelly Gellatly, *Rosalie Gascoigne* (Melbourne: National Gallery of Victoria, 2008), 20.
30   MacDonald, *Rosalie Gascoigne*, 15–16.
31   Rosalie Gascoigne, Interview by Robin Hughes, 12 November 1998.
32   MacDonald, *Rosalie Gascoigne*, 17.

Experiments in Modern Living

Figure 5.3 Rosalie Gascoigne, *Loose Leaf*, 1991. Sawn 'Schweppes' soft drink crates

Image: Rosalie Gascoigne Archives

Other items that she hoarded during the Stromlo period included skulls, bones and rocks. But Rosalie was not the only one: on family outings her children—Martin, Thomas ('Toss') and Hester—also started to collect found objects. Martin recalled how bringing 'a good stone or a nicely shaped piece of wood' home was the way to his mother's heart, and how he and his siblings became quite good at it.[33] All of the items that were brought home were carefully placed in various locations around the house:

---

33   Ibid., 18.

It was just something to have on the mantelpiece. I needed things to look at, you see…So if I put an old kerosene tin lid on because I thought it was a lovely orange or something, and put it there, well that was something for me to look at. See, it's sort of need of the pleasures of the eye. I needed it badly.[34]

This is where the importance of that other type of space—the private, enclosed spaces of her house—becomes apparent. Intimate spaces inside and underneath the Mount Stromlo house provided Rosalie with an opportunity to remove the found objects from their original setting, to introduce them to her own context, and to contemplate them over time. But nothing happened immediately: 'It was very gradual. I had to bring things into my house to look at.' Any available horizontal surface became a potential display space:

As vision grows I see more, I bring back materials from the landscape and place them around. Little things on ledges, or laid out on the floor or in the garden. They are then available to be looked at in my space. As things are moved about, there are more discoveries, more is revealed.[35]

The domestic spaces where Rosalie studied her findings became 'intensely private' places, inner sanctums where she attempted to create order out of chaos. In there she would rearrange objects until she reached a point where they recalled 'the feeling of an actual moment in the landscape'.[36] Rosalie became involved with flower arranging. From September 1955 she entered her displays in the annual Canberra Horticultural Society shows—often held in the Albert Hall on Commonwealth Avenue—or at events organised by the Country Women's Association. At these, she had significant success—regularly winning prizes right through until the mid-1960s—and developed a reputation for her arrangements in the Canberra region.[37]

While living on Mount Stromlo, the Gascoignes became friendly with Jack Deeble, Executive Secretary of the Academy of Science, and his family, who were there from 1956 to 1958. One day in 1959 Deeble phoned Rosalie and asked her if she would like to prepare some of her art arrangements for a major conference that was to be held in the Academy building. Rosalie was delighted, and accepted the challenge. She prepared arrangements for the main entrance foyer, the stair halls and the Fellows' room. The experiment was so successful that in 1960 Rosalie was formally commissioned to provide art installations for the main public areas of the Academy building, an arrangement that continued

---

34   Rosalie Gascoigne, Interview by Robin Hughes, 12 November 1998.
35   Rosalie Gascoigne, in Edwards, *Rosalie Gascoigne: Material as Landscape*, 8.
36   Edwards, *Rosalie Gascoigne: Material as Landscape*, 8.
37   Ian North, 'Signs of Light', in *Australia Venice Biennale 1982: Works by Peter Booth and Rosalie Gascoigne* (Visual Arts Board of the Australia Council, 1982), 48–9.

through until 1964. From Rosalie's point of view, the most significant aspect of this commission was that it provided her with an opportunity to work on a much larger scale than what she was able to achieve within her home environment.

In 1960 the Gascoignes left Residence 19 on Mount Stromlo and moved to a much smaller house, owned by The Australian National University, at 22 Dugan Street, Deakin. While this leafy suburb is now considered to be established and central, when they moved there the house was one of the first in the area, and was still surrounded by farmland. Rosalie described the house as 'very badly designed', a 'terrible house' with 'no room in it'.[38] But the surrounding paddocks and slopes of Red Hill became her new domain—and an abundant source of found objects for an artist whose eyes were becoming 'attuned to the landscape'.

In 1962 Rosalie began attending formal lessons in ikebana under Norman Sparnon, Director of the Australian branch of the modern Sogetsu School. Considered to be a fine art in Japan, Sogetsu was considered sculpture rather than decoration.[39] While Sparnon's ikebana classes helped to develop her compositional eye, Rosalie eventually found them to be too restrictive. Ceasing to attend in 1972, she progressed to pure sculpture.

But the confined spaces of the Deakin house were a limitation. The only place where she could accumulate material was the garden: 'But when I wanted to do something, there was nowhere to do it in the house. There was one sitting room, lots of passageways. Two bathrooms. A lot of passage…[but] there was nowhere to settle in the house.' At this point, Rosalie became convinced that she and Ben would have to build their own house.[40]

When it came to finding an architect, the Gascoignes did their research. Rosalie knocked on the door of houses that she liked, asking the owners who had designed them. They were attracted to Ken Woolley's Pettit and Sevitt Houses, which, by the late 1960s, were appearing around Canberra suburbs. They visited the Lovering House—just around the corner in Beauchamp Street, Deakin—that Woolley had designed for the ANU geologist John Lovering and his wife, Kerry, and inspected Noel Potter's Birch House.[41] But it was when Louisa Pike invited the Gascoignes to see their Bischoff-designed house at 3 Garsia Street, Campbell, that they really took notice. For clients who were concerned with views, and who valued natural light, the Pike House was a revelation. Bischoff had designed it as a series of cellular, rectangular spaces separated by a 'star

---

38 Rosalie Gascoigne, Interview by Robin Hughes, 12 November 1998.
39 The Sogetsu School was created in 1926 by Sofu Teshigahara. Kasumi Teshigahara, *The Sogetsu Text on Moribana* (Tokyo, 1969).
40 'You can't have what you want unless you build it yourself'. Rosalie Gascoigne, Interview by Robin Hughes.
41 Hester Gascoigne, In discussion with the author, 26 July 2009, Canberra.

pattern' of variously proportioned open courtyards that flooded the adjacent spaces with natural light. Spread round a square, central court that contained a fountain, there were five courtyards in total.

Further aspects of the Pike House that the Gascoignes liked were the wide circulation gallery surrounding the central court and the sensible solar orientation. Ben remembered how the house 'took advantage of the site…the sun came around on the right side', and 'it had a certain eastern aspect to catch the early morning sun, which in Canberra's important because the winters, of course, can be mighty cold'. After their experience with the Mount Stromlo house, he was determined that they would have a house with a northern, or north-eastern, aspect.[42] Some time later, Ben and Rosalie noticed an article in *The Canberra Times* about the Pike House, which they cut out and saved for future reference. Ben, no doubt, was intrigued by the optical theme of Ann Whitelaw's article: 'Courtyard and Fountain Provides Bright Focal Point.'[43]

Whether Ben was also aware that Bischoff had generated his plan from a 'star pattern' of courtyards is not clear; but there was already enough evidence to convince the Gascoignes that they had found the right architect, and Bischoff was engaged to design their new house.

An Informed Brief

> After all, houses are important: it's where you live, and it's worth giving serious thought to.
>
> — Ben Gascoigne[44]

The one activity that underscored and informed all aspects of the Gascoignes' involvement with their house was observation. In terms of relative dimension between observer and object, Ben and Rosalie—as astronomer and artist—approached this from opposite poles. But despite these extremes of focal length, it was the act of observation in its broadest dimension—of studying physical objects in three-dimensional space—that united the Gascoignes in their approach to their surroundings, and in their perception of domestic space. That the fundamental purpose of observation, for Ben, was to find an essential truth, or quality, in the physical environment was a truism. Yet the same objective also

---

42 Ben Gascoigne, Interview by the author, 26 November 2007.
43 Ann Whitelaw, 'Courtyard and Fountain Provides Bright Focal Point', *The Canberra Times* (4 June 1968): 12, clipping held in Papers of Ben Gascoigne, 1938–2007, Box 4 (House).
44 Ben Gascoigne, Interview by the author, 26 November 2007.

applied to Rosalie, for whom 'the bottom line in art' was honesty—a quest for 'eternal truths in nature, the rhythms, cycles, seasons, shapes, regeneration, restorative powers, spirit'.[45]

Ben and Rosalie had strong ideas about what kind of house they wanted. In accordance with their contrasting approaches—as Martin observed, 'their personalities were famously [unalike]'—these ideas came from widely differing perspectives.[46] Ben's approach, naturally, was rational and scientific, based on an analysis of known facts, the establishment of problems and the formulation of specific responses in the form of design criteria. These were requirements that, to a competent architect, could be clearly understood—and even quantifiable in the completed building. Rosalie's approach, in contrast, was more instinctive and intuitive: a combination of gut instinct and practicality, expressed in the form of poetic aphorisms. Rosalie's instructions to Bischoff were informed by her experience of working within the larger volumes of the Academy building: 'don't shut us in…I need space…lots of air: high ceilings and wide windows to allow the elements in and frame views of the distant hills.'[47]

All of the problems that the Gascoignes had experienced with Residence 19 were filed away in Ben's memory. From there they resurfaced as the generating force behind his brief to Bischoff. Added to that was his analysis of other houses for sale in the Australian Capital Territory. Ben was appalled by their neglect of aspect: 'They all faced the same way—they all faced out onto the road and they had little verandahs or porches, so you could sit out there. [But] nobody ever did!'[48] In early July 1967, soon after the Gascoignes obtained the lease for an elevated site in Anstey Street, Pearce, for the sum of $2200, Ben wrote to Bischoff to explain his requirements, adding that it had been '[i]mpossible to do anything until we had settled on a block'.[49]

Gascoigne's extensive notes reveal that the concept of the Gascoigne House was based on maximising the potential for observation. Both external and internal environments were to be framed and defined by the house, which was to become a form of habitable optical instrument. In regard to looking outwards, views of varying depth were to be provided through the garden and over the Woden Valley to the distant Black Mountain. In the other direction, the house was to turn its back to the street:

---

45   Janet Hawley, 'A Late Developer', [Good Weekend], *Sydney Morning Herald* (15 November 1997): 44.
46   Martin Gascoigne, *New Zealand Lives: The New Zealand Families of Rosalie Gascoigne and Ben Gascoigne*, 8.
47   Rosalie Gascoigne, in MacDonald, *Rosalie Gascoigne*, 22.
48   Ben Gascoigne, Interview by the author, 26 November 2007.
49   Ben Gascoigne to Bischoff, 2 July 1967, Bischoff, Theo, ACT Heritage Library, HMSS 0159, Box 4, Project Files, 'Prof. Gascoigne House, Anstey St., Pearce, 1968–1970'. Decimal currency was introduced to Australia on 14 February 1966.

The block is on the NE slope of Mt Taylor, and has a NE aspect and views E and N. It runs N–S, with a fall of about 1 in 15. We bought it chiefly because of the aspect and view, of which we want to take full advantage, and with this in mind envisage a house with its back to the road and living rooms looking out N or NE, across a terrace to a native garden in the lower part of the block.[50]

Rather than being detached from its setting, the house was to be a natural extension of the site—to appear 'as if it grew out of the block'. It was, nevertheless, to maintain a distinction between inside and outside, and a reasonable degree of privacy. Inside, the emphasis was on facilitating the display of art. The overriding function of internal spaces was to provide naturally illuminated wall surfaces for hanging pictures, and horizontal benches for constructing and displaying ikebana arrangements. The dining space—which was to double as Rosalie's ikebana studio—was to be a simple room, possibly enclosed by white-painted, bagged brick walls, with plenty of natural light. It was to be a long room, with a large table and strong shelves for supporting vases and containers. Views from the kitchen were particularly important. Ben envisaged the various spaces being linked together by a well-lit hall, possibly containing a skylight, which would also double as a gallery space. Along with these written instructions to his architect, Ben included an outline sketch plan and schedule of areas.[51]

Protégé

Like Grounds and Boyd, Bischoff was a native Victorian and a graduate of the School of Architecture at the University of Melbourne. But while his mentors both remained in Melbourne, Bischoff decided early in his career that the best opportunities were to be found by relocating to Australia's rapidly developing capital city. In a career that spanned 30 years in Canberra, he designed, documented and supervised a large number of buildings, ranging from private houses to CSIRO laboratories and facilities for government departments. After initially working in private practice, Bischoff joined the ACT Region of the Commonwealth Department of Works.

---

50 Ibid.
51 Although the sketch is referred to in Ben Gascoigne's letter, there is no copy of it in the Bischoff or Gascoigne archives.

Born in Oakleigh, Melbourne, in 1927, Bischoff attended the Murrumbeena State School from 1932 to 1937. He received a Daffyd Lewis Trust scholarship, which allowed him to enrol at the University of Melbourne. Not knowing whether to enter surveying or architecture, Bischoff eventually settled on the latter, and entered the School of Architecture, headed by Leighton Irwin, in 1945. In early 1947, Irwin was replaced with Brian Lewis, who became the inaugural *Age* Professor of Architecture. Lewis's pedagogical approach emphasised the practice of architecture, based on a sound knowledge of building construction, complemented with an appreciation of fine arts. But in late 1947, Lewis left his position at the School of Architecture to become consulting architect for The Australian National University. Arranging for Grounds to replace him, Lewis recruited a series of part-time lecturers including Boyd, Raymond ('Ray') Berg, George Mitchell and John Mockridge.[52] Other lecturers whom Bischoff encountered during his studies included Frederick Romberg, Fritz Janeba, Keith Mackay and structural engineer Norman Mussen.[53]

In the spirit of his immediate predecessor, Grounds emphasised a 'back-to-basics' approach to teaching architecture. A natural showman, he devised novel ways of introducing students to building materials—sometimes with unexpected results. On one occasion, after asking students to bring in two bricks each the following day, he found himself bricked inside his office.[54] Grounds developed a reputation as an architectural guru, often inviting students back to his Toorak house or to spend weekends engaged in 'talk-fests' at his country house at Ranelagh, Mount Eliza.[55] Bischoff established bonds with Grounds, and with Mussen and Mackay, whose office—Mussen, Mackay and Potter, Architects and Engineers—he worked in after graduating with a Bachelor of Architecture degree in 1951. Phoebe Bischoff, who married Theo in the same year, remembered Mussen, Mackay and Potter working together on projects with Grounds—or later with Grounds, Romberg and Boyd—when they set up their partnership in 1953. She also recalled the two of them being invited to stay at Grounds' country retreat in Marysville.[56]

When Mussen, Mackay and Potter replaced Lewis as architects for the John Curtin School of Medical Research building in 1953, Mussen and his wife, Ruth, moved to Canberra to set up a branch office in a room of Lewis's newly completed University House. Bischoff, who had worked for the firm for barely two years, was offered a position as supervising architect for the John Curtin School—an opportunity he gladly accepted. There were a number of advantages associated

---

52 Geoffrey Serle, *Robin Boyd: A Life* (Melbourne: Melbourne University Press, 1995), 104.
53 Conrad Hamann, Modern Architecture in Melbourne: The Architecture of Grounds, Romberg and Boyd, 1927–1971 (PhD dissertation, Visual Arts Department, Monash University, 1978), 45–6.
54 Serle, *Robin Boyd: A Life*, footnote, 104.
55 Ibid., 63, 104.
56 Phoebe Bischoff, In discussion with the author, 13 January 2009.

with working in the University House office. These included the proximity to the building site—a mere 300 m away—and the opportunity to meet potential university clients such as Pike and Marshall.[57]

After the John Curtin School building was completed and occupied in 1957, Bischoff joined Mussen, who had by then established his own practice in Canberra as a consulting engineer. A brilliant mathematician, Mussen published widely—and sometimes in unexpected locations. When Peter Burns published Mussen's 'There are Only Numbers' in the first edition of *Architecture and Arts* in July 1952, he thought the topic was so unusual that he claimed: 'Here, possibly for the first time, an article on mathematics is included in an art magazine. Only after reading this absorbing article, will it be realised why some people place the art of mathematics before all others.'[58] Mussen introduced his essay with a brief polemic on the advantages of a cool, detached mind that was oblivious to the subjectivities, shortcomings and frailties of the specific individual—in other words, a scientific mind. Mussen's approach, which essentially called for an appreciation of beauty in numbers, was close to that of Philip—for whose house Mussen had been structural engineer. While in Mussen's office, Bischoff discovered a building site in Griffith that was part of a disused quarry. With no-one else interested in purchasing it, the Bischoffs took over the lease and Theo designed a house for his own family. Completed in 1959, the Bischoff House at 47 Carstensz Street, Griffith, contained many ideas that would become part of his domestic vocabulary: rectangular plan, northern orientation, concrete floor slab, unpainted brick walls and low-pitched, gable roof of galvanised iron.

In 1960 Bischoff left Mussen to set up his own Canberra practice. By that time Grounds, Romberg and Boyd were expanding their Canberra operation, and he began to assist them on various projects. In 1960 he helped Boyd with the leaking roof on the Fenner House, and with tenders for the Philip House. He assisted Grounds, Romberg and Boyd with the Japanese Ambassador's Residence at 114 Empire Circuit, Yarralumla—which was designed by the Japanese Government Architect, I. Shimoda—and supervised the Forrest Townhouses at 2 Tasmania Circle and 3 Arthur Circle. In 1964 Bischoff formed a partnership with John Scollay and Tony Pegrum. A flexible arrangement, it allowed each partner to work on individual projects while providing an opportunity to collaborate on larger commissions when required.

Bischoff was a rigorous, methodical and highly organised designer who believed that a thorough understanding of the technical aspects of architecture was one of the keys to successful design. He had an intimate knowledge of the properties of timbers and other building materials, and of the principles

---

57 Marshall, a microbiologist, and his wife, Kathleen, worked under Fenner in the John Curtin School.
58 *Architecture and Arts* 1, no. 1 (July 1952).

behind construction techniques and mechanics. His sketch plans and working drawings—hand-drawn in ink, with notation in a combination of stencil and hand lettering—were so precisely executed that they appeared as precursors of computer drawings.

Bischoff's domestic architecture reflected all of this. Precise, reductive, simply planned and practically detailed, these houses were, at the time they were built, amongst the most refined and understated modernist designs in Canberra. He impressed many clients with his eye for detail. Wendy Benson, a client whose house Bischoff designed at 61 Quiros Street, Red Hill, in 1962, described how he 'even measured wall spans to ensure that small pieces of brick were not needed, only whole or half pieces'.[59] But Bischoff was far from a detached technocrat. Like his friend and mentor Grounds, he was motivated primarily by client needs. He believed in getting to know his clients well before he started designing, and was careful to incorporate appropriate spaces to meet their individual needs. Dorothy Clark, whose house at 210 Dryandra Street, O'Connor, Bischoff designed in 1958, confirmed that their architect had listened to their wishes, providing her and her husband, George, with their 'exact needs and tastes'.[60] Douglas and Louisa Pike's son Andrew recalled Bischoff coming to meet his family on a number of occasions in 1965 to discuss the planning of their house. He and his brother—both teenagers at the time—were impressed that Bischoff took the time to ask them what requirements they had for their bedrooms.[61]

Like Grounds, Bischoff generally worked with a limited vocabulary of forms and material. Following detailed discussions with clients in the preliminary stages, he tested various permutations and combinations of these forms until the final resolution was reached. The end result was a varietal family of different plan forms that Bischoff recalled in the form of tiny, almost iconic 'general layout' sketches.

Whitelaw regularly interviewed Bischoff and his clients, featuring the results in her weekly 'Homes and Building' columns. In these articles, she reinforced how Bischoff attempted to understand his clients' requirements. She explained how he designed houses that were not 'foregrounds'—elaborate, formal statements that dominated the site—but were 'backgrounds'. Neutral, recessive and in harmony with the site, they provided backdrops to their clients' lives. Whitelaw stated that the Watson House, at 13 Waller Crescent, Campbell, not only provided comfort and convenience, it also formed 'an encouraging background' to the Watsons' way of living, and 'grew from the owners' requirements, the particular site conditions and the materials and methods of construction'. In the

---

59   *Canberra Homes*, Undated copy held by Phoebe Bischoff; author not named.
60   Ibid.
61   Andrew Pike, In discussion with the author, 8 September 2007, Canberra.

same way that Grounds used natural materials and natural colours to visually anchor his buildings to their site, Bischoff specified that the brick walls of the Watson House were to be bagged and 'left the natural sandy colour of the mortar'.[62]

Whitelaw described 'a timeless quality' in the house that Bischoff designed for medical practitioner Dr Aubrey Tow at 56 Vasey Crescent, Campbell—a house that was completed in 1964 and is currently owned by members of the Gascoigne family.[63] The Tow House, which she described as 'twentieth-century Georgian', was similar to the Philip House in its modernist interpretation of that style. A two-storey house with a symmetrical street frontage, and with the horizontal lines of the cantilevered first-floor slab and roof eaves countered by regularly spaced, slender steel columns, the Tow House, like its predecessor, made gentle allusions to Georgian precedents. It was constructed of similar materials and finishes to the Philip House: face brickwork in a blue–brown colour, low-pitched metal deck roof, and ceilings and deep eaves soffits lined with matching limed ash boarding. The main departures from the Philip House were in the external proportions—longer and lower—and the direct, central external access stair. Ben and Rosalie Gascoigne retained a copy of Whitelaw's article on the Tow House for future reference.[64]

The Gascoigne House, which Bischoff designed in 1967 and 1968, was one of his last domestic commissions.[65] Throughout the briefing, design and construction stages, he made a concerted effort to ascertain the clients' wishes, to formulate appropriate design responses, and to clearly communicate his intentions.

In July 1967, a short time after Bischoff had received Ben's written brief, he met with his clients at their Dugan Street house. He made detailed notes of the family: 'Parents, 2 grown-up boys, girl 17'; the number of bedrooms: 'Parents', Girl, Boys and Study'; and the total spaces required: '3 bedrooms, 1 study, separate entrance hall, separate dining room, kitchen, living room'. Opposite these room names, he jotted down cryptic notes to remind himself of specific requirements: 'many paintings'; 'ikebana display—inside, working space inside and outside'; below, he repeated in capitals '*IKEBANA in various states of disarray*'; 'lots of callers but only a few parties'; 'no steps'; 'neutral and light and informal'; '*house on the ground, easy access to garden*'; 'strong, plain statement'; 'not formal, not novel'; 'outside brown inside white'; 'Car 2'; and 'storage (mainly of ikebana)'.[66]

---

62 Ann Whitelaw, 'House and a Half at Campbell', *The Canberra Times* (25 October 1963).
63 Ann Whitelaw, '20th Century Georgian: Timeless Quality of Simple Lines', *The Canberra Times* (16 April 1968). The house is currently owned by Toss and Lyn Gascoigne.
64 Papers of Ben Gascoigne, 1938–2007, Box 4 (House).
65 The Gascoigne House was completed in 1969. Two years later, Bischoff's practice with Scollay and Pegrum was dissolved and he joined the Commonwealth Department of Works.
66 Theo Bischoff, Handwritten note on file, Undated [but most likely between 2 July and 20 July 1967], Bischoff, Theo, 'Prof. Gascoigne House, Anstey St., Pearce, 1968–1970'.

Experiments in Modern Living

After discussing the above requirements, Bischoff asked: 'Do you have any other ideas about the house?' Ben replied: 'well, we see a house running across this way, and perhaps a kitchen here and a dining room there, living room there and a bedroom there.'[67]

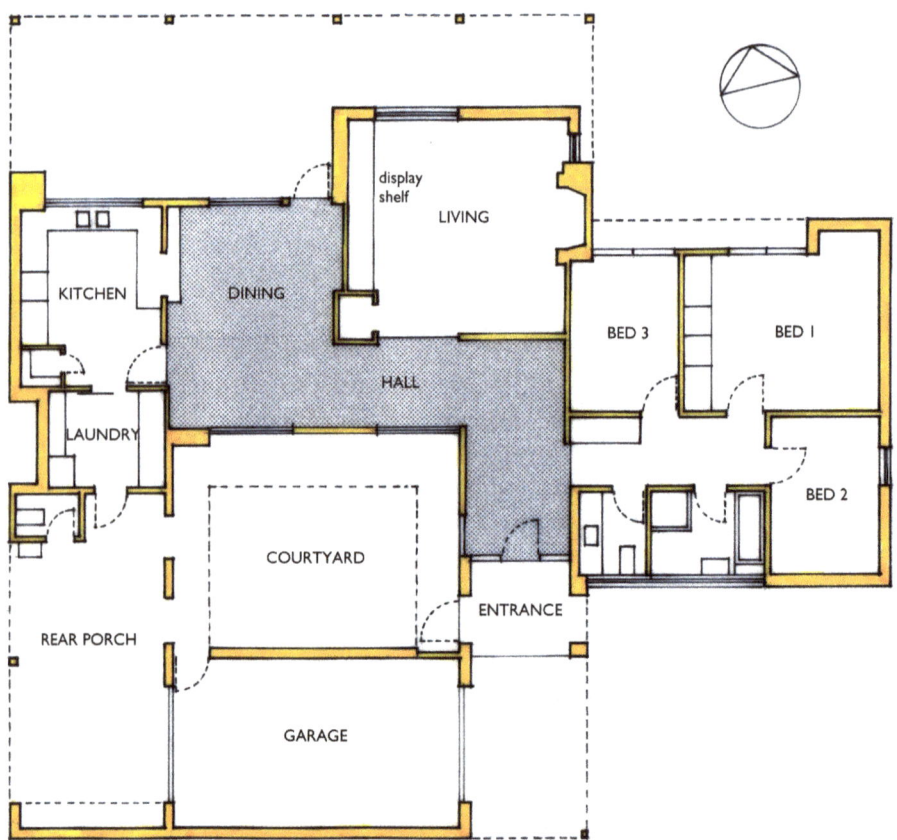

Figure 5.4 Gascoigne House, floor plan

Image: redrawn by the author from Theo Bischoff. Courtesy of Phoebe Bischoff

In January 1968, Bischoff wrote to Ben confirming the discussion, and describing his preliminary design. Bischoff explained that the main rooms were to face north, and would open off a gallery that extended around a courtyard, enclosed on the street side by a garage and store. The main rooms would open onto a terrace along the northern side, and would overlook the main garden, with a distant view across the Woden Valley. The house was to be constructed of concrete floors and face brickwork, with a timber-framed roof covered with steel decking. There was to be an emphasis throughout on natural finishes:

---

67 Ben Gascoigne, Interview by the author, 26 November 2007.

windows, doors and selected internal walls were to be timber, while the standard of finish was to be similar to that of the Pike House. Bischoff estimated the cost of the proposed house to be $21 000. Like Seidler, he recommended to his clients that the best option would be to negotiate a price with a selected builder. He suggested Hubert Roetzer of 54 Girraween Street, Braddon, who had 'successfully completed a number of houses' for his clients.[68] Ben approved the completed documents in June 1968, and in July a tender of $21 670 was received from Roetzer. After ensuring that finances were approved, Ben signed the contract documents on 22 August 1968.[69]

'Entry into the Art World'

> To me, as to all of us, her work was so intimately associated with her domestic setting…the house really marked her entry into the art world. It gave her space, and she wanted space in which you could assemble things.
>
> — Ben Gascoigne[70]

By Christmas of 1968, Roetzer was making good progress on site. Until that time it had largely been Ben who had driven the project. But now Rosalie—who never drew or planned her own work in advance, but preferred to work directly with the materials themselves—could see the internal spaces taking shape, and began to have ideas of her own.[71] Following Rosalie's instructions, Bischoff provided sketches and quotations for a series of horizontal surfaces for constructing and displaying sculpture in various locations throughout the house and garden. These included a 450 mm wide by 975 mm high 'polished dark wood shelf' to the living room, a 300 mm by 50 mm 'rough-work' bench to the west terrace, and a 3000 mm by 750 mm workbench on legs to the garage. Ben claimed that the living-room shelf, which was ideal for big, heavy vases, was 'a brilliant idea' that had 'made the house'.[72]

---

68 Papers of Ben Gascoigne, 1938–2007, Box 4 (House).
69 Bischoff, Theo, 'Prof. Gascoigne House, Anstey St., Pearce, 1968–1970'.
70 Ben Gascoigne, 'The Artist-in-Residence', in *From the Studio of Rosalie Gascoigne* (Canberra: The Australian National University, Drill Hall Gallery, 2000), 12; Ben Gascoigne, Interview by the author, 26 November 2007.
71 Marie Hagerty, In discussion with Mary Eagle, in *From the Studio of Rosalie Gascoigne*, 20.
72 Ben Gascoigne, Interview by the author, 26 November 2007.

Figure 5.5 Rosalie Gascoigne with *Ikebana*, Gascoigne House, c. 1969

Photograph: National Archives of Australia. NAA: A1501, A9510

The Gascoignes had asked Bischoff for a house that was 'neutral and light and informal', but was also a 'strong, plain statement'. They required a building of mass: solid walls for paintings, and heavy timber shelves and benches for sculptures. Views to the outside were important, where required, and so was the admission of natural light. But, as Rosalie had requested, these were to be framed views rather than expansive areas of glass. The predominant condition was to be solidity, with a clear demarcation between inside and outside. And so the house was primarily constructed of masonry: concrete floor slab and brick walls.

When it was completed, the house generated two unexpected responses. The first was that a neighbour lodged an objection to the corrugated-iron roof—an objection that the Department of the Interior dismissed. The second response was that Ben was 'alarmed by it, and rather appalled because it was empty'. With nothing to cover the internal surfaces and no objects to focus the eye, the building materials themselves became dominant, and the plain surfaces and natural materials assumed an institutional appearance. As Ben explained: 'And just being plain brick walls, and this courtyard out there like a prison yard…I thought "by golly, you know, this could just about be a branch of the prison!"'

But Bischoff had not done his clients a disservice, and Ben's fears soon dissipated. Once Rosalie began to bring in her artworks and materials, the house took on a different appearance: 'Once we got it going and we got our furniture and hung a few things on the wall…it certainly became very integral to what we did.'[73]

The increased space for storing materials provided Rosalie with more opportunities for hoarding—a situation she fully exploited. As Ben recalled:

> She began collecting on an ever-increasing scale, and over what now seems a very short period she had accumulated an incredible variety of stuff (there is no other word)—telephone pole insulators, swan feathers from Lake George, sheets of corrugated iron (especially from the old brickworks), postcards and old photographs, discarded beer-cans, bleached bones, sea shells, battered enamel-ware, dried grasses and other vegetation, bric-a-brac from old country fair sideshows, and boxes, always more boxes.[74]

With Ben now travelling frequently for work, Rosalie felt more than ever that she needed 'something to fill the vacuum'. This was when she decided to get 'into art in a big way'—a process she instigated by making things 'all over the house'.[75] As her reputation in the art world spread, journalists and writers visited her at home to report on her progress. The articles they published after these visits confirm just how important the house was to Rosalie's art. In 1970 one writer noted that Rosalie had displayed 'an arrangement of two pieces of dried fern and a berry branch in an old motorcycle petrol tank in her elegant entrance hall'.[76] Two years later, an article in *Vogue Living* described the house as a 'gallery and studio: extremities piled with rusting iron shapes, logs, twigs, bundles of seed heads, cartons of broken glass; and shelves and mantels inside showplaces for the sculpture and other art works these things ultimately become'.[77]

---

73 Ibid.
74 Ben Gascoigne, 'The Artist-in-Residence', 10.
75 MacDonald, *Rosalie Gascoigne*, 25.
76 Author and publication unknown, from a cutting of an article titled 'Ikebana Fad Spreading in Australia', in Rosalie Gascoigne's scrapbook, cited by MacDonald, *Rosalie Gascoigne*, 19.
77 *Vogue Living* (May 1972).

Figure 5.6 Gascoigne House, hall with artworks by Rosalie Gascoigne, c. 1975

Photograph: Rosalie Gascoigne Archives

By the time Matt Abraham visited, the artist's collection had spread in all directions. He observed how 'Rosalie Gascoigne has a house full of junk. Old newspapers, pieces of wood, bunches of twigs and grass stalks, faded tobacco tins, empty shotgun shell, feathers and rusty corrugated iron are among the discards of man and nature which litter every room of her Canberra home.' He was shocked to find that one artwork, made from newspaper and titled *Paper Squares*, almost reached the ceiling. Even the outside walls of the house were not exempt: there the artist had placed other works to weather over time.[78] Jacqueline Rees, writing for *The Canberra Times*, also noted how Rosalie's work was not limited to the interior of the house. She observed '26 yards or so of threaded sheep bones' in the Pearce garden.[79] Rosalie only constructed two of these monumental bone sculptures, which formed a transition between ikebana and her later installation works. Perhaps that was just as well, because they became the subject of some consternation from a neighbour.[80]

The house became a central character in Rosalie's own narrative. When Martin left Canberra to take up his first overseas posting in late 1971, she began writing

---

78 Matt Abraham, *The Advertiser* [Adelaide] (28 February 1980).
79 Jacqueline Rees, *The Canberra Times* (20 June 1974).
80 MacDonald, *Rosalie Gascoigne*, 22.

to him regularly, explaining in minute detail what she was thinking and doing. After finding '300 wooden blocks' at Captains Flat in June 1972, she proceeded to place them in rows 'on top of the wrought iron table' in the dining room. In May of the following year, she discovered an abandoned apiary near Gundaroo, and brought back 22 weathered wooden bee boxes of 'faded pink, green, brown and white paint'. That night she piled them up in the 'gallery between [the] sitting room and courtyard and was amazed at how good they looked'. Her only concern was to prevent Ben from 'making an unguarded left turn when he returned home' and discovering her latest acquisitions. She later stacked the crates on the terrace outside the dining room, but believed they did not look so good there, and required the 'confinement of a gallery and not so much sky'. In February 1976, after finding an entire circus sideshow discarded at the Bungendore dump, she wrote enthusiastically to Toss: 'I have the house to myself for a fortnight, and am busy sorting out my circus…The place looks like sideshow alley at the Queenbeyan [sic] show.'[81]

In early 1978 Rosalie described how: 'The pale beer cans [*Early Morning*] are sitting on a corner of mantelpiece above Jim's flower bucket [*Bucket of Flowers*] and beside the lino on wood panels [*River Banks*] and it looks very good to me.' In some of these descriptions the house appeared to take on the role of an active, although not always cooperative, participant—one that was sometimes capable of thwarting her ambitions. When she found herself watching 'a large arrangement [of dismantled drink boxes] over the fire place', Rosalie claimed to 'have also held the window corner with a corner piece of the same height but can't get the reading I want as the window is recessed after the chimney breast'. On other occasions, the house was simply too small to cope with the scale and vibrancy of the works. This was the case with *Parrot Country*, another work constructed from dismantled drink boxes. Consisting of three large panels of horizontal red, green, yellow and white painted boards (which she later modified to become four panels), *Parrot Country* took up 'the whole width of the white alcove' in the living room. Although Rosalie found it 'very dashing—all sideways flight', she admitted to feeling 'quite ill sitting in the room with it', and concluded that it would be more appropriate in a gallery space. She quickly removed the cause of her nausea—which eventually found a more fitting home in the cavernous spaces of the Jasmax Architects-designed Museum of New Zealand, Te Papa Tongarewa, in Wellington—and replaced it with a smaller work constructed entirely of white boxes. This she found to be 'quite beautiful and restful'.[82]

---

81 Rosalie Gascoigne to Toss Gascoigne, 8 March 1976, Rosalie Gascoigne Archive.
82 The letters were written between 1971 and 1980. Extracts from some of these were selected and edited by Mary Eagle, *From the Studio of Rosalie Gascoigne*, 29–61. For quoted extracts, see pp. 35, 37, 41, 52, 55, 60 and 61.

Experiments in Modern Living

In another letter, Rosalie explained how she was observing an installation of thistle stalks that she had found in the new suburb of Erindale: 'I have it cleaned and piled in the passage between the courtyard and the sofa.' In a reference to the quality of natural light that would have pleased her architect, she described how the installation reflected the light, producing 'a beautiful metallic grey'.[83]

As a setting in which Rosalie could collect objects, assemble them and observe them, the Gascoigne House was an unqualified success. Part of the reason for this might have been Bischoff's empathy for his client: Phoebe Bischoff believed there was an affinity between Theo and Rosalie due to Theo's parallel interests in fossicking and art.[84] Rosalie herself believed that her architect was 'very sympathetic' to what she did.[85] In fact, the house was so closely tailored to her requirements, the floor plan can be considered as a virtual diagram of her activities. Rosalie's domain was a spine, measuring up to 2.3 m wide, which extended from the specially designed, wide front door—through which she carried her materials—around an 'L'-shaped hall and gallery space where she displayed her work, and into the dining room, her main work area.

Bischoff covered the floor of this zone with 150 mm square semi-glazed tiles, and clad the walls with continuous vertical boards of tongue-and-groove, 'V'-jointed alpine ash. The combination of these materials separated this area, visually and aurally, from the remainder of the house, and enhanced its location as a central domain. The remainder of the house and garden were extensions of this central zone. From her work table, Rosalie could observe the courtyard where she stored her materials and works in progress. Through the courtyard, she could access a series of semi-enclosed working spaces on the southern side of the house (the rear porch and west terrace). From the dining room, she could look to the north, across the garden towards the Woden Valley, and could walk out onto the open north terrace. In this reading of the Gascoigne House, the kitchen, laundry, living room and separate bedroom and bathroom wing were ancillary to this central zone of activity.

In addition to providing spaces in which Rosalie could view her assemblages, the Gascoigne House allowed visitors to view the completed works in carefully constructed settings—a development that contributed significantly to her rapid ascension within the art world. The house, with her works in progress all around, was where she met fellow artists such as Michael Taylor. It was Taylor, a painter who lived at Bredbo, NSW, and taught at the Canberra School of Art, who, perhaps more than anyone else, convinced Rosalie that she could become

---
83 Ibid.
84 After arriving from Victoria, the Bischoffs explored the countryside, rubbish tips, roadsides and antique shows for various items, particularly Australian items. Theo was also a self-taught watercolourist. Phoebe Bischoff, Correspondence with the author, 19 October 2010.
85 Rosalie Gascoigne, Interview by Robin Hughes, 12 November 1998.

a successful artist. As Martin recalled, Rosalie's work provided the background to their conversations. 'Her thinking revolved around what she was making and the objects—made and half made—were in the room while they talked, for her house was her studio.' Taylor was instrumental in setting up Rosalie's first exhibitions: a solo exhibition at the Macquarie Galleries in Canberra in 1974, and a group show titled 'Artists' Choice' at Gallery A in Sydney the following year.[86]

Figure 5.7 Gascoigne House, living room with various artworks, c. 1975

Photograph: Rosalie Gascoigne Archives

When Rosalie's work was removed from the house and exhibited in galleries, some writers stressed the importance of its domestic origins. Hannah Fink believed that Gallery A, a stripped-back sandstone terrace house at 2 Gipps Street, Paddington, was an appropriate setting for that reason:

> As it turned out, the formalist context of Gallery A Sydney showed Rosalie's originality in greater relief. There was still a sense in the gallery of the house it had once been, a domestic scale that suited works made in a living room and on a dining room table.[87]

---

86 Martin Gascoigne, 'Rosalie's Artists', in Gellatly, *Rosalie Gascoigne*, 35. Taylor helped to convince Anna Simons, the Director of Macquarie Galleries, to show Rosalie's first solo exhibition.
87 Hannah Fink, 'The Life of Things: Rosalie Gascoigne at Gallery A Sydney', in *Gallery A Sydney 1964–1983* (Campbelltown, NSW: Campbelltown Arts Centre and Newcastle Region Art Gallery, 2009), 150.

A number of commentators observed how Rosalie's art and career flourished during the years that she lived and worked in the Pearce house. Some believed that the house—and a studio built on the southern (street) side of the garage in 1983 to a design by Trevor Gibson—was a fundamental reason for her success. In Rosalie's obituary, Daniel Thomas highlighted two factors that contributed to her success: her husband and her Pearce house and studio. 'Rosalie Gascoigne is survived by her husband, Ben…who long ago brought her down from Stromlo, built her a house for making art in and then a studio.'[88]

In 1982 Rosalie's work was chosen to represent Australia at the Venice Biennale. After that she exhibited extensively in Australia, England, France, Switzerland, Sweden, Korea, Japan, Taiwan and New Zealand. Her art has been purchased by major galleries in Australia and New Zealand, and by the Metropolitan Museum of Art in New York. At the time this chapter was written—approximately 10 years after her death—the Ian Potter Centre of the National Gallery of Victoria was showing a major retrospective of her work.[89]

But while the Gascoigne House influenced Rosalie's art, what of the reverse effect—that of her art upon the house? What is important here is not so much that the house itself was changed through this—as discussed previously, the house did assume different qualities when inhabited by her art—but that Rosalie allowed the art to affect her experiences of working within its spaces. A large part of her early years in Australia was spent exploring the wide, open spaces of Mount Stromlo and the Monaro region. While her working environment at home improved after she left the mountain, the work itself, which was essentially always about landscape, was still informed by the natural qualities of those vast spaces. As Rosalie explained:

> After seventeen years living on Stromlo and later in suburban Deakin, I felt defenceless. On Stromlo, there was a feeling of emptiness…I needed art as an extension of what I honestly did like, air, hills, freedom, grass mowing; I am so moved by natural things. Living on Stromlo was lonely, but it provided good quality experience. Standing on the mountain, looking to the Brindabellas is so beautiful. I always wanted to possess it, to set it in time.[90]

And so Rosalie, living and working in the confines of suburban Pearce, attempted to experience a sense of what it was like to be in an open landscape through the process of making her art installations. Her landscape assemblages were a form

---

88 Daniel Thomas, *The Australian* (29 October 1999). The studio, which was completed in 1983, was designed by architect Trevor Gibson.
89 See Gellatly, *Rosalie Gascoigne*.
90 Rosalie Gascoigne, 'In Her Own Words', James Mollison and Steven Heath, in Edwards, *Rosalie Gascoigne: Material as Landscape*, 7.

of surrogate spatiality—constructed objects whose large scale and weathered colours provided a sense of openness within the walls that Bischoff had built around her. Rosalie's art became a physical affirmation of her desire to 'possess space'. Attempting to express this in words, the fiercely independent Rosalie appeared, for once, to have borrowed a metaphor from her astronomer husband: 'Nature selects, makes, abandons, is big. We need to be reminded of this because suburbia is boxed in; we need confirmation of an expanding universe.'[91]

---

91 Ibid., 8.

6. The Origins of Form: Grounds, Bischoff and the Frankel House

The Frankel House, at 4 Cobby Street, Campbell, was designed by Grounds in 1969 and realised by the same team that produced the Gascoigne House: Bischoff, who worked closely with the Frankels to develop the design and prepare contract documents from late 1969 to early 1970, and Roetzer, who constructed the house during 1971 and 1972. This was the third architect-designed house commissioned by the Frankels, and the second in Canberra. The first house, in Christchurch, New Zealand, was designed by Ernst Plischke, while the second, designed by Oscar Bayne, was adjacent to the CSIRO at 40 Nicholson Crescent, Acton.

Figure 6.1 Frankel House, Opawa, Christchurch, c. 1940

Photograph: Manuscript Collection, Adolph Basser Library, Australian Academy of Science. Frankel, Sir O. H., FAA (1900–2007), MS 106, Box 13

Figure 6.2 Frankel House, Cobby Street, Campbell, view from south-west

Photograph: Ben Wrigley, 2011

When the National Capital Development Commission (NCDC) decided to widen Nicholson Crescent to form part of Barry Drive—a major new road intended to connect the expanding suburbs of Belconnen to the city centre—one obstacle stood in their way: the Frankels' first Canberra House.[1] This was not so much a physical impediment as a political one: Otto—already 'Sir Otto'—and Margaret had significant clout. Not wanting to become embroiled in a drawnout battle, officers of the NCDC offered the Frankels an alternative building site in Campbell in return for their undertaking to vacate Nicholson Crescent.[2] But it was not just any site that they offered the Frankels; in Otto's words, it was

> quite unlike anything a normal citizen could aspire to…It is three-quarters of an acre on a very favoured and secluded site in a prestige area in Campbell and we are able to select our particular site…it is rather dramatic with a view of mountains and lake and bushland.[3]

---

1   In 1958 Frankel discussed the road widening with Ruddock, Associate Commissioner and former member of Coombs' Department of Post-War Reconstruction, and Grounds, who was site architect for the CSIRO. The original road alignment, which they marked up on a site plan, would not have affected the Frankels' house.
2   The Frankels enjoyed living in the Nicholson Crescent house, and put a lot of work into the gardens. They initially considered staying in the house and fighting the NCDC, but decided that it would be in their best interests to cooperate. The NCDC gave the Frankels an undertaking that they could occupy the Nicholson Crescent house until the new one was available. Frankel, Sir O. H., FAA (1900–1998), Manuscript Collection, Adolph Basser Library, Australian Academy of Science, Canberra, MS 106, Box 13, Item C.
3   Otto Frankel to Roy Grounds, 31 July 1968, Frankel, Sir O. H., FAA (1900–1998), 13/C.

In mid-1968, when Frankel asked Grounds to design his house, both men had received knighthoods and were in the twilight of their careers. Although Frankel was involved in many professional activities—both within Australia and overseas—he had been retired from the CSIRO for two years.[4] Because Grounds was fully committed to the Victorian Arts Centre and National Gallery projects, Frankel was not sure if he would accept the commission.[5] So he began his request in such a way that the architect could hardly have refused: 'There is nothing we would wish better than for a house designed by you', he wrote. Frankel explained how he and Margaret should have commissioned Grounds for their existing house in Nicholson Crescent. He disclosed how Bayne had confided to him that he regretted not recommending Grounds back in 1953, and felt that his own design was 'too unadventurous'. (Frankel did not know Grounds in 1953; that was before the Academy of Science building.)

Figure 6.3 Frankel House, Nicholson Crescent, Acton, 1955

Photograph: National Archives of Australia. NAA: A1200, L19496

Believing that praise would get him everywhere, Frankel continued:

> But genius apart, which we take for granted, with no-one else, would we be so sure of intrinsic quality of design and thoughtfulness of detail. Besides, you know us so well that we would scarcely have to use more

---

4 Frankel was Vice-President of the International Biological Program (IBP).
5 In 1966 Grounds designed a house in Canberra for the plant physiologist Sir Rutherford Robertson, which was not built. The only other domestic projects that he appeared to be involved with at this stage of his career were the M. A. Nicholas House at 22 Hill Street, Toorak (near his own house), and the Ken Myer holiday house and Kraal structure at Penders, in southern New South Wales. Conrad Hamann, Modern Architecture in Melbourne: The Architecture of Grounds, Romberg and Boyd, 1927–1971 (PhD dissertation, Visual Arts Department, Monash University, 1978), vol. 2, Bibliography and Catalogue, Part II, Grounds, 66–9.

than shorthand in conveying our own ideas; and I believe that both parties would enjoy the collaboration as of course we did on earlier occasions.[6]

Buoyed by Grounds' initial response—'I'd be a bastard to say no'[7]—but aware of the architect's other commitments, Frankel offered a compromise. He was prepared to permit others in Grounds' office to carry out the details, so long as Grounds was the major contributor. But just in case there was any doubt as to what level of commitment he expected, Frankel added: 'the burden on you would be there and this has to be reckoned with by both parties.' And there was yet another condition: to prevent the Frankels from having to move house twice, the design drawings were required urgently.[8]

On one level, it is a wonder that Grounds accepted the invitation. After all, he was based in Melbourne and was fully committed to a major architectural project. Given that Frankel was aware of this, it is surprising that he bothered to ask Grounds. There was no shortage of available architects in Canberra at the time: officers of the NCDC—which, by the late 1960s, had seized control of the design and construction industry in Canberra—had advised Frankel that they could 'bring an element of pressure to bear on Canberra architects, most of whom they employ in one way or another', to obtain a house design for him at short notice.[9]

But none of this takes into account one overriding factor: the close professional and personal relationship that had developed between Frankel and Grounds. It was a friendship that had been nurtured through the design and construction of the Australian Academy of Science building in the late 1950s, and had developed through the Phytotron project. Although they came from different countries and professions, they had much in common—not the least of which was a shared interest in conservation of the natural environment. Frankel's area of expertise was the conservation of genetic plant resources, which were becoming increasingly depleted through development. He addressed a UN committee on genetic conservation, and was instrumental in founding an international 'genetic bank' of plant gene pools, through which plant breeders contributed to the collection, conservation and exchange of rare specimens.[10]

Grounds believed that he inherited his interest in conservation through his association with Frankel and his colleagues. He claimed to have 'got very close

---

6   Frankel to Grounds, 31 July 1968, Frankel, Sir O. H., FAA (1900–1998), 13/C.
7   Ibid.; Frankel to C. H. Davis, Acting Assistant Secretary (Land Administration), Department of the Interior, 29 June 1970, Frankel, Sir O. H., FAA (1900–1998), 13/C; Lloyd Evans, Handwritten notes, 27 June 1990, Frankel, Sir O. H., FAA (1900–1998), 15/E, 114 (p. 2, point 5).
8   Frankel to Grounds, 31 July 1968, Frankel, Sir O. H., FAA (1900–1998), 13/C.
9   Ibid.
10 'Interview—A Scientist in Stockholm', *Australian Country* (June 1968): 40; *Coresearch* [CSIRO newsletter] 161 (August 1972).

to nature through the scientists of the Academy of Science', and in the last 15 years of his life spent much of his spare time returning the flora of Penders, on the NSW South Coast, to its natural state.[11]

Personal qualities shared by Frankel and his architect included supreme confidence in their own judgment and an uncompromising determination to pursue their goals. Both saw themselves as pragmatists, and both had agrarian connections. Frankel liked to portray himself as a practical person who had become an agriculturalist due to his mother's background. A farming family from Galicia—'the Austrian part of Poland'—they had given him his 'peasant instincts', he claimed.[12] Grounds, who also prided himself on his practicality, could claim an even stronger connection to the land, having spent two years working as an orchardist and dairy farmer in country Victoria.[13]

So significant was the alliance established between these two that not only did Grounds accept the commission; he promised to do it for free.[14] But there were other reasons why he agreed. In Canberra, he had an excellent accomplice in Bischoff, who had worked on a number of previous Grounds, Romberg and Boyd projects. There was also the question of convenience: Bischoff's office—which he shared with John Scollay and Anthony Pegrum—was located in the townhouses that Grounds had designed on the corner of Tasmania Circle and Arthur Circle, Forrest, and where he retained an apartment as a Canberra *pied-à-terre*.[15]

The Origins of Form

> [Otto] had a very attractive French nursemaid, who took him for a walk in the park every afternoon. On one occasion, a young man turned up, gave Otto a pink sugar mouse to suck quietly on the park bench, and then whisked the maid behind the bushes. But Otto finished the mouse too soon, and when he found out what was going on, he decided that he too must become a geneticist.
>
> — Lloyd Evans, speech on Frankel's eightieth birthday, 4 November 1980[16]

---

11   Roy Grounds, De Berg Tapes, National Library of Australia, Recorded in Melbourne, 11 October 1971.
12   Lloyd Evans, 'Otto Herzberg Frankel, 4.11.0–', Frankel, Sir O. H., FAA (1900–1998), 12/A. But, as Evans stated, Frankel was 'some peasant!' Evans's speech at Otto Frankel's eightieth birthday celebration, 4 November 1980, Frankel, Sir O. H., FAA (1900–1998), 12/A, 1.
13   Hamann, *Modern Architecture in Melbourne: The Architecture of Grounds, Romberg and Boyd, 1927–1971*, vol. 1, 45.
14   Grounds to Theo Bischoff, 13 February 1970, Bischoff, Theo, ACT Heritage Library, Woden, Canberra, HMSS 0159, Box 5, 'Frankel House, Campbell', File 2/2.
15   Otto Frankel, 'Sir Roy Grounds, 1905–1981', *Historical Records of Australian Science* 5, no. 3 (1982): 89–91.
16   Frankel, Sir O. H., FAA (1900–1998), 12/A, 1–2.

So what was it about Grounds' architecture that had Frankel so clearly hooked, so keen to have him design his house, in spite of all the obstacles? The path towards that answer must be navigated through two separate but overlapping routes: an examination of the way in which Grounds regarded science, and the way in which Frankel thought about architecture. But a simplistic reversal of their professional stereotypes—with Grounds recast as rationalist and Frankel as aesthete—will not lead to a satisfactory answer. Grounds, as demonstrated in Chapter 4, was highly sceptical of the so-called 'scientific age' and all the jargon that went with it.[17] Frankel, on the other hand, came from a background where acute visual awareness and observational skills were just as important as scientific accuracy.

To get to the core of the answer it is necessary to uncover Frankel's roots as a geneticist, and to examine how his aspirations and ideologies in that field informed his perceptions of the physical environment. Previous connections have been established—somewhat precariously—between genetics and architecture. In *The Monumental Impulse: Architecture's Biological Roots*, art historian George Hersey cited a number of examples. Hersey believed that Vitruvius, by individually naming and specifying the measurements and proportions of the elements required to construct a temple in *De architectura*, allowed other architects to 'reproduce' his designs. Jean-Nicolas-Louis Durand, a nineteenth-century French architectural theorist, had similar intentions with his variations on facade design.[18]

In 1930, Hans Sedlmayr explored a potential link between genetics and architecture. An Austrian art historian and contemporary of Frankel, Sedlmayr was influenced by the experiments of Gregor Mendel, an Austrian Augustinian priest and scientist. Mendel had proven that characteristics of offspring followed specific laws that could be represented in mathematical form.[19] While Mendel calculated that there were seven pairs of possible characteristics that might appear in the offspring, Sedlmayr concluded that the walls of Borromini's San Carlo alle Quattro Fontane were composed from a 'gene-pool' of five elements: convex segment, concave segment, triangular moulding, large column and small column. It was the appearance of these inherited traits as dominant elements—or, on the other hand, their non-appearance as recessive elements—that constructed the total body of the architectural organism, as interpreted by Hersey in Figure 6.4.[20]

---

17 Roy Grounds, *Architecture and Arts* 1, no. 1 (July 1952): 13.
18 George Hersey, *The Monumental Impulse: Architecture's Biological Roots* (Cambridge, Mass.: MIT Press, 2001), 158–60.
19 Although Gregor Mendel (1822–84) published during Darwin's lifetime, his work was neglected until the early twentieth century when its reappraisal led to the foundation of the science of genetics. Waddington described how Mendel 'discovered that from crosses between certain types of parents particular categories of offspring were born in definite proportions which could be stated as simple arithmetic ratios'. Conrad Waddington, *The Nature of Life* (London: George Allen & Unwin, 1961), 12.
20 Hersey, *The Monumental Impulse: Architecture's Biological Roots*, 158–62.

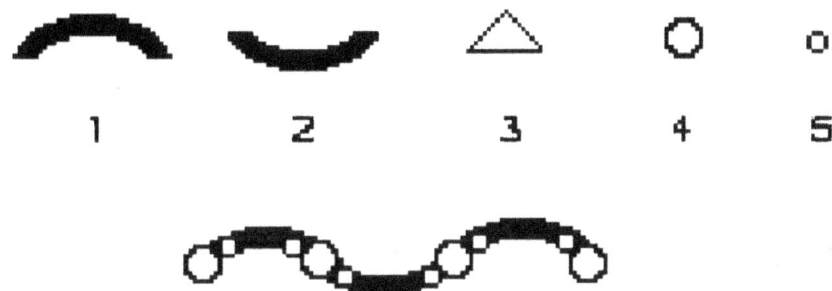

Figure 6.4 Hans Sedlmayr, the five 'genetic elements' of Borromini's architecture

Image: redrawn by George Hersey after Sedlmayr and Borromini, from Hersey, *The Monumental Impulse: Architecture's Biological Roots*, The MIT Press, 161

While the similarity between Sedlmayr's concave segment and the Frankel House plan shape was purely coincidental, the close resemblance reflects Grounds' search for a plan form that was reduced to a singular, elemental concept.

One day in 1922, Frankel attended a lecture in Berlin by Erwin Baur on plant genetics, and a whole new world opened up. Frankel was particularly challenged by Baur's Mendelian claim that he could 'work with genes and the genetic combinations' of plants in the same way that a chemist worked with 'atoms and molecules'. Frankel's enthusiasm was infectious: even though he was only in his second year of study, Baur allowed him to enrol in a PhD on the snapdragon (*Antirrhinum*), which Frankel claimed included 'the first review on linkage in plants'.[21]

In his study of the German genetics community between 1900 and 1933, Jonathan Harwood identified two distinct styles of thought: the 'pragmatists' and the 'comprehensives'. The pragmatists—exemplified by Baur—believed that genetics was a highly specialised subject requiring specific knowledge and skills for solving practical problems. Comprehensives, on the other hand, favoured a broader approach that encompassed development, evolution, heredity and morphology. Alfred Kühn, a contemporary of Baur and Professor of Zoology at Göttingen, encouraged a scholarly and holistic approach to biology based on sound observation skills. Kühn wrote: 'For the biologist who genuinely notices the diversity of organisms in nature, the question of their transformation is

---

21 Otto Frankel, Interview by Gavan McCarthy, Frankel, Sir O. H., FAA (1900–1998), 12/A; Evans, 'Otto Herzberg Frankel, 4.11.0–'; Jonathan Harwood, *Styles of Scientific Thought: The German Genetics Community 1900–1933* (Chicago: University of Chicago Press, 1993), 245; Otto Frankel, Interview by Dr Max Blythe, 15 September 1993, Frankel, Sir O. H., FAA (1900–1998), 12/A.

simply inescapable...the description and comparison of forms deserves a place alongside the experimental work.'[22] Kühn possessed a highly developed visual and aesthetic sensibility, and was fascinated not only by animal morphology, but also by architecture and art—particularly the Italian Renaissance and expressionism. He believed that an appreciation of art led to a broader scientific perspective, and claimed that 'the most insightful scholars are those who have also been interested in art'.[23]

In the circles in which Kühn, Baur and Frankel moved, many scientists were accomplished in fine arts, music and writing. On a lecture tour of the United States in 1938, Fritz von Wettstein visited every major art museum he could find and, like Fenner, filled his diary with details of the collections he observed. Karl Pirschle studied Egyptian art, Richard Goldschmidt and William Bateson collected fine art, Johannes Holtfreter, Carl Correns, Edmund Sinnott and Theodor Boveri were gifted artists, while Karl Henke wrote articles on contemporary art.[24] But, as Harwood explained, these activities were not just hobbies. It was impossible, he argued, to separate aesthetic sensibility from scientific research: for these biologists, artistic intuition was intrinsic to their work.[25] Underlying the connections between art, architecture and biology within that fraternity was the notion of ontological holism—a search for the nature, origins and meaning of form.[26]

Of all the twentieth-century biologists who ventured into the realms of art and architecture, it was Conrad Waddington who became the most well known. And it was Waddington who, through a long professional and personal association with Frankel, was the one most likely to have influenced his way of thinking. Frankel first met Waddington in the late 1920s when he spent nine months at the Plant Breeding Institute in Cambridge, where Waddington was a lecturer in zoology and Fellow of Christ's College. From there, their paths continued to cross. One connection was through their wives. Waddington's second wife, the architect Justin Blanco White, was the daughter of the feminist writer Amber Reeves, and grand-daughter of the New Zealand politician and social reformer William Pember Reeves, who had represented Christchurch in Parliament. The Reeves family had built Risingholme, which they later sold to the Andersons,

---

22 Alfred Kühn (1950, 178), cited by Harwood, *Styles of Scientific Thought: The German Genetics Community 1900–1933*, 235. Alfred Kühn was no relation to Thomas Kuhn.
23 Ibid., 240–1.
24 Other biologists who were known for their visual sensibility included Otto Bütschli, Ernst Haeckel and Carl Chun. Fritz Baltzer, Viktor Hamburger, Hilde Mangold and Fritz Süffert were of a similar inclination. Ibid., 255, 257, 358.
25 Ibid., 255.
26 'The aesthetic appeal of biological form, combined with the intellectual puzzle as to how it is generated in development and modified in the evolutionary process, made biology especially attractive to this generation.' Ibid., 257. 'This ability can be understood as a part of the sense of form which makes a good naturalist and morphologist.' Richard Goldschmidt, *Portraits from Memory: Recollections of a Zoologist* (Seattle: University of Washington Press, 1956), 62–3.

Margaret Frankel's family. (It was on part of the Risingholme estate that the first Frankel House, designed by Plischke, was built.) In later years, Waddington and Frankel sat on the committee of the International Biological Program.

Waddington was so well connected in cultural and artistic circles that a colleague once described him as more of an artist than a scientist.[27] His friends included Walter Gropius, the artists John Piper, Henry Moore, Barbara Hepworth, Ben Nicholson, Alexander Calder and László Moholy-Nagy, the physicist and novelist Charles Snow, and the scientists Sir Julian Huxley and John Bernal.[28] He published prolifically, and spent a large part of his career exploring the overlapping territories between biology and the visual aspects of art and architecture. In 1941 Waddington published *The Scientific Attitude*, in which architects and architecture were given special prominence. Along with the best architectural polemicists of the period—such as Le Corbusier—Waddington complemented his text with evocative, black-and-white photographs of images of the modern world.[29]

Waddington gave many public lectures, including one titled 'Biological Form and Pattern' at the Architectural Association at Bedford Square, London, in May 1958. A study of biological form in relation to geometry, this talk covered ontological aspects such as symmetry, repetition, rhythm and periodicity, and ended with a similar analysis of painting and sculpture.[30] A series of lectures at the University of Wales led to Waddington's most comprehensive and best-known exploration of the nexus between science and art: *Behind Appearance*, published in 1969.[31]

Waddington and Frankel had much in common. Both were geneticists, and although Frankel had trained in the pragmatic school, the wider knowledge that he received through subsequent experience indicated a strong comprehensive tendency. Both had married women of New Zealand extraction who worked in the closely related professions of architecture and art. Both located themselves at the centre of artistic and cultural communities, and in doing so became

---

27 John Bernal, 'Vote of Thanks' [to Waddington after his talk at the Architectural Association], *Architectural Association Journal* LXXIV, no. 825: 77.
28 Conrad Waddington, *The Scientific Attitude* (Pelican Books, 1941), 10; Conrad Waddington, *Behind Appearance: A Study of the Relations Between Painting and the Natural Sciences in this Century* (Edinburgh: Edinburgh University Press, 1969), Foreword.
29 Waddington claimed: 'Of all the artists, it is probably the architects who have realised most fully both the scientific character of the point of view to which they have come, and the existence of an essentially poetic element in scientific thought.' The reason for this was simple: architecture was 'half scientific', and in order to fully understand the potential of new materials such as reinforced concrete and glass, the architect needed to become like an 'applied scientist'. Waddington, *The Scientific Attitude*, 49.
30 Conrad Waddington, 'Biological Form and Pattern', *Architectural Association Journal* LXXIV, no. 825: 71–6.
31 Waddington, *Behind Appearance: A Study of the Relations Between Painting and the Natural Sciences in this Century*.

exposed to contemporary attitudes in art, design, architecture and literature. But Frankel differed from Waddington in one key respect: in spite of his lifelong patronage of modern art and architecture, he was always perceived as a scientist—nobody accused Frankel of being 'too much of an artist'. Unlike Waddington, whose publication record reflected his position as a leader of the comprehensive school, Frankel generally limited his research and publication activities to scientific fields.

But there was one notable exception. In 1981, following Grounds' death, Frankel published a tribute to his friend in the *Historical Records of Australian Science*. In this acknowledgment of Grounds' contribution to Australian domestic architecture, Frankel explained how the architect had been a true comprehensive. Grounds, he said, had aimed to

> integrate the nature of the site, its possibilities and challenges, the chosen materials, the surroundings, and, foremost, the requirements, ideas, idiosyncrasies of the client, to result in a building in which simplicity and efficiency in construction and operation were combined with evident effort (and with evident success) to perpetuate the kind of good taste which some modern architects neglected.[32]

Frankel noted that while Grounds responded to a range of criteria before he settled upon a design solution, he always limited himself to a set range of materials, components and spatial permutations: 'Interior brick walls and floors, hardwood wall covering fixed vertically, muted colours, a minimum of paint. Space was broken up to the least possible extent, allowing the most adaptable use and providing pleasing aspects throughout the building.' Adding that 'the planning of form and space' became a dominant theme, Frankel elaborated on three Grounds houses. The architect's own house in Hill Street, Toorak, of 1954, was 'a square unit with a round, glassed-in courtyard-garden in the centre, and wide-open living space in between'; the 1951 Leyser House in Kew was triangular; while the 1952 Henty House in Frankston (the second house for that client) was circular and 'attracted wide publicity'.[33]

Frankel was aware that his creative architect was influenced by a wide range of sources, and that his designs were not generated purely through an analysis of site conditions or client requirements. For instance, even though Grounds had stated that the circular plan of the Academy of Science building was 'strongly influenced by the shape of the site' and that 'the domed shape was a corollary of the rounded hills and mountains which enclose the valley of Canberra', Frankel doubted that these were the main reasons for the architectural form. He knew that Grounds had visited Saarinen's Kresge Auditorium in Cambridge,

---

32 *Historical Records of Australian Science* 5, no. 3 (1982): 89–91.
33 Ibid.

Massachusetts, which was completed in 1955. Constructed of a concrete shell, sheathed in copper, which formed a one-eighth segment of a sphere, the structure was enclosed by glass curtain walls and attached to a circular brick platform at only three points. Grounds had been particularly impressed by Saarinen's auditorium, and the similarities between it and the Academy of Science building led Frankel to conclude that the architect's references to the rounded hills of Canberra 'may have been an afterthought'. Conrad Hamann shared this view.[34]

Frankel was unaware what form his Cobby Street house would assume. He did not know whether it would respond to some aspect of the surroundings or simply follow Grounds' intuition. But he was familiar with the gene pool of characteristics—including materials, colour and articulation of internal space—that his architect operated with. When Frankel wrote to Grounds asking him to design their house, he claimed that he and Margaret were 'thoroughly happy' with the 'architectural language' that Grounds had developed, and how this language had 'led to the elements we have come to like and admire'.[35]

While an attempt has been made to locate Frankel's attitude to architecture, what of Grounds' perception of science? It has been established that he was sceptical of the so-called 'age of science'. But how did the way in which Grounds viewed science impact upon his relationship with Frankel, and how did it affect the design of the Frankel House? There was one particular aspect of science that motivated Grounds, and it had nothing to do with the popular practices of borrowing scientific methodology or metaphors. What interested Grounds were the scientists themselves—in particular, the way in which they thought. Remembering the Academy of Science building, Grounds recalled:

> What I was concerned about was in the main that the scientists were a group to me of very mysterious men. Sir Mark Oliphant was chairman of the building committee, a loveable man, a very dominating character, a very wilful man and a very loveable human being, and I became very attached to him and his colleagues.[36]

---

34 Ibid., 89–91. Hamann believed the fact that Grounds had 'tried and failed to get a hemispherical house built five years earlier' was a more plausible reason for the form of the Academy of Science building than was its supposed relationship to the 'rolling hills of the Canberra countryside'. Hamann, Modern Architecture in Melbourne: The Architecture of Grounds, Romberg and Boyd, 1927–1971, 295. For an analysis of the influence of geometry on Victorian architects during this period, see Philip Goad, 'Form and the So-Called Melbourne Geometric School', in The Modern House in Melbourne 1945–1975 (PhD dissertation, University of Melbourne, 1992), 5/39–5/62. In a later essay on domes, Goad stated that the most commonly cited source for Grounds' Academy of Science dome was an amalgam of Saarinen's Kresge Auditorium with the same architect's adjacent Kresge Chapel. Philip Goad, 'Shells, Spires and a Dome: Science and Spirit in the Space Age', in Ann Stephen, Philip Goad and Andrew McNamara, eds, *Modern Times: The Untold Story of Modernism in Australia* (Melbourne: Miegunyah Press, 2008), 141.
35 Frankel to Grounds, 31 July 1968, Frankel, Sir O. H., FAA (1900–1998), 13/C.
36 Roy Grounds, De Berg Tapes, National Library of Australia, Recorded in Melbourne, 11 October 1971.

Grounds came to two important conclusions. The first was that scientists understood art better than artists understood science. The second was that scientists were 'intensely creative' people. To Grounds, there was something rational and disciplined—but at the same time opaque and enigmatic—about the Academy of Science clients. It was with this dialectic in mind that he proceeded to design their building:

> I wanted a sense of enormously disciplined order, which is the way their minds work, and I wanted it to have a big emotional impact, because they are very emotional people. They're intensely creative but they don't know how to create in an abstract way. That was my task. And so it was a blending of forces: they were emotional, they were intellectual, they were intensely personal, and I decided that I must produce a building that combined all of those factors.

An impossible brief, it would seem, given the complexity and contradictions within the above statement. But then Grounds proceeded to conceal his design process under a shroud of mystery, describing it as a creative act that defied rational explanation: 'There was no preconception, there was no anything, and so it grew out of me, out of them.' In case there was any doubt remaining about the elusive and indeterminable origins of the Academy of Science building, he finished with '[t]here is no other reason why that building…it can't be rationalised'.[37] But perhaps, to some extent, it could. While Grounds was correct that there was no rational connection between the form of the Academy of Science building and the clients' needs—it did not represent discipline, emotion, intellect or the personal—there was a simpler explanation for its origin: Frankel, for one, clearly believed that the structure owed much to Saarinen's Kresge Auditorium.

The Mathematics of [Re]Production

> But I must not teach my grandmother what to do with the eggs!
>
> — Otto Frankel, letter to Roy Grounds[38]

There is some irony in the fact that the last house designed and built by the environmental conservationists Grounds and Frankel—and indeed the final house of this book—should have owed so much to a road. In fact, the Frankel

---

37 Ibid.
38 This was a very detailed letter in which Frankel explained how he, Margaret and John Philip had redesigned a significant portion of the house. The 'eggs' reference was associated with their questioning of the size of the shower cubicle in the main bathroom. Frankel to Grounds, 6 November 1969, Frankel, Sir O. H., FAA (1900–1998).

House was indebted not just to one road, but to three. Directly attributable were both origin and form: the house would not have been required if it were not for the arrival of Barry Drive; it was the shape of Cobby Street that generated its architecture, while it was the threat of yet another proposed road—Monash Drive—that influenced the landscape design.[39]

The way in which the house, and the constructed elements of its landscape, reproduced the form of Cobby Street and sought to provide shelter from a potential environmental threat, can be compared with the biological term mimicry, where plants and animals assume physical resemblances to their surroundings as a means of self-protection. This was further enhanced by the Frankels' choice of materials and colours: 'darkish brownish in harmony in bush.'[40]

The mimetic form was nothing new for Grounds. As Hamann explained, the architect had experimented with relating building form to some aspect of site shape from an early stage in his career. The walls of his 1940 Quamby Flats in Toorak were set out radially from the centre-point of Glover Court, so that each flat became a segment of a circle. A project for Sir Lawrence Hartnett responded to a conical site in a similar way. In a number of houses designed for unorthodox-shaped sites—including the 1948 Hall House and the 1949 Neale House—Grounds allowed the boundaries of the site to dictate the outline of the house.[41] Of all the Grounds houses, however, the one that was closest in form to the Frankel House was an unbuilt proposal for Australian Prime Minister Harold Holt, designed in 1960. Although it was a much larger house, built over two levels, the Holt House was based on the same arc shape with cross walls set out in a radial pattern.[42]

After Grounds agreed to take on the Frankel House, Otto sent him a very detailed brief. Four pages of typewritten notes, divided into separate subheadings for each space, specified room relationships, fenestration, furniture and storage. Six metres of bookshelves were required, while Margaret's pottery kiln could be relocated to Campbell only once their current house in Nicholson Crescent had been demolished around it. It appears that, even at that early stage, Frankel had

---

39 Monash Drive was a road proposed on the Territory Plan to link Canberra's easternmost suburbs in a north–south direction, and would have cut across the lower slopes of Mount Ainslie. It was not built and was finally removed from the Territory Plan in 2009.
40 Theo Bischoff, Handwritten notes at meeting with Grounds and the Frankels, 3 February 1969, 'Point 5, "Exterior"', Bischoff, Theo, Box 5, 'Frankel House, Campbell', File 2/2.
41 Hamann, Modern Architecture in Melbourne: The Architecture of Grounds, Romberg and Boyd, 1927–1971, 61, 286.
42 Ibid., vol. 2, Bibliography and Catalogue, Figure 7, 15.

some inkling of what the final form of the house might be. Amongst his written specifications was the following comment: 'If the house is L (or U) shaped, one should think of a future wall as protection should Monash drive eventuate.'[43]

The Frankel House site, which Grounds studied in late 1969 when he began to prepare the sketch plans, was irregularly shaped. Located at the end of Cobby Street where it branched off Rosenthal Street and curved sharply, the site was fan-shaped—like a segment of a circle with the apex removed. The shortest boundary, facing onto Cobby Street, was curved to follow the line of Cobby Street, whose centre-point it shared. The two side boundaries radiated out from the same centre-point, while the boundary to the rear of the block was formed by another curve—one that was generated from a different centre-point. The Cobby Street frontage of the block faced south-west.

In October 1969, Grounds prepared a plan of the house. He proposed a single-level, rectangular-shaped house, curved along its major axis to form a shallow arc shape, with the concave side facing the street. The curvature of the arc was generated from the same centre-point as Cobby Street, with the radius of the internal (street-facing) wall being 6.4 m.[44] While the longitudinal external walls were both curved, both end walls, and all internal cross walls, were radial. Internal longitudinal walls were generally faceted (broken down into shorter, straight sections).

The internal layout was tripartite, divided into separate zones by radial cross walls. The north-western zone contained 'service' functions—garage, utility (pottery workshop) and tool shed; the middle zone contained the living, dining and kitchen areas; while the south-eastern area contained three bedrooms, two bathrooms and a study. The south-eastern zone was designed to accommodate a live-in nurse to care for the Frankels in their later years. The nurse was to use the guest bedroom for sleeping and the study—which had its own external access via a raised porch and steps—as a sitting room. This idea of the live-in nurse—which never eventuated—also explains the reason for the two adjacent bathrooms described as 'main' and 'guest'.[45]

With the combined lengths of the service zone and the living zone approximately equalling that of the bedroom wing, and the recessed entrance porch placed between, the Frankel House was symmetrical when viewed from Cobby Street. The central location of the front door recalled Grounds' own house in Toorak.

---

43 'Original brief supplied to RG', Undated document consisting of four typed pages with handwritten notes added, Bischoff, Theo, Box 5, 'Frankel House, Campbell', File 2/2.
44 In 1969, the imperial system of measurement was still in place. Australia changed over to the metric system between 1970 and 1988. For consistency, all original measurements specified by the architects have been left in the imperial system.
45 Stephen Frith, In discussion with the author, 4 Cobby Street, Campbell, 18 August 2009.

6. The Origins of Form: Grounds, Bischoff and the Frankel House

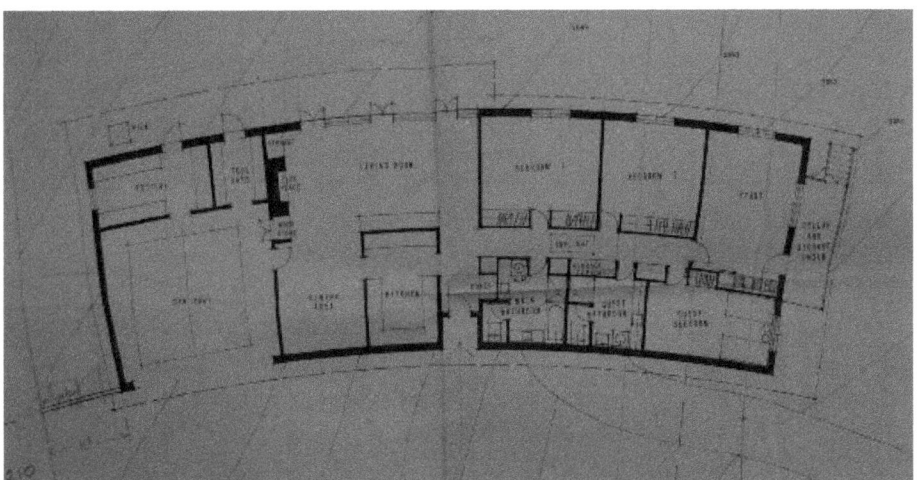

Figure 6.5 Frankel House, preliminary floor plan, October 1969. Service functions to the left, living zone in the centre, bedrooms on the right. Cobby Street is to the bottom of the sheet

Image: ACT Heritage Library, Bischoff, Theo – Architectural Records, 0159. Courtesy of Victoria Grounds and Phoebe Bischoff

The plan of the Frankel House indicated that geometric form was Grounds' primary consideration. By reproducing the curve of Cobby Street in the footprint of the house, he relegated issues such as natural site contours and solar orientation to secondary priority. The site is located on the lower slopes of Mount Ainslie, and falls from north to south. But Grounds' arc cuts across the natural site contours rather than following them. Based on a finished floor level of 100.00, the highest natural point of the site (RL 103.00) is at the northernmost corner of the utility room, while the lowest is the guest bedroom in the opposite corner, at RL 95.5. With no changes of level throughout the house to accommodate the fall, the difference between the highest and lowest levels—2.3 m—meant that a significant amount of cut and fill was required in order to achieve a single-level house.[46]

The problems regarding the shape and orientation of the Frankel House were further compounded in terms of solar orientation. In this regard, the house was reasonably positioned, but far from ideal. With its major facades facing north-east and south-west, and with the service zone in the north-western corner, the pottery workshop—which Grounds initially showed with no windows to the north—and tool shed occupied the sunniest parts of the house. If the house had

---

46   Theo Bischoff, Drawing B107-4p, 'Preliminary slab layout, showing building work below top of floor, draft only, 24.2.70', Bischoff, Theo, E 1 FF 14-25.

followed an east–west principal axis, with the rooms facing north, it would have been a much more successful solution for solar orientation, and for minimisation of cut and fill.

All of this indicates the lengths to which Grounds was prepared to go in order to mimic the road—whose form was, after all, an arbitrary one created by NCDC road engineers. The simple gesticulatory flourish with which Grounds bent his wrist and allowed his pencil to follow the curve of the street was a familiar creative process, and one he had successfully employed on previous projects. Perhaps expediency was part of the reason: having completed the National Gallery project, Grounds was turning his attention to the Cultural Centre and Concert Hall, and would have had little time for other projects.

Frankel had no problem with Grounds' methodology. He was aware that geometrically derived solutions were a modus operandi of his architect. But the internal layout of the house was an entirely different matter, and one in which both Otto and Margaret became heavily involved. Having praised Grounds before he accepted the commission—'you know us so well that we would scarcely have to use more than shorthand in conveying our own ideas'[47]—his clients had no hesitation in criticising the layout once they received it. The dining room was 'in a dark corner' and had an undesirable entrance directly off the garage, which would 'be behind somebody's chair'. Margaret preferred a sideboard in the dining area with direct access to the kitchen, where they could 'serve and carve'. The living area, they believed, was 'rather diffuse'. With the dining room so close, it would not be quiet enough for people sitting around the fireplace, while the depth of the living room—between the fireplace and bedroom one—was too large and 'scarcely usable', particularly now they no longer held 'stand-up' parties.[48]

The Frankels then proceeded to redesign the living areas of the house—a task for which they enlisted the advice of John and Frances Philip. The kitchen was turned through 90 degrees, so that instead of protruding into the living space it was set back parallel to the Cobby Street facade and opened up extra space towards the centre of the house. This allowed the fireplace unit to be detached from the radial wall and left as a freestanding unit to separate the dining and living spaces—where it was more effective both thermally and spatially. This resulted in the dining room becoming located on an external wall, facing northeast, where it was more clearly defined as a separate space to the living area. The living space was more practical in size, and the door from the garage opened onto a circulation space rather than into the centre of a room. There was a stronger connection between the kitchen and the dining space, whereby the connecting

---

47 Frankel to Grounds, 31 July 1968, Frankel, Sir O. H., FAA (1900–1998), 13/C.
48 Frankel to Grounds, 6 November 1969, Frankel, Sir O. H., FAA (1900–1998), 13/C.

doorway was at the end of the dining area rather than in the middle—where, like the door from the garage, it would have clashed with a dining chair. A generous servery was accessible from a major circulation route, rather than from the dining room itself. All of these improvements, plus possible solutions to address the lack of a dedicated laundry space, were set out in a letter from Frankel to Grounds.[49] Attached were revised plans and detailed instructions about the preferred location for a variety of items: firewood, art books, pottery, after-dinner drinks and coffee cups.[50]

In December 1969, Grounds incorporated the suggestions into a revised plan that represented a significant improvement on his rather crude and unresolved preliminary sketch. The new plan reflected a better understanding of the ways in which the spaces were to be used, and was more successful in terms of functional relationships, articulation of space and circulation flow. If it were not for the intervention of Grounds' clients—both current and former—the Frankel House would have been both impractical and uncomfortable, and could well have been a disaster.

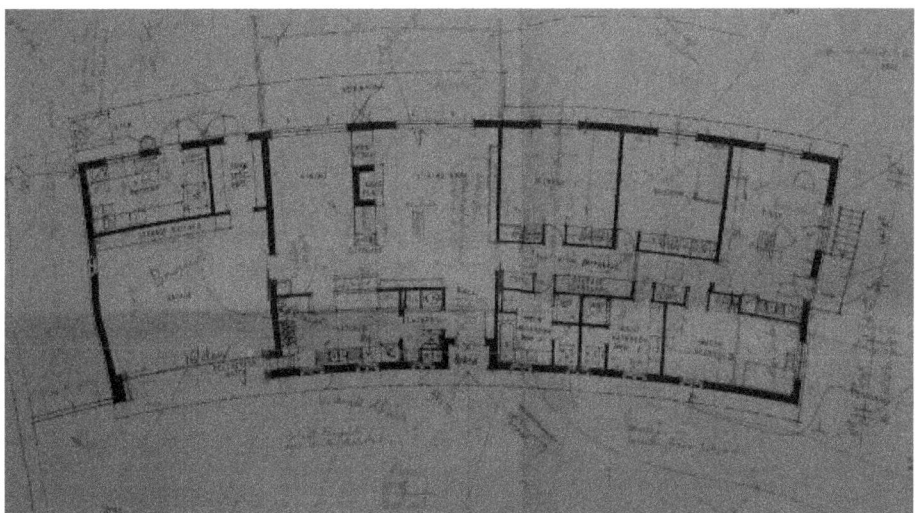

Figure 6.6 Frankel House, revised plan, December 1969

Image: ACT Heritage Library, Bischoff, Theo – Architectural Records, 0159. Courtesy of Victoria Grounds and Phoebe Bischoff

This entire intervention occurred before Bischoff appeared on the scene.[51] At 10.40 on the morning of 3 December 1969, Grounds arrived at the Canberra

---

49   Otto quoted Margaret as stating that Grounds' proposal for clothes to be washed in the main bathroom was 'rather slummy'. Ibid.
50   Ibid.
51   Grounds sent Bischoff a print of the preliminary schematic plan in November 1969, noting that, while it indicated 'the general location and shape of the proposed house sketch plans were currently undergoing

Aerodrome on TAA Flight 406. Bischoff greeted him there and they drove to meet the Frankels, to whom Grounds presented the revised sketch plans. It was a relatively short meeting—Margaret Frankel was a jury member for the C. S. Daley Architecture Award, which was being judged that afternoon[52]—but there was ample time for Bischoff to jot down a few salient points. The house was to be of brick veneer to allow for a 'timber interior', with 'ply face in corridor'. The exterior was to be 'darkish brownish in harmony [with] bush', the budget was $50 000 overall, and the program was tight: tenders were to be called within three months and the construction period was to be six months.[53] After returning to his office and writing 'superseded' across the original plan, Bischoff studied Grounds' new drawings—three sheets containing revised plan, elevations, roof details and brick grille details—and began to consider how the Frankel House would be documented and built.

Bischoff held a number of subsequent meetings with the Frankels and discussed further details of the layout, materials and colours. The Frankels confirmed that internal walls were to be of plywood, the floor was to be carpet, and the ceilings of ash boards spaced apart, running in a radial direction. Otto told Bischoff that the boarded ceilings should be continued through to the kitchen.[54] Details of the pottery room were finalised, the garden layout was discussed, and external materials were selected. In keeping with the desire for the house to reproduce the darker colours of the bush,[55] the Frankels chose 'Tan Manganese Nutex' bricks to be 'raked with dark mortar', a fascia of 'Burnt Copper' and bronze anodised aluminium windows.[56]

In late February 1970, Bischoff sent prints of the working drawings—comprising 10 A2-sized drawings—to Grounds in Melbourne for his approval. In the accompanying letter, he stated that the project had 'proven quite a difficult undertaking'.[57] The reason for this was the curved form of the house: what appeared to be a simple gesture in plan form had implications for almost every component. To begin with, the mathematical setting out of the arc was

---

development'. Grounds to Bischoff, 20 November 1969; Bischoff reply, 26 November 1969; Bischoff, Handwritten notes, 3 February 1969, Bischoff, Theo, Box 5, 'Frankel House, Campbell', File 2/2.
52   Bischoff to Grounds, 26 November 1969, Bischoff, Theo, Box 5, 'Frankel House, Campbell', File 2/2.
53   Theo Bischoff, Handwritten notes, 3 February 1969, Bischoff, Theo, Box 5, 'Frankel House, Campbell', File 2/2.
54   Bischoff, Handwritten notes at meeting with Grounds and the Frankels, 3 February 1969, 'Point 1, "Site & character"'; Handwritten notes at meeting with the Frankels, 1 May 1970, Bischoff, Theo, Box 5, 'Frankel House, Campbell', File 2/2.
55   Bischoff, Handwritten notes at meeting with Grounds and the Frankels, 3 February 1969, 'Point 5, "Exterior darkish brownish in harmony in bush"', Bischoff, Theo, Box 5, 'Frankel House, Campbell', File 2/2.
56   Ibid. Bischoff met with the Frankels on 9 December 1969, 3 February 1970 and 20 February 1970, when they chose a dark-coloured brick from the trade catalogue of Multibricks, a Queanbeyan supplier. 'Nutex Face' referred to the surface texture of the brick, which was lightly pitted in a random pattern (also available was 'Rustic Face', a rough, patterned surface, and 'Vertex Face', whose parallel vertical marks expressed the wire-cut process).
57   Bischoff to Grounds, 25 February 1970, Bischoff, Theo, Box 5, 'Frankel House, Campbell', File 2/2.

complex, particularly given that it was carried out without the aid of computer technology. The thorough and methodical Bischoff—who, as a former employee of structural engineer and mathematician Mussen, was experienced in this area—filled at least 14 foolscap-sized pages with handwritten trigonometric calculations. He manipulated sines, chords and arcs until he found the right combination and shape.[58]

Just how thorough Bischoff was can be seen in his dimensioning of the Cobby Street wall. In addition to the radius, which was taken from the Grounds plan, Bischoff also dimensioned the wall as an arc (the 'true' length of the wall taken around the line of the curve) and as a chord (a straight line drawn between the two end points). The plans contained 'notes on setting out', in which Bischoff confirmed that all cross walls were to be radial, while walls along the length of the building were concentric with the street boundary. Also concentric was a 17 m long garden wall that was set back 12 m from the rear of the house to provide privacy from Monash Drive. To make sure that his instructions were fully understood, Bischoff requested the builder mark out the position of the walls on the top of the concrete slab before proceeding.[59]

No element of the Frankel House escaped the tyranny of the centre-point. A landscaping plan prepared by Bischoff showed how not only were the house and garden walls set out in ever-expanding arcs from the same centre-point; beyond them, a row of fruit trees, a concrete path and a vegetable garden were all concentric.[60]

The geometric setting out of the materials and components was the most difficult part of the documentation. Bischoff pondered over whether linear materials should be set out in a radial or tangential direction, and whether curved elements were to be literally curved or made up of short, straight segments. He resolved that the external brick wall veneer was to be circular in form, as were the fascia and eaves. Internal curved walls were to be made up of straight chords joining concentric points, and clad with plywood on timber framing. Ceilings were to be ash boards, spaced apart over foil paper, running in a radial direction. The front faces of kitchen benches and cupboards were to be constructed in straight segments. Although the fascias were to be curved and skylights set out radially, the Brownbuilt steel ribbed roofing, and majority of the framework, was to be on the orthogonal.

For some of these issues, Bischoff sought Grounds' opinion. One question was the direction of the ash boards to the eaves soffits. After initially believing that they

---

58   Ibid.
59   'Working drawings, Frankel House', Bischoff, Theo, E 1 FF 14-25.
60   This was a rough sketch, which is why it is not reproduced here. 'Landscaping Plan, Frankel House', Bischoff, Theo, B107-1 b, E 4 CC 10. Ray Margules was a landscaping consultant.

should be set out radially—like the internal ceilings—Bischoff changed them to be concentric generally, but radial on the wide eaves to the rear terrace and street entrance.[61] Grounds agreed, except for the main entry, where he believed they should run concentrically like the rest of the eaves on that elevation. He also added that the house was going to be 'really first class'. In a later note to file, Bischoff proudly recorded his mentor as saying the documents, which he had laboured over so carefully, were 'a sheer delight'.[62]

But the difficulties associated with building an arc-shaped house did not end with the documentation. Bischoff had a fight on his hands to make sure that the subtlety of the curved line was not compromised through poor workmanship. Bricklayers normally set their bricks out with the aid of a string line. Nothing more than a piece of string secured at both ends and pulled tight, it is a traditional and very simple solution to the problem of how to define the outer face of a brick wall during construction. But it is not possible to set out a curved wall with a string line, and the smooth profile of the finished wall is testament to the skill and patience of Roetzer's bricklaying team.

Bischoff's other concern was reproducing the curve of the arc on the fascia, which formed the edge of the roof. Constructed of Brownbuilt 12-inch Mark III profile galvanised-steel roofing trays laid horizontally with the ribs facing inwards, it was a similar detail to commercial and industrial buildings. Bischoff was not satisfied with the way the fascias had been fitted, and met Roetzer and the roofing contractor on site, on 27 April 1971, to relay his concerns. The list of defects he identified included 'joints, dips at corners, making good, touch up…pop rivet front capping, birdproofing end cappings, slope rear cappings, fixing down of lap fronts'.[63] By late May, with the situation still not rectified, he issued a handwritten reminder: 'NOTE. AS FIRST ADVISED, BUILDING APPEARANCE DEPENDS ON A WELL EXECUTED FASCIA.'[64]

Two days later, Bischoff fired off a letter to the roofing contractor: 'As has been stated to you a number of times, the fascia has been and remains critical to the appearance of the house and to the building progress.' But sadly, in spite of his best efforts to fix the problem, Bischoff was denied a satisfactory outcome; a later file note read: 'Fascia: not satisfactorily completed but accepted deduction to be made.'[65]

---

61 Bischoff to Grounds, 25 February 1970; 26 February 1970, Bischoff, Theo, Box 5, 'Frankel House, Campbell', File 2/2.
62 Roy Grounds, Letter to Theo Bischoff, 11 March 1970; Theo Bischoff, Note to file, 24 April 1970, Bischoff, Theo, Box 5, 'Frankel House, Campbell', File 2/2.
63 Bischoff, Note to file, 27 April 1970, Bischoff, Theo, Box 5, 'Frankel House, Campbell', File 2/2.
64 Bischoff, Note to file, 29 May 1971, Bischoff, Theo, Box 5, 'Frankel House, Campbell', File 2/2.
65 Bischoff to roofing contractor, 31 May 1971, Undated file note, Bischoff, Theo, Box 5, 'Frankel House, Campbell', Files 1/2 and 2/2.

An Artistic Gesture

> We prefer our own company to that of others.
>
> — Otto Frankel[66]

The above comment was Frankel's favourite response to a question he was often asked: why did his house have no windows facing the street? But he was joking; Otto and Margaret were hospitable entertainers who welcomed many people into their house. The question remains, however: why did the house appear so private, so withdrawn and detached from the street? And why did the Frankel House provoke so many comments, such as that made by Peter Frith, son of the current owner, who rather unflatteringly compared the family house with a public toilet block?[67]

The provision of private space was a common thread that linked all three Frankel houses. The form of the Plischke-designed Christchurch house—an 'L'-shape built around a private, walled garden—was generated by the desire to provide maximum privacy from both road and neighbours. Plischke envisaged this house—his first in New Zealand—to be a prototype for a new model of urban living. In *Design and Living*, he described the Frankel House: 'Far from being a show-piece on the street front the garden is domestic and private. It becomes even more private if the neighbouring houses have similar shaped plans, enabling the bedroom wings of the houses to create enclosed living courtyards.' But this house type was possibly too private, and too urbane, for its time and context in 1930s New Zealand.[68]

When Frankel wanted his second house, in Canberra, to be built on a corner of the CSIRO's land, close to his laboratories, Ian Clunies-Ross questioned whether that was an appropriate environment for the head of the Division of Plant Industry. Frankel's abrupt response was: 'We don't mind. We make our own environment.'[69] Some years later, when Otto and Margaret were offered the

---

66 Frankel, quoted by Lloyd Evans, In discussion with the author, May 2009.
67 Stephen Frith, In discussion with the author, 18 August 2009. Frith said that Peter came to this conclusion after noticing similarities between the house and a toilet block in the Canberra showgrounds at EPIC.
68 Ernst Plischke, *Design and Living* (Wellington: Department of Internal Affairs, 1947). Douglas Lloyd Jenkins wrote that the Frankel House in Opawa remained an 'essentially isolated' example of modernism in New Zealand, and that it 'alluded to a more expansive, more urbane world than was typical of domestic life in the 1930s (it simply doesn't look like New Zealand in the 1930s), this promise did not survive translation into the built structure'. Douglas Lloyd Jenkins, *At Home: A Century of New Zealand Design* (Auckland: Godwit, 2004), 82, 109.
69 Lloyd Evans, 'The Man: Sir Otto Herzberg Frankel, 4 November 1900–21 November 1998', [Obituary for the Royal Society, London, 1999], Frankel, Sir O. H., FAA (1900–1998), 12/C.

new site in Campbell, Otto wrote to Grounds describing how the few existing houses in the precinct 'could be readily screened by fast growing eucalypts and wattles'.[70]

In Frankel's ideal environment, the protection of views looking outwards was just as important as the prevention of other people looking in. Lloyd Evans recalled an issue that arose one day in Frankel's Black Mountain office:

> He was working up a head of steam once, looked out the window, saw the washing (to the rear of Bruce Hall, an Australian National University student residence across the road) and immediately wrote a letter… complaining that CSIRO did not relish being in the backyard of an 'Italianate slum'.

As a result of Frankel's complaint, the university constructed a brick screen wall that later became known as 'the Frankel fence'.[71] Another indication of the Frankels' need for privacy was evident during the construction phase of the Cobby Street house, when they requested that their names be omitted from the signboard.[72]

While the plan form and orientation of the Frankel House were not ideal for site topography or solar orientation, those same aspects were highly functional when it came to the question of privacy. Essentially an impervious wall, two rooms deep, the Frankel House formed a barrier between the street and the rear garden. The concept of the house as a protective shield between public and private was dramatised through a lack of visible fenestration on the public side—the principal reason the house elicited so many comments about its appearance. Grounds' only concession to the concept of 'windows' on the Cobby Street elevation were seven repetitive grilles, formed by leaving geometric openings in the stretcher bond brickwork. While windows were placed in the cavities behind these grilles—some as operable louvres, others as fixed glass with a mechanical fan—they were not visible from the outside of the house.

In spite of the private aspect to the rear, fenestration to that elevation was limited to two sliding doors (one each to the dining and living areas), and relatively modest bedroom windows. A potential lack of natural light to the interior was offset with a series of small roof-lights: three to the passage, two to the kitchen and one to each bathroom. This aspect of the Frankel House marked a departure

---

70   Frankel to Grounds, 31 July 1968, Frankel, Sir O. H., FAA (1900–1998), 13/C.
71   Lloyd Evans, Handwritten notes, 'Otto Dinner 4.3.80', Frankel, Sir O. H., FAA (1900–1998), Box 15, Item D, 17.
72   Frankel to Grounds, 6 November 1969, Frankel, Sir O. H., FAA (1900–1998), 13/C; Bischoff, Note to file, 24 April 1970, Bischoff, Theo, Box 5, 'Frankel House, Campbell', File 2/2; Drawing no. B107-14, Bischoff, Theo, E 1 FF 14-25. In accordance with their instructions, Bischoff sketched a signboard specifying himself as 'Executive Architect', Grounds as 'Consulting Architect' and Roetzer as builder.

from most other Grounds houses, where a clear distinction between public and private aspects was articulated through fenestration. The architect's own Hill Street house, for instance, also presented a solid, impervious shell to the street, but opened up in the centre to a fully glazed, private courtyard. One possible reason for the lack of windows on the private side of the Frankel House was the uncertainty surrounding Monash Drive.

The external materials were typical for a Grounds building: industrial-style bricks, anodised aluminium windows, metal roof and metal fascia. Yet in terms of materials and finishes, the house incorporated a further departure from his previous houses: a clear disjunction between outside and inside. In the Vasey Crescent houses, for instance, the interior was a continuation of the exterior: walls of concrete block extended inwards, and timber boarding on eaves soffits continued inside to become ceilings. Grounds' own house in Hill Street followed a similar principle; although it contained timber ceilings and timber joinery, the remaining internal surfaces were lightly bagged and painted brickwork walls that reflected their external counterparts. The Frankel House, with its complete internal sheathing of timber, broke the tradition of a seamless continuity between exterior and interior.

From the understated and anonymous Cobby Street facade, nothing of the interior was revealed. The true function of the building, the disposition of its internal spaces and the activities that took place therein were all hidden. In this respect the Frankel House was one of the most private of the Grounds houses, even more so than his Hill Street house, which, although it presented a private face to the street, provided glimpses of the interior through a continuous strip of windows at a high level.

Once inside the Frankel House, the transformation between private and public was complete: the house revealed itself as a beautifully crafted vessel that cosseted its occupants in a lush, private, internal world. The spaces, materials and detailing all contributed to the impression of a cocoon-like interior that enveloped its occupants in a warm and private inner sanctum. The brick grilles—which, from the outside, gave away no clues about the interior— suddenly assumed a whole new significance. From the safety and anonymity provided by the house, the inhabitant was able to observe the outside world without being detected.[73]

---

73 This aspect of the house was emphasised by Stephen Frith, the current owner.

Figure 6.7 Frankel House, view from dining room

Photograph: Ben Wrigley, 2011

This feeling of being wrapped in a protective cushion and insulated from the outside world was accentuated by a low ceiling height of 2.5 m throughout the house, and further enhanced by the warm glow of the timber surfaces: 'Hanbro' rotary-cut, Victorian ash-faced plywood veneer to the walls and doors, and 75 x 25 mm ash boards to the ceilings. All of these timber surfaces were finished in clear, matt polyurethane.

In the comprehensive documentation, Bischoff included a number of measures to maintain clean, uninterrupted surfaces and spaces. To ensure that nothing could detract the eye from the sensuous, curved lines of the internal spaces, he instructed the builders that 'there are generally no skirtings or cornices, and, except in Bathroom area, no architraves'. Bischoff maintained visual continuity by coordinating the height of doorknobs and light switches to a uniform 1 m above the finished floor level. A variety of storage spaces—for specific items such as toilet paper—was ingeniously recessed into the brick cavities and covered with sliding or hinged flush ply panels that matched the surrounding wall surfaces.[74]

There were other measures to create privacy. A short, radial section of trellis constructed of 25 mm square timber verticals fixed to both sides of horizontal

---

74   Bischoff, Working drawings, Frankel House, April 1970, Bischoff, Theo, E 1 FF 14-25.

timber rails was provided outside the dining area. This was to divide the rear terrace into two separate zones, for dining and for pottery, and to screen views from the dining terrace into Margaret's work area. Bischoff maintained acoustic privacy by specifying sound-insulated walls between the living space, bedrooms and study.

The interaction between Grounds and the Frankels on this, the final house in the book, reveals more about relationships between architecture and science. It also helps to unravel the separate threads of artistic expression and scientific rationality that weave through this investigation of Canberra houses. When Frankel asked Grounds to design this house, it is clear he had complete faith in his architect. He described the site to Grounds, and explained its potential to provide the private spaces that he and Margaret desired. In the same way that dominant characteristics of offspring could be predicted according to Mendelian theories, Frankel could predict the types of materials, finishes and spatial configurations from Grounds' architectural 'gene pool' that were most likely to appear in his house.

Yet in spite of this, and in spite of his extensive knowledge of the physical environment and previous experience in building houses, Frankel could not imagine the complete form of the house, or its location or orientation on the site. He had no desire to do so—that was what Grounds was for. Grounds was fully aware of the boundary between Frankel's area of expertise and his own, having previously noted that the scientists involved in the Academy of Science project were creative and well informed about art, yet incapable of abstract thought. Understanding what was expected of him, Grounds delivered the Frankels the artistic statement they wanted: with one sweep of his hand across the site plan, he mimicked the form of Cobby Street and produced the single, powerful idea that provided the concept and generated the plan form of the house. The fact that this solution inherited a number of practical limitations was not as important to Grounds—or to his clients—as was the fact that it was an exceedingly simple, iconic shape that could be developed into a house. The simplicity of that solution provided Grounds and Bischoff with a further series of challenges as they worked through the house in increasingly smaller scales to consider how to build it. The care with which this process was carried out, and the intellectual rigour that was applied to all aspects of the detailing and construction, resulted in the house becoming a finely crafted artefact.

The Frankels—and their surrogate planning consultants, John and Frances Philip—did not question the form, orientation or location of the house. Nor did they comment on its external architecture. For that, they required an architect—someone who could apply conceptual thought to the problem of designing a house and give three-dimensional form to a series of disparate ideas. It was not essential for that process to be based on rationalism; reproducing the shape of the adjacent road seemed, to Frankel, to be as valid as any other methodology. It was the integrity of the artistic gesture that was important.

But when it came to the internal configuration of that prescribed form, they had no hesitation in questioning Grounds' judgment, and no qualms about redesigning the living areas in accordance with their own functional criteria.

It would seem that, within the mixture of aspirations and ideologies that led to the creation of the Frankel House, art was of equal value to the scientist-clients as was scientific rationality to the architects. Both the remaining Frankel houses continued to delight architects and artists for decades after they were built. When Otto and Margaret visited the Christchurch house in the 1970s, some 35 years after they had commissioned Plishcke to design it, they were pleased to find it being lived in by an architect 'who loved it and cared for it'.[75] Following Margaret's death in 1997, and Otto's during the following year, their friend and colleague Lloyd Evans was appointed executor of the will (the Frankels did not have children), and was given instructions regarding the estate. On 16 February 1999, the Frankel House was sold by public auction at Olim's Hotel in Braddon. Like their Christchurch house, it was purchased by an architect: Stephen Frith, Professor of Architecture at the University of Canberra. And, like Margaret, Frith's wife, Catherine, was a potter.

There was one final twist in the story of the Frankel House—one that will forever equate Grounds' creation with art. Evans was instructed by the Frankels that the proceeds from the sale were to go to the National Gallery of Australia in order to purchase a painting. But not just any painting; they stipulated that they wanted to donate a significant New Zealand painting to the gallery's collection. When Margaret was involved with The Group in Christchurch some 60 years previously, she had befriended and helped a struggling young artist named Colin McCahon. In the intervening years, McCahon had become New Zealand's most renowned modernist painter, with a considerable international reputation for his powerful and iconic 'biblical landscapes' in which he attempted to explore questions of his own faith in relation to the New Zealand context.[76] In 2004, with funds from the Sir Otto and Lady Margaret Frankel Bequest, the National Gallery of Australia purchased McCahon's *Crucifixion: the apple branch*, a large oil-on-canvas painting that McCahon had painted in Christchurch during April 1950—the year before the Frankels departed that city for Canberra. An intensely personal painting that depicted the artist, his family and a crucifixion scene all set within a diptych of South Island landscapes, it had been exhibited only once

---

75 Lloyd Evans, Handwritten notes, 4 November 1989, Frankel, Sir O. H., FAA (1900–1998), Box 15, Item E, P. 130, 2.
76 Lloyd Evans, In discussion with the author, 14 June 2009, Canberra.

in McCahon's lifetime: in The Group exhibition, with Margaret Frankel, in 1950. After that time, the painting had remained with the artist, in his studio, until his death in 1987.[77]

The acquisition and hanging of this painting completed a number of cycles within the story of the Frankel House. New Zealand, the country where Otto and Margaret met, began their patronage of art and architecture, and spent a significant portion of their lives together, would forever be represented in Australia, the country in which Otto had achieved his considerable success as a scientist. Otto and Margaret, with some help from a fellow scientist (John Philip), had collaborated with Grounds to build a house that owed more to the freedom of artistic intuition than it did to any notion of scientific rationality—a house that, after their deaths, was sold to purchase a work of art.

When the National Gallery of Australia hung McCahon's masterwork—unseen by anyone except McCahon and his closest associates for more than 50 years—within the cavernous spaces of Col Madigan's concrete labyrinth, the cycle from private house to public exhibition was complete.

---

77 Deborah Hart, *Colin McCahon: Focus Exhibition* (Canberra: National Gallery of Australia, 2007), 5–7.

Afterword: Before and After Science[1]

The processes of design and construction for these houses were grounded as much in the subjectivity of art and creativity as they were in the objectivity of any 'pure' scientific rationality. All of the clients' requests regarding technical and functional aspects were faithfully incorporated into the finished designs. But these requirements did not, in themselves, generate the design of any of the houses; they were simply added to the mix. Each house was based, primarily, on an architectural concept that originated from a variety of sources—overseas examples, a contemporary reworking of traditional designs or the geometry of a road.

Although most of the clients were directly involved in many aspects of their design, all left the formulation of the concept entirely to their architects. This was where the binuclear plan, the one-box square plan, the building blocks, the courtyard plan and the crescent-shaped plan originated. So robust were these sketch concepts that the clients could adjust various aspects to improve functionality—internal circulation, materials and details—without destroying the integrity of the idea.

While Fenner and Zwar believed that functional and environmental considerations were important, they were not the main reasons they rejected accepted architectural styles and adopted Boyd's and Seidler's visions of modernity. The principal reason was the aesthetic imperative: the visual appearance of modern architecture, art and design. What was important to these scientists was that their new houses incorporated forms, materials, details and equipment that represented particular physical attributes of the modern world. Whether or not these related to the functional requirements of a suburban house was often of secondary importance. Fenner's chance encounter with Lever House in New York—details of which he sketched in his diary because he believed they might be appropriate for his Red Hill house—reinforces the importance of this aspect.

Boyd's approach to architectural design was similarly subjective. The 1950s was a highly creative period for him, and his houses contained influences from a wide variety of sources. Breuer's binuclear plan, which he presented in modified form as the Fenner House, was just one of many concepts that he experimented with during that period. In one respect, Boyd's architecture could be termed experimental because of this inclusiveness, but at the same time his approach was the antithesis of the true scientific experiment, where problems are solved through the careful observation of limited interventions on a specific model.

---

1 *Before and After Science* was the name of British musician Brian Eno's fifth studio album, released in 1977.

Seidler, on the other hand, believed that his version of transplanted European modernism was the only way for architecture to progress, and he worked with a limited architectural vocabulary derived from that single source. While this was seen to be a limitation, it was also his strength: it allowed him to pursue a sustained and incremental modification of that model. In doing so, Seidler avoided some of the dilemmas that obsessed his fellow practitioners: how to design houses that were 'Australian', or 'regional', in style.

Seidler's approach to the Zwar House could be compared with a scientific experiment in which scientists acknowledge and build upon the findings of previous researchers. The importance of the Zwar House, like the experiment, was not related to it status as an original, site-specific object, but its importance as a single increment in the long-term evolution of a house type. Part of a process of refinement in different architectural offices—and on different continents—the modestly proportioned Zwar House reclaimed one of the philosophical cornerstones of modern architecture: the idea that houses should be affordable for clients on average incomes.

These harbingers of a new era, however, contained significant technical flaws. It was as if the enthusiasm for the images and iconography of modernism had overtaken the architects' and builders' abilities to construct them as fully functioning houses. It was not that the brave new world promised by the early post–World War II houses lacked courage. It was more that, in regard to technological performance, some promised more than they delivered.

Grounds was highly sceptical about the existence of an 'age of science'. Architecture, for him, was tied up in the mystery of the creative process. Clients' needs were recorded and adhered to, but the design process was primarily an artistic venture. Grounds believed that the best designs transcended analysis. His substantial connections to scientist-clients—he was the most prolific, and most successful, designer of buildings for scientists in Canberra during the period of this study—were forged through a mutual understanding that architectural design was fundamentally a creative act.

The facts that two of the clients for the Vasey Crescent Group were scientists and that this ambitious attempt at cooperative design was so successful are important. The Vasey Crescent clients dispelled the notion that architectural design must be an individualist statement. They did not buy into the accepted orthodoxy that each house must, like a work of art, reflect originality, a sense of uniqueness or some identifying mark of its designer or owner. What was more important to them was the pursuit of a coordinated, symbiotic form of environmental design in which the houses worked in unison to create architecture whose whole was greater than the sum of its parts. The Vasey Crescent Group was a carefully calculated experiment whose success owed much to the commitment of all those involved. Grounds and Boyd deserve credit not only for the rigour of the original concepts, but also for their patience and willingness to compromise in order to address the myriad concerns raised by their demanding clients.

As significant as the cooperative efforts behind the Vasey Crescent Group was the fact that the Philip House demonstrated a more accurate understanding of the science of building. While material from the Commonwealth Experimental Building Station had been available for some years, it had not been incorporated accurately into houses such as the Fenner and Zwar houses. While Boyd and Seidler demonstrated an understanding of the general principles involved, they often fell short when it came to the detail. It is possible that when considering issues such as sun angles and thermal properties of materials, Boyd and Seidler followed their own intuition rather than placing their trust in mathematical calculations.

But it was not Boyd, or Grounds, who could claim credit for the success of the Philip House in relation to environmental design. It was John Philip—a mathematician and environmental scientist—who was most responsible. Therein lies another twist. Philip did not begin his approach to domestic design with scientific calculations. Nor was he seduced—as much as some of his predecessors had been—by the appearance of modern architecture or design. Instead, Philip began his consideration of the kind of house that he wanted to live in with an analysis of existing Australian building types. Both John and Frances Philip saw merit in the ways in which older Australian buildings responded to the local climate. This was the closest that any of the scientist-clients had come to acknowledging the existence of traditional architectural style. While Fenner, Zwar and Frankel all considered the idea of building in anything that resembled a historical style to be abhorrent, the Philips were not so dismissive. But they were not interested in style in terms of aesthetic appearance. The merits that they saw in Australian vernacular buildings were related to how they operated in functional terms. In their search for an appropriate house, the Philips followed scientific methodology by building on established practice and knowledge rather than attempting to design from scratch.

After Grounds presented the Philips with a design solution that was an adept, modernist interpretation of historical precedents, John Philip introduced physics into the process. Backed up with mathematical calculations, he recommended that his architect make significant alterations to the design, including the location of rooms and the dimensions of eaves overhangs. The Philips later helped the Frankels to replan their Campbell house according to functional considerations. By being the principle protagonists for the Vasey Crescent Group, and by contributing so much to the design of their own house and to the Frankel House, John and Frances Philip's contribution to scientists' houses in Canberra was significant.

Like Philip and Frankel, Ben Gascoigne provided his architect, Bischoff, with a list of requirements for his house. Gascoigne's was the most systematic, and the most detailed, of all the briefs, and was formulated upon his experiences of living in environmentally deficient houses in the Australian Capital Territory. Gascoigne specified the way in which the house was to be orientated for sun and light, how it was to provide specific views outwards into the landscape, and how it was to contain suitable spaces for Rosalie Gascoigne to construct and view her artwork.

The idea that subjective qualities of artistic expression and creativity are central to this study became more apparent as the study progressed. While the Gascoigne House was essentially a series of crisp, modern and well-lit spaces for art, the Frankel House itself became the art object. No longer part of a search for a rational, postwar house that followed correct siting and planning procedures to optimise sun, light or view, this house was a perfectly executed, built diagram of a singular artistic gesture.

The connections to art continued long after the original clients vacated the houses. When the Zwar House was first completed, Seidler presented his clients with *Seclusion*, a Josef Albers print, to hang on the wall. More than half a century later, with the Zwar House demolished, *Seclusion*—now displayed in Zwar's townhouse—is the only remaining element of Seidler's integrated vision for a new way of living. After Candida Griffiths helped her mother, Frances, to restore the Philip House, the property was sold. It is now the home of Ron Radford, Director of the National Gallery of Australia. The idea that these houses equate, in some way, with art became unequivocal when Otto and Margaret stipulated that the Frankel House was to be sold after their deaths to purchase a painting.

The nexus between rationality and creativity, and between science, art and architecture, that lies at the core of this book was expertly navigated by Grounds more than 50 years ago when he worked with Oliphant, Frankel and Eccles on the Academy of Science building. Scientists, he decided, knew more about art than artists knew about science.

Grounds' theory is backed up by an intriguing statistic. Of the five scientists whose houses are discussed in the preceding chapters, four were married to artists. Heather Zwar and Margaret Frankel were potters; the latter was also a painter. Frances Philip was a painter whose portraits line the walls of the Academy of Science and The Australian National University. But of all the artist wives it was Rosalie Gascoigne who became the most celebrated. In the later years of her life, due to a number of factors—including Ben's support and the spaces that Bischoff provided for her in her Anstey Street house—Gascoigne came to be regarded as one of Australia's leading contemporary artists.

Afterword: Before and After Science

The above statistic reveals that the scientists whose houses are studied in this book chose partners who complemented their own ways of thinking and working. In life, and in architecture, they chose allies and accomplices whose abilities compensated for their own lack in certain areas. These personal and professional unions formed mutually beneficial partnerships that combined objectivity with subjectivity, and scientific rationality with artistic creativity. The houses that the scientists built for themselves and their families reflect a number of aspects of these dualities. Within their fabric there is evidence of a passion for the modern world, of optimism, and of an underlying rationalism—all of which contributed to the overwhelming idea that the national capital location represented a new beginning, and these clients were building a new world.

Bibliography

Primary Sources

Archival Records and Personal Papers

ANU Archives: University Records, The Australian National University, Canberra, ANUA 53, Correspondence files.

Bischoff, Theo, ACT Heritage Library, Woden, Canberra, HMSS 0159.

Commonwealth Department of Works and Railways, 'Commonwealth Observatory Mount Stromlo Erection—Notes on Projected Commonwealth Observatory, Stromlo, Federal Territory', 19 February 1923, National Archives of Australia, Canberra, NAA Series A199, Item FC 1926/206.

Duffield, Doris, 'Woods' Australian Diary, 1925, Duffield, Walter Geoffrey (1879–1929), Manuscript Collection, Adolph Basser Library, Australian Academy of Science, Canberra, MS 095.

Duffield, Walter Geoffrey (1879–1929), Manuscript Collection, Adolph Basser Library, Australian Academy of Science, Canberra, MS 095.

Fenner, F. J., FAA (1914–2010), Manuscript Collection, Adolph Basser Library, Australian Academy of Science, Canberra, MS 143.

Fenner, Frank, 'Collins' Trip Book, 1953, Fenner, F. J., FAA (1914–2010), Manuscript Collection, Adolph Basser Library, Australian Academy of Science, Canberra, MS 143.

Frankel, Sir O. H., FAA (1900–2007), Manuscript Collection, Adolph Basser Library, Australian Academy of Science, Canberra, MS 106.

Grounds, Romberg and Boyd Records (1927–1979), Manuscript Collection, State Library of Victoria, Melbourne, MS 13363.

Harry Seidler Collection of Architectural Drawings, 1948–1987, Manuscripts, Oral History and Pictures Catalogue, State Library of New South Wales, Sydney, PXD 613.

Papers of Ben Gascoigne (1938–2007), Manuscript Collection, National Library of Australia, Canberra, MS Acc08/33.

Papers of John Eccles (1911–1997), Manuscript Collection, National Library of Australia, Canberra, MS 9330.

Papers of John Philip (1927–1999), Manuscript Collection, National Library of Australia, Canberra, MS 9801.

Papers of Malcolm Moir (1903–1971), Manuscript Collection, National Library of Australia, Canberra, MS 9169.

Papers of Manning Clark (1907–1992), Manuscript Collection, National Library of Australia, Canberra, MS 7550.

The Tocumwal Archive, ACT Heritage Library, Woden Library, Canberra.

PhD Theses

Favaro, Paola, Drawn to Canberra: The Architectural Language of Enrico Taglietti (PhD dissertation, Faculty of the Built Environment, University of New South Wales, 2009).

Goad, Philip, The Modern House in Melbourne 1945–1975 (PhD dissertation, University of Melbourne, 1992).

Hamann, Conrad, Modern Architecture in Melbourne: The Architecture of Grounds, Romberg and Boyd, 1927–1971 (PhD dissertation, Visual Arts Department, Monash University, 1978).

Conservation Plans

Emmet, Peter, *Rose Seidler House, Wahroonga 1948–50: Conservation Plan* (Sydney: Historic Houses Trust of New South Wales, 1999).

Tanner Architects, *Conservation Management Plan, Mount Stromlo Observatory, Australian Capital Territory*, February 2004, Prepared for the Research School of Astrophysics and The Australian National University, Canberra.

Reports

Barnes, J. R., *Report No. R. 2: Thermal Conductivities of Building Materials* (Melbourne: CSIRO Division of Building Research, March 1946).

Freeman, Peter and Kumar, Trish, *Malcolm Moir: His Life and Work* (Canberra, 1997).

Langer, Karl, *Sub-Tropical Housing* (Brisbane: University of Queensland Press, 28 May 1944).

Lepschi, Brendan J., *Canberra Post-War Houses Project: No. 12 Yapunyah Street, O'Connor* (Canberra, November 2005).

Morse, R. N., *Report No. E. D. 1: The Design and Construction of Solar Water Heaters* (Melbourne, April 1954).

Phillips, R. O., *CEBS Technical Study 23 (D. D. 23): Sunshine and Shade in Australasia*, 2nd edn (Sydney, 1951).

Newspapers

The Advertiser

The Age

The Australian

The Canberra Times

New Zealand Herald Free Lance

New Zealand Woman's Weekly

Sydney Morning Herald

Interviews and Discussions

Bischoff, Phoebe, In discussion with the author, Canberra, 13 January 2009.

Boyd, Robin, National Library of Australia Oral History Program, August 1962.

Evans, Lloyd, In discussion with the author, Canberra, May 2009, 14 June 2009.

Fenner, Frank, Interview by the author, Canberra, 18 October 2007.

Fenner, Frank, Interviews by Ann Moyal, National Library of Australia Oral History Section, Canberra, 8 March 2001, 4 April 2001.

Frankel, Otto, Interview by Gavan McCarthy, Australian Academy of Science, 1985.

Frankel, Otto, Interview by Dr Max Blythe, Australian Academy of Science, 15 September 1993.

Gascoigne, Ben, Interview by the author, Canberra, 26 November 2007.

Gascoigne, Rosalie, Interview by Robin Hughes, *Australian Biography*, 12 November 1998, <http://www.australianbiography.gov.au/subjects/gascoigne/interview>

Griffiths, Candida, Interview by the author, Canberra, 27 June 2008.

Griffiths, Colin, Interview by the author, Sydney, 31 October 2008.

Grounds, Roy, De Berg Tapes, National Library of Australia, Melbourne, 11 October 1971.

Potter, Noel, Interview by Margaret Park, National Library of Australia, 16 August 2004.

Power, Mike, In discussion with the author, Canberra, 2007.

Rolland, Henry M., Interview by Donald Brech, Commonwealth Archives Office, Canberra, 24 November 1967.

Rolland, Henry M., Second interview by Donald Brech, Commonwealth Archives Office, Canberra, 27 November 1967.

Seidler, Harry, Interview by Hazel de Berg, National Library of Australia Oral History Program, 13 January 1972.

Seidler, Harry, Interviews by Russell Henderson, National Library of Australia Oral History Program, 21 April 1986, 21 May 1986.

Slatyer, June, In discussion with the author, Canberra, 28 October 2008.

Zwar, John, Interview by Brendan Lepschi, Canberra, 2005.

Zwar, John, Interview by the author, Canberra, 26 September 2008.

Secondary Sources

Books and Essays

Agrest, Diane, Conway, Patricia and Weisman, Leslie K., eds, *The Sex of Architecture* (New York: Harry N. Abrams, 1996).

Alberti, Leon Batista, *Ten Books on Architecture. Book IX*, 1755, reprint (London: Alec Tiranti, 1955).

An Architectural Guide to Australia's Capital, Canberra (Canberra: Royal Australian Institute of Architects, ACT Chapter, 1982).

Apperly, Richard, Irving, Robert and Reynolds, Peter, *A Pictorial Guide to Identifying Australian Architecture: Styles and Terms from 1788 to the Present* (North Ryde, NSW: Angus & Robertson, 1989).

Australia: The Official Handbook (Melbourne: Speciality Press, 1947).

Banham, Reyner, *Age of the Masters: A Personal View of Modern Architecture* (London: Architectural Press, 1975).

Benjamin, Walter, 'Paris, Capital of the Nineteenth Century', *Reflections, Essays, Aphorisms, Autobiographical Writings*, Translated by Edmund Jephcott (New York: Helen and Kurt Wolff, 1978).

Bhathal, Ragbir, *Australian Astronomers: Achievements at the Frontiers of Astronomy* (Canberra: National Library of Australia, 1996).

Birks, Tony, *Lucie Rye* (Somerset: Marston House, 1987).

Blake, Peter, ed., *Marcel Breuer: Sun and Shadow, the Philosophy of an Architect* (New York: Dodd, Mead, 1955).

Blondel, Jacques Francois, *Cours d'Architecture* (Paris: Desaint, 1777).

Boesiger, Willy, ed., *Richard Neutra 1923–50: Buildings and Projects* (London: Thames and Hudson, 1964).

Boyd, Robin, *Victorian Modern: One Hundred Years of Modern Architecture in Victoria* (Melbourne: Architectural Students' Society of the Royal Victorian Institute of Architects, July 1947).

Boyd, Robin, *Australia's Home: Its Origins, Builders and Occupiers* (Melbourne: Melbourne University Press, 1952).

Boyd, Robin, *The Australian Ugliness* (Melbourne: F. W. Cheshire, 1960).

Bunning, Walter, *Homes in the Sun: The Past, Present and Future of Australian Housing* (Sydney: W. J. Nesbitt, 1945).

Canberra, ACT (South Australia: C. A. Pitt & Co., c. 1950).

Canberra: Australian Federal Capital (Mentone, Vic.: Nucolorvue Productions, c. 1978).

Charlton, Ken, Garnett, Rodney and Fowler, Martin, *Federal Capital Architecture Canberra 1911–1939* (Canberra: National Trust of Australia, 1984).

Charlton, Ken, Jones, Bronwen and Favaro, Paola, *The Contribution of Enrico Taglietti to Canberra's Architecture* (Canberra: Royal Australian Institute of Architects, ACT Chapter, Register of Significant Twentieth Century Architecture Committee, 2007).

Clark, C. M. H., *A History of Australia* (Carlton, Vic.: Melbourne University Press, 1962).

Cockburn, Stewart and Ellyard, David, *Oliphant: The Life and Times of Sir Mark Oliphant* (Adelaide: Axiom, 1981).

Collins, Peter, 'The Biological Analogy', *Architectural Review* 126 (December 1959): 303–6.

Collis, Brad, *Fields of Discovery: Australia's CSIRO* (Crows Nest, NSW: Allen & Unwin, 2002).

Colomina, Beatriz, 'The Split Wall: Domestic Voyeurism', in Colomina, Beatriz, ed., *Sexuality and Space* (Princeton, NJ: Princeton Architectural Press, 1992), 73–128.

Colquoun, Alan, 'Typology and Design Method', *Perspecta* 12 (1969): 72.

Conner, J. R., *A Guide to Canberra Buildings* (Sydney: Angus & Robertson in association with the Royal Australian Institute of Architects, 1970).

Coombs, H. C., *Trial Balance* (South Melbourne: Macmillan, 1981).

Creighton, Trevor, Freeman, Peter and Russell, Roslyn, *Manning Clark House: Reflections* (Canberra: Manning Clark House, 2002).

Cuffley, Peter, *Australian Houses of the Forties and Fifties* (Melbourne: Five Mile Press, 1993).

Daley, Charles S., *As I Recall: Reminiscences of Early Canberra* (Canberra: Mulini Press, 1994).

Drew, Philip, 'He Built this City', [Domain Home], *Sydney Morning Herald* (16 March 2006): 8–9.

Driller, Joachim, *Breuer Houses* (London: Phaidon, 2000).

Edquist, Harriet and Black, Richard, *The Architecture of Neil Clerehan* (Melbourne: RMIT University Press, 2005).

Edwards, Deborah, *Rosalie Gascoigne: Material as Landscape* (Sydney: Art Gallery of New South Wales, 1998).

Fairfax, Vicki, *A Place Across the River: They Aspired to Create the Victorian Arts Centre* (South Melbourne: Macmillan, 2000).

Fenner, Frank, ed., *The Australian Academy of Science: The First Fifty Years* (Canberra: Australian Academy of Science, 2005).

Fenner, Frank, *Nature, Nurture and Chance: The Lives of Frank and Charles Fenner* (Canberra: ANU E Press, 2006).

Fenner, Frank and Curtis, David, *The John Curtin School of Medical Research: The First Fifty Years 1949–1998* (Gundaroo, NSW: Brolga Press, 2001).

Forty, Adrian, *Words and Buildings: A Vocabulary of Modern Architecture* (London: Thames and Hudson, 2000).

Foster, Hal, ed., *The Anti-Aesthetic: Essays on Post-Modern Culture* (Port Townsend: Bay Press, 1983).

Foster, Stephen G. and Varghese, Margaret M., *The Making of The Australian National University 1946–96* (St Leonards, NSW: Allen & Unwin, 1996).

Frame, Tom and Faulkner, Don, *Stromlo: An Australian Observatory* (Crows Nest, NSW: Allen & Unwin, 2003).

Frampton, Kenneth and Drew, Philip, *Harry Seidler: Four Decades of Architecture* (London: Thames and Hudson, 1992).

Freeland, John M., *Architecture in Australia: A History* (Melbourne: F. W. Cheshire, 1968).

Freeman, Donald, ed., *Boston Architecture* (Boston and Cambridge, Mass.: The Boston Society of Architects and MIT Press, 1970).

Freeman Peter, ed., *The Early Canberra House: Living in Canberra 1911–1933* (Canberra: The Federal Capital Press of Australia, 1996).

Freestone, Robert, 'Living in a Garden Suburb', in Troy, Patrick, ed., *A History of European Housing in Australia* (Cambridge: Cambridge University Press, 2000), 136.

Friedman, Alice, *Women and the Making of the Modern House: A Social and Architectural History* (New York: Harry Abrams, 1998).

Gascoigne, Martin, *New Zealand Lives: The New Zealand Families of Rosalie Gascoigne and Ben Gascoigne* (Canberra: Private publication, 2005).

Gascoigne, Rosalie, *From the Studio of Rosalie Gascoigne* (Canberra: Drill Hall Gallery, The Australian National University, 2000).

Gellatly, Kelly, *Rosalie Gascoigne* (Melbourne: National Gallery of Victoria, 2008).

Gibbney, Jim, *Canberra 1913–1953* (Canberra: Australian Government Publishing Service, 1986).

Giedion, Sigfried, *Walter Gropius: Work and Teamwork* (New York: Reinhold, 1954).

Giedion, Sigfried, 'R. J. Neutra, European and American', in Neutra, Richard, *Richard Neutra 1923–50: Buildings and Projects* (London: Thames and Hudson, 1964).

Giedion, Sigfried, *Space, Time and Architecture: The Growth of a New Tradition* (Cambridge, Mass.: Harvard University Press, 1967).

Goad, Philip, 'The Influence of the Case Study House Programme in Australia', *UME* 14 (2002): 28.

Goad, Philip, 'An Interview with Penelope Seidler, The Architect's Studio, 1948–49', in Ann Stephen, Philip Goad and Andrew McNamara, *Modern Times: The Untold Story of Modernism in Australia* (Melbourne: The Miegunyah Press, 2008), 114–19.

Goldschmidt, Richard, *Portraits from Memory: Recollections of a Zoologist* (Seattle: University of Washington Press, 1956).

Harwood, Jonathan, *Styles of Scientific Thought: The German Genetics Community 1900–1933* (Chicago: University of Chicago Press, 1993).

Hatje, Gerd, *Encyclopaedia of Modern Architecture* (London: Thames and Hudson, 1963).

Hersey, George, *The Monumental Impulse: Architecture's Biological Roots* (Cambridge, Mass.: MIT Press, 2001).

Hoyningen-Huene, Paul, 'Paul Feyerabend and Thomas Kuhn', in John Preston, Gonzalez Munévar and David Lamb, eds, *The Worst Enemy of Science? Essays in Memory of Paul Feyerabend* (New York: Oxford University Press, 2000).

Jenkins, Douglas L., *At Home: A Century of New Zealand Design* (Auckland: Godwit, 2004).

Kepes, Gyorgy, *The New Landscape in Art and Science* (Chicago: Paul Theobold, 1956).

Keynes, John M., *The General Theory of Employment, Interest and Money* (London: Macmillan, 1936).

Kuhn, Thomas, *The Structure of Scientific Revolutions* (Chicago: University of Chicago Press, 1996).

Lavin, Sylvia, *Form Follows Libido: Architecture and Richard Neutra in a Psychoanalytic Culture* (Cambridge, Mass.: MIT Press, 2004).

Lax, Eric, *The Mould in Dr Florey's Coat: The Story of the Penicillin Miracle* (New York: Henry Holt, 2004).

Lech, Alison, ed., *The Savoy Food and Drink Book* (London: Pyramid, 1988).

Le Clerc, George Louis ['Count of Buffon'], *Natural History of Birds, Fish, Insects and Reptiles*, 6 volumes (London: H. D. Symonds, 1808).

Leet, Stephen, *Richard Neutra's Miller House* (New York: Princeton Architectural Press, 2004).

Linnaeus, Carl, *Species Plantarum*, [facsimile of 1st edition, 1753] (London: Ray Society, 1959).

McCartney, Karen, *50/60/70, Iconic Australian Houses: Three Decades of Domestic Architecture* (Sydney: Murdoch Books, 2007).

McCoy, Esther, *Modern California Houses: Case Study Houses 1945–1962* (New York: Reinhold, 1962).

McCoy, Esther, *Blueprints for Modern Living: History and Legacy of the Case Study Houses* (Cambridge, Mass.: MIT Press, 1990).

MacDonald, Vici, *Rosalie Gascoigne* (Paddington, NSW: Regaro, 1998).

Mennis, Mary, *The Book of Eccles: A Portrait of Sir John Eccles, Australian Nobel Laureate and Scientist, 1903–1997* (Queensland: Lalong, 2003).

Metcalf, Andrew, *Architecture in Transition: The Sulman Award 1932–1996* (Glebe, NSW: Historic Houses Trust of New South Wales, 1997).

Metcalf, Andrew, *Canberra Architecture* (Sydney: Watermark Press, 2003).

Miller, Jo, *Josef Albers: Prints 1915–1970* (Brooklyn: The Brooklyn Museum, 1973).

Myerscough-Walker, R., *Choosing a Modern House* (London: The Studio, 1939).

North, Ian, 'Signs of Light', *Australia Venice Biennale 1982: Works by Peter Booth and Rosalie Gascoigne* (Visual Arts Board of the Australia Council, 1982).

Ockman, Joan, ed., *Architecture Culture 1943–1968* (New York: Rizzoli, 1993).

Pevsner, Nikolaus, *The Sources of Modern Architecture and Design* (London: Thames and Hudson, 1969).

Plischke, Ernst, *Design and Living* (Wellington: Department of Internal Affairs, 1947).

Plischke, Ernst, *On the Human Aspect in Modern Architecture* (Vienna, 1969).

Rowse, Tim, *Nugget Coombs: A Reforming Life* (New York: Cambridge University Press, 2002).

Schedvin, Boris, *Shaping Science and Industry: A History of Australia's Council for Scientific and Industrial Research, 1926–49* (North Sydney: Allen & Unwin, 1987).

Seidler, Harry, *Houses, Interiors and Projects* (Sydney: Associated General Publications, 1954).

Seidler, Harry, *Houses, Buildings and Projects 1955/63* (Sydney: Horwitz, 1963).

Semper, Gottfried, *Style in the Technical and Tectonic Arts; or, Practical Aesthetics*, Translated by Harry F. Mallgrave and Michael Robinson (Los Angeles: Getty Publications, 2004).

Serle, Geoffrey, *Robin Boyd: A Life* (Melbourne: Melbourne University Press, 1995).

Shakespeare, William, *As You Like It* (1599–1600).

Sparke, Eric, *Canberra 1954–1980* (Canberra: Australian Government Publishing Service, 1988).

Spigelman, Alice, *Almost Full Circle: Harry Seidler, A Biography* (Rose Bay, NSW: Brandl & Schlesinger, 2001).

Steadman, Philip, *The Evolution of Designs: Biological Analogy in Architecture and the Applied Arts* (Cambridge: Cambridge University Press, 1979).

Stephen, Ann, McNamara, Andrew and Goad, Philip, *Modernism & Australia: Documents on Art, Design and Architecture 1917–1967* (Melbourne: Miegunyah Press, 2006).

Stephen, Ann, McNamara, Andrew and Goad, Philip, *Modern Times: The Untold Story of Modernism in Australia* (Melbourne: Miegunyah Press, 2008).

Stirling, James, *James Stirling: Buildings and Projects 1950–1974* (London: Thames and Hudson, 1975).

Taglietti, Enrico, *EnrioTaglietti: Architect in Australia* (Milan: Lodigraf, 1979).

Teshigahara, Kasumi, *The Sogetsu Text on Moribana* (Tokyo, 1969).

The Work of Bunning & Madden: Architects and Town Planners (Sydney: Bunning & Madden, 1970).

Troy, Patrick, ed., *A History of European Housing in Australia* (Cambridge: Cambridge University Press, 2000).

Waddington, Conrad H., *The Scientific Attitude* (Harmondsworth, UK: Penguin Books, 1941).

Waddington, Conrad H., 'Biological Form and Pattern', *Architectural Association Journal* LXXIV, no. 825 (September–October 1958).

Waddington, Conrad H., *The Nature of Life* (London: George Allen & Unwin, 1961).

Waddington, Conrad H., *Behind Appearance: A Study of the Relations Between Painting and the Natural Sciences in this Century* (Edinburgh: Edinburgh University Press, 1969).

Ward, Fred, *Fred Ward: A Selection of Furniture and Drawings* (Canberra: Drill Hall Gallery, The Australian National University, 1996).

Waterhouse, Jill, *University House as They Experienced It: A History 1954–2004* (Canberra: The Australian National University, 2004).

Williams, Trevor, *Howard Florey: Penicillin and After* (Oxford: Oxford University Press, 1984).

Journals

ANU News

Architecture

Architecture and Arts [Australia]

Architecture in Australia

Architectural Association Journal

The Architectural Review [London]

Arts and Architecture [California]

Australian Country

Australian Home Beautiful

Australian House and Garden

Canberra Historical Journal

Canberra Homes

Coresearch

Historical Records of Australian Science

Home Builders Annual

Lines

People

The Australian Women's Weekly

Transition

Vogue Living

Woman's Day and Home

Web Sites

Bowron, Greg, Firth, 'Cedric Harold 1908–1994, Builder, Architect, Writer', *Dictionary of New Zealand Biography*, <http://www.dnzb.govt.nz>

Gascoigne, Rosalie, Interview by Robin Hughes, *Australian Biography*, <http://www.australianbiography.gov.au/subjects/gascoigne/interview>

Miles, Martin, *Canberra House: Mid-Century Modernist Architecture*, <http://www.canberrahouse.com>

Index

Acton 9, 14n.26, 17n.43, 41, 95n.60, 116n.46, 161, 163
Ada, Gordon 37
aesthetics 26, 38–9, 47, 54, 78, 83, 93, 113, 115, 118, 121–3, 125, 166, 168, 189, 191
affordable housing 51–2, 83, 98, 100, 190
Ainslie 1, 105
Albers, Josef 98, 192
Albert Hall 102, 141
Albert, Adrien 16, 17, 21, 36n.104
Ancher, Mortlock and Woolley 37
Aranda 1, 37, 40
architectural
    advice 14, 16n.35
    aesthetics 26
    commissions 38
    competition 11
    culture 28
    design 27, 189, 190
    discourse 46, 48, 61, 63, 64, 66, 90, 100, 166, 169
    firms 14, 40, 102, 103
    fraternity 45
    language and form 39, 99, 104, 105, 170, 171, 190
    patronage 38, 102
    practice 104, 116
    precedents 123, 125
    publications 54, 67, 88
    style 122, 124, 128, 133, 191
    tastes 5, 7
    zeitgeist 51
architecture 11, 28, 34, 41, 89, 98, 100, 113, 114, 115, 118, 146, 147, 190, 193
    and 'counterpoint' 80, 94–6
    and environmental issues 62
    and gender 65, 72, 74
    attitudes towards 5, 77, 122, 166, 171
    'Australian' 67, 99, 122
    big-business 56
    British 13
    classification 48, 49, 50, 51
    contemporary 90
    criticism of 49, 60, 75
    domestic 22, 24, 47, 49, 52, 75, 78, 88, 95, 99, 103, 108, 122, 148, 170
    experimental 51, 52, 54, 189
    history 77
    in Canberra 20, 24, 38, 47, 75, 78, 95, 103, 126
    modern 28, 36, 55, 60, 61, 77, 87, 91, 98, 102, 104, 189, 190, 191
    New Zealand 31
    overlap with science 4–5, 7, 16, 48, 56, 63–6, 86–8, 100, 109, 116, 127, 131–59, 166–9, 171–2, 185, 186, 187, 189–93
    postwar recovery 56
    regressive style 25
    see also Australian architecture, names of individual styles, typology
Architecture and Arts 38, 66, 147
Arts and Crafts style 18, 60, 67n.63
Australian Academy of Science 25, 27, 101, 114, 132, 165, 172, 185, 192
    Adolph Basser Library vii, viii, 5n.7
    building 19, 25, 26, 27, 28, 34, 38, 103, 109, 110n.26, 115, 116n.46, 117, 163, 164, 170–2, 192
Australian
    architecture 46, 48n.10, 49, 64, 66, 67, 78n.2, 89, 90, 99, 190, 191
    buildings and climate 41, 64, 65n.56, 66, 70n.71, 89, 92, 93n.52, 122, 134n.10, 191
    culture 18, 90
    design 18
    landscape 33, 34, 37
Australian Home Beautiful 19, 61, 64n.56, 78n.2, 107, 111, 119
Australian House and Garden 24–5
Australian National University, The (ANU) 3, 4, 19, 20, 25, 101, 138, 182, 192
    buildings 24, 35, 39, 52, 116n.46

Design Unit 19
formation of 7–25, 55
Rock Mechanics Laboratory 17
staff and faculty 23, 31, 38, 43, 62, 66, 133, 142, 146
staff housing 14, 15, 17, 37, 132, 141
University House 17, 18, 20, 26n.73, 38, 146, 147
see also Canberra University College, John Curtin School of Medical Research

Balinese style 47
Barnard House (Campbell) 38
Barry Drive 162, 173
Bauhaus School 26, 83, 88, 98
Baur, Erwin 167, 168
Bayne, Oscar 1n.2, 25–6, 161, 163
Belconnen 162
Benjamin House (Deakin) 38, 39
binuclear plan 22, 43, 49–52, 65, 66, 72, 75, 78n.2, 89, 92, 189
Birch House (Yarralumla) 23, 24 143
Birch, Sir Arthur 3n.4, 4n.6, 23, 24, 36n.104
Bischoff House (Griffith) 147
Bischoff, Frederick Theodore ('Theo') 1, 36, 37n.106, 38, 71, 131–3, 143–52, 156, 159, 161, 165, 177–80, 182n.72, 184, 185, 192
Bischoff, Phoebe 146, 156
Black Mountain 22, 41, 134n.12, 145
Black Mountain Laboratories (CSIRO) 40, 41, 95, 114, 116n.46, 182
Blakers House (Campbell) 101, 104, 105, 120n.58
see also Vasey Crescent Group
Blakers, Catherine 105, 119n.57
Blakers, Gordon 102, 103, 106, 107, 127
Bland House (Coogee) 84, 85, 91n.42
Blondel, Jacques Francois 48n.12, 64n.52
Boardman House (Forrest) 40
Boyd, Arthur 2, 101

Boyd, Robin 21, 38, 48, 54, 55, 74, 77, 89, 93, 101, 145, 146, 189
and Australian climate 66, 67, 68
and Fenner House 43–75, 118, 147
and Manning Clark House 22, 43n.3, 52
and Seidler 49, 50, 52
and Vasey Crescent Group 101–28, 191
clients 21, 36, 52
criticisms by 46–7, 49, 60, 66, 75
evolution of style 51, 52, 89
houses 1, 101
publications 18, 22, 46, 49, 50, 60, 66
response to Canberra 53, 67
see also Grounds, Romberg and Boyd
Breakspear House (Clontarf) 83
Breuer, Marcel 49, 50n.21, 51, 52, 65, 66, 72, 88, 89, 90, 91, 98, 99, 100, 189
Bunning and Madden 4n.6, 23
Bunning, Walter 64n.56, 67, 109
Butler, Walter 67

C. S. Daley Architecture Award 24, 178
Californian bungalow style 46
Californian Case Study Houses 72
Campbell 1, 4n.6, 17, 38, 39, 81n.10, 101, 102, 115, 133n.6, 133n.7, 143, 148, 149, 161, 162, 173, 182, 191
Canberra Times, The 1, 3, 4, 102, 133, 143
Canberra University College 22
cantilevering 13, 68, 81, 88n.29, 104, 118, 119, 123, 149
Carlingford (NSW) 84
Chain, Ernst 10–11, 88
Chifley, Ben 7, 8, 9, 10
Christchurch (NZ) 28, 29, 30, 32, 161, 168, 181, 186
Clark, Dymphna 22, 43n.2, 52, 43n.2, 52
Clark, Manning 3n.4, 4n.6, 22, 43n.2, 52, 101
see also Manning Clark House
classical style 25, 95

climate 34, 40, 41, 62, 64, 65, 66, 67, 75, 80n.8, 92, 113n.36, 122, 134n.10, 136, 191
  see also Australian—buildings and climate, solar orientation, sunlight, penetration of
Clunies-Ross, Ian 33, 41, 181
Collard, Max 17
colour 37, 47, 61, 62, 67, 73, 74, 80n.8, 81, 82, 96, 98, 107–12, 136, 137, 149, 159, 170, 171, 173, 178
Commonwealth Experimental Building Station (CEBS) 64n.56, 66, 86, 191
Commonwealth Scientific and Industrial Research Organisation (CSIRO) 3, 4, 19, 25, 28, 33, 34, 36, 38, 40, 64n.56, 71, 77, 87, 101, 114, 116n.46, 118, 145, 161, 162n.1, 163, 181, 182
Coombs, Herbert Cole ('Nugget') 7, 8, 9, 10, 11, 33, 36, 41, 162n.1
Copland, Lady 15
Copland, Sir Douglas 15, 16, 41
Council for Scientific and Industrial Research (CSIR) 8, 33, 95
'counterpoint', *see* architecture—and 'counterpoint'
Curtin 1, 37, 38, 133

Daley, Charles 14, 24
Dalheim Constructions 110, 111
Darwinism 64, 114, 166n.19
Deakin 1, 4n.6, 36n.105, 37, 38, 40, 43, 78, 132, 133n.7, 138, 141, 142, 158
Dedman, John 9, 33n.94
demolition of significant houses vii, 1, 20n.51, 37n.109, 47, 85, 98, 192
Department of Post-War Reconstruction (Commonwealth) 7, 9, 162n.1
Department of the Interior (Commonwealth) 19, 20, 54, 102, 103, 106, 115, 138, 152
Department of Works (Commonwealth) 20, 135, 145, 149n.65

Dickson, Bertram 95
Duffield, Geoffrey 134, 135

Eccles, Sir John ('Jack') 3n.4, 20, 21, 22, 25, 36n.104, 41, 73, 192
Elizabethan style 46
Ennor House (Red Hill) 1n.2, 20
Ennor, Arnold ('Hugh') 16, 20, 21, 23, 36n.104, 41
Erindale 156
Europe 36, 56, 91, 93, 100
European modernism 31, 81n.9, 88, 89, 90, 190
Evatt, Dr Herbert Vere ('Doc') 7

Falk House (Aranda) 40
Federal Capital Advisory Committee (FCAC) 135
Federal Capital Commission (FCC) 4n.6, 95n.59, 95n.60, 135, 136n.17
Fenner House (Red Hill) 4n.6, 5, 43–76, 79n.6, 98, 99, 109, 118, 125, 147, 189, 191
Fenner, Charles 48, 62
Fenner, Frank 3n.4, 16, 21, 36, 37, 41, 48, 62, 71, 73, 74, 98, 102, 147n.57, 168, 189, 191
Firth, Cedric 31
Firth, Raymond 9, 11, 31
Fleming, Alexander 11, 88
Florey, Sir Howard 7, 9, 10, 11, 12, 13, 16, 17, 20, 35, 36, 41, 62, 75, 88
Forrest 1, 4n.6, 22, 37, 40, 73n.84, 116n.46, 147, 165
Frankel House (Campbell) 4n.6, 5, 39, 41, 133n.6, 161–87, 191, 192
  first house 1n.2, 162
Frankel, Margaret 29, 30, 31, 38, 162, 163, 168, 169, 171, 172n.38, 173, 176, 177n.49, 178, 181, 185, 186, 187, 192
Frankel, Mathilde ('Tilli') 28, 29, 30, 32n.90

Frankel, Sir Otto 3n.4, 4n.6, 25, 26–8, 29, 30–4, 38–42, 78, 101, 102, 162–73, 176–8, 181, 182, 185–87, 191, 192
Freeman House (Deakin) 38
functionalists 51
functionality 31, 35, 36, 44, 50, 59, 62, 64, 72, 78, 84, 93, 95, 100, 102, 118, 122, 145, 177, 182, 186, 189–91

gardens 23n.65, 54, 106, 107, 117, 128, 142, 145, 149, 150, 151, 154, 156, 170, 178, 179, 181, 182
Garran 38
Gascoigne House (Pearce) 5, 131–59, 161
 see also Residence 19
Gascoigne, Hester 140
Gascoigne, Martin 140, 142, 144, 154, 157
Gascoigne, Rosalie 131, 132, 133, 136–45, 149, 151, 152, 154–9, 192
Gascoigne, Sidney ('Ben') 3n.4, 131, 132, 133, 136, 137, 138, 142, 143, 144, 145, 149, 150, 151, 153, 155, 158, 192
Gascoigne, Thomas ('Toss') 114n.40, 133n.7, 140, 149n.63, 155
Geller House (I and II) 49, 51, 52, 72n.81, 99
gender, see architecture—and gender
Georgian style 40, 122, 123, 135, 149
Giedion, Sigfried 35n.102, 54n.28, 90, 91n.38, 100
Giurgola, Romaldo ('Aldo') 25
Griffin, Walter Burley 75, 126
Griffing House (Campbell) 4n.6, 39, 101, 102n.1, 104–5, 110, 111, 120n.58, 121
 see also Vasey Crescent Group
Griffing, Bruce 4n.6, 39, 102, 103, 125n.77
Griffing, Penny 39, 102, 103n.6, 110, 112
Griffiths, Candida 103n.2, 113, 115, 119, 123n.72, 125, 127, 192
Griffiths, Colin 78n.2, 83, 84, 85, 86, 89, 93, 94

Gropius, Walter 26, 62, 78, 86, 87, 88, 89, 90, 91, 99, 100, 169
Grounds, Betty 109, 110n.26, 126
Grounds, Romberg and Boyd 4, 27, 61, 70n.71, 71, 101, 103, 107, 113, 115, 120, 121, 126, 146, 147, 165
Grounds, Sir Roy 15, 21, 25–6, 27, 34, 39, 40–2, 75, 145, 146, 148, 149, 170, 173, 190, 191, 192
 and Frankel 39, 170–2
 and Frankel House 161–7, 171, 173–4, 175–80, 182–3, 185–7
 and Philip House 41, 101–28, 191
 houses 1, 39–40, 170, 183
 see also Grounds, Romberg and Boyd
Gunn, Graeme 70n.71, 102n.1

Hancock House 20
Hancock, Courtney and Renfree 38
Hancock, William ('Keith') 9, 13, 17, 23n.62, 36n.104, 38, 41
Hannan House (Red Hill) 38
Haseler, Tom 20, 73
heating 41, 43n.3, 66, 69, 91, 92, 93, 94, 99, 100, 118, 119, 120, 138
 see also insulation
Heyden House (Miranda) 83
historical style 4, 40, 46, 54, 75, 123, 124, 125, 191
Hohnen, Ross 37, 38n.112, 52, 53
Hughes 15

insulation 65, 66, 90, 121, 138
 acoustic 185
 see also heating, temperature, thermal
International Congress for Modern Architecture (CIAM) 9
International Style modernism 49, 51, 56

jazz style 46
Jelinek, Alex 38

John Curtin School of Medical Research 4, 16, 17, 19, 20, 21, 35, 36, 37, 50, 51, 52, 55, 62, 63, 65, 146, 147

Krastins, Rudi 19n.48, 40
Kresge Auditorium (Boston) 114, 170–1, 172
Kühn, Alfred 167, 168

Lake Burley Griffin 15, 103n.2
language and form, *see* architectural—language and form
Le Corbusier, Charles 54–5, 116, 169
Lever House (New York) 56, 59, 60, 189
Lewis, Brian 11, 12, 13, 14, 15, 16, 17, 18, 20, 21, 38, 146
Lovering House (Deakin) 37, 142
Luursema House (Castlecrag) 84

McCahon, Colin 186, 187
McCormick, James 102n.1, 118, 123
Macdonald House (Aranda) 40
Manning Clark House 23, 53
    see also Clark, Manning
Marcus Seidler House (Turramurra) 83
Marshall House (Curtin) 36, 37n.106, 133
Marston, Hedley 25, 26
Mendel, Gregor 166, 167, 185
modernism 5, 18, 28, 31, 54–5, 60, 61, 77, 78, 88, 90, 95, 98, 99, 100, 104, 122, 123, 125, 133, 148, 149, 181n.68, 186, 190, 191
    see also European modernism, International Style modernism
Moir and Sutherland 14, 40
Moir, Malcolm 14, 26n.73
Monash Drive 173, 174, 179, 183
Mount Ainslie 22, 134n.12, 173n.39, 175
Mount Mugga 134n.12
Mount Stromlo 4, 132, 134–5, 136, 137, 138, 139, 140, 141, 143, 158
Mussen, Norman 112, 146, 147, 179

Narrabundah 37
National Capital Development Commission (NCDC) 115, 162, 164, 176
National Capital Planning and Development Committee (NCPDC) 15
National Gallery of Australia 30n.83, 132, 142, 163, 176, 186, 187, 192
'New Regionalism' 90
New Zealand 8, 9, 28, 29, 30, 31, 33, 132, 136, 155, 158, 161, 168, 169, 181, 186, 187
Nicholson House (Campbell) 4n.6, 39
North America 5n.8, 36, 56, 88, 89, 91, 93n.52, 104
    see also United States of America

O'Connor 1, 4n.6, 14, 15, 19, 39, 40, 41, 78, 94, 95, 133n.7, 148
Oliphant, Ken 8n.5, 15
Oliphant, Rosa 13, 14
Oliphant, Sir Mark 3n.4, 8, 9, 11–17, 19, 21, 25, 26, 27, 35, 36, 37, 41, 101, 171, 192
ontology 168, 169
open plan 51, 52, 65, 66

Palladian style 47
Paral House (Narrabundah) 37
Paterson House (Aranda) 37
Pearce 1, 37, 98, 131, 144, 154, 158
Pegrum, Anthony 147, 149n.68, 165
Pegrum, Roger 37, 38, 40
Pennant Hills (NSW) 84
Philip House 4n.6, 5, 39, 101–29, 147, 149, 191, 192
    see also Vasey Crescent Group
Philip, Frances ('Fay') 39, 41, 101–3, 106, 107n.13, 114, 115, 117, 118, 121, 123, 124, 129, 176, 185, 191, 192

Philip, John 3n.4, 4n.6, 39, 41, 81n.11, 101–7, 109–10, 113–15, 117–21, 123–4, 126–28, 147, 172n.38, 176, 185, 187, 191, 192
'Phytotron' 34, 35, 38, 116n.46, 164
Picturesque movement 11
Pike House (Campbell) 38, 133n.7, 143, 147, 148, 151
Plischke, Ernst 31, 32, 38, 161, 169, 181
Potter, Noel 4n.6, 23, 25, 143, 146
privacy, provision of 31, 37, 52, 54, 65, 141, 145, 179, 181, 182, 183, 184
Pryor, Lindsay 54, 75

Red Hill 1, 2, 4n.6, 20, 22, 38, 43, 55, 133n.7, 141, 148, 189
regionalism 49, 90, 91
   see also 'New Regionalism'
Residence 19 (Mt Stromlo) 132, 134, 136, 138, 141, 144
Robertson House 39, 163n.5
Roche, Dr Hilary 4n.6, 36, 70
Roetzer, Hubert 151, 161, 180, 182n.24
Rolland, Henry 4n.6, 95n.59, 135
Romberg, Frederick 70, 146
   see also Grounds, Romberg and Boyd
Rose Seidler House (Turramurra) 49, 78n.2, 88, 89, 91, 96, 98–9
Royal Australian Institute of Architects (RAIA) 16n.36, 24, 26, 37n.107, 46, 83, 127, 133n.6
   2006 Tour Guide 4, 133n.6
   ACT Chapter Medallion 46, 61, 70, 72, 73
   Small Homes Bureau 83

Saarinen, Eero 114, 170, 171, 172
Sanders, Gordon 16, 17
Schreiner, Karl 20, 43, 46, 55
science, see architecture—overlap with science
Scollay, John 38, 40, 46, 147, 149n.68, 165

Sedlmayr, Hans 166, 167
Seidler, Harry 38, 128, 151, 189, 190, 191
   and Zwar House 41, 77–96, 98–100, 190, 192
   houses 1, 49, 50, 52
   see also Marcus Seidler House, Rose Seidler House
Skidmore, Owings and Merrill (SOM) 56, 60
Small Homes Service (SHS) 50
Sogetsu School 142
solar orientation 31, 40, 41, 62, 64n.56, 83, 91, 95, 104, 118, 119–20, 127, 143, 175, 176, 182
   see also sunlight, penetration of
Spanish Mission style 46
'Spanish' style 40
Stewart House (O'Connor) 40
style, see architectural—style, names of individual styles
Suendermann, Fritz 113, 121
Sulman Medal 18, 27, 78n.2, 115
sunlight, penetration of 31, 62, 64, 68–9, 75, 85, 89, 91, 94, 100, 118, 119–20, 134n.10, 137, 138, 143, 175, 191, 192
   see also climate, solar orientation

Taglietti, Enrico 20n.51, 37
temperature 66, 67, 70, 92, 93, 100, 114, 120
   see also heating, insulation
thermal 64n.56, 67, 90, 94, 100, 121, 176, 191
   see also heating, insulation
Thompson House 88–9
Titterton, Sir Ernest 3n.4, 36n.104, 37, 41, 66
Tow House (Campbell) 133n.7, 149
Trudinger House (O'Connor) 4n.6, 39
'Tudor' style 40
Turner 41
Tuscan style 47

typology 48, 49, 50, 51, 52, 53, 54, 63, 64n.52, 83, 100, 105, 139, 190, 191

United States of America 46, 50, 55, 70, 88, 91, 99, 134, 168
see also North America
Universal House 83, 92n.44
University House, *see* Australian National University—University House
University of Canberra 186
University of Melbourne 11, 15, 18, 112n.34, 113, 145, 146
University of Sydney 23

Vasey Crescent Group 101–7, 109–10, 112, 115, 118, 119, 121–3, 125–7, 183, 190, 191
see also Blakers House, Griffing House, Philip House
Verge House 2
'Victorian Type' 49, 51

Waddington, Conrad 65, 66, 87, 88, 90, 100, 166n.19, 168, 169, 170
Wamboin (NSW) 37
Ward, Fred 18, 19, 20
Warren, Robert 1n.2, 20, 26, 27n.76
water penetration 70, 71, 74, 89, 114, 125
Waterhouse, Doug 3n.4, 40, 101
Weetangera 14
Wellington (NZ) 31, 32n.90, 155
Weston, Charles 135, 137
Woden Valley 145, 150, 156
Woolley, Ken 114, 142
Wright, Frank Lloyd 32, 127
Wrigley, Derek 37, 38, 41

Yarralumla 4n.6, 23, 147

Zwar House (O'Connor) 1n.2, 5, 77–100, 125, 190, 191, 192
Zwar, John 41, 77, 78, 79, 80, 81, 82, 87, 92n.47, 93, 94, 95, 96, 98, 102, 189, 191, 192

www.ingramcontent.com/pod-product-compliance
Lightning Source LLC
Chambersburg PA
CBHW040935240426
43670CB00033B/2982